# Social and Cultural Foundations in Global Studies

From the *Foundations in Global Studies* series, this text offers students a fresh, comprehensive, multidisciplinary entry point to the study of the social and cultural aspects of global studies. After a brief introduction to global studies, the early chapters of the book survey the key concepts and processes of globalization and also take a critical look at its meaning and role. Students are guided through the material with relevant resource boxes and text boxes that support and promote further independent exploration of the topics at hand. The second half of the book features interdisciplinary case studies, each of which focuses on a specific issue, including:

- Global News Media
- NGOs, Humanitarianism, and the Cultural Construction of Global Hierarchy
- Climate Change and Changing Global Imaginaries
- Transnational LGBT Identities
- The Islamic Veil and the Global Politics of Gender
- Yoga in America

**Eve Stoddard** is Charles A. Dana Professor of Global Studies at St. Lawrence University. She is the author of *Positioning Gender and Race in (Post)colonial Plantation Space* and co-editor of *Global Multiculturalism*.

**John Collins** is Professor of Global Studies at St. Lawrence University. He is the author of *Global Palestine* and *Occupied by Memory* and co-editor of *Collateral Language: A User's Guide to America's New War*.

**Foundations in Global Studies**
Series Editor: *Valerie Tomaselli, MTM Publishing*

**Recent Books in the Series**

**East Asia in the World: An Introduction**
*Editor: Anne Prescott, Five College Center for East Asian Studies at Smith College*

**The Middle East in the World: An Introduction**
*Editor: Lucia Volk, San Francisco State University*

**South Asia in the World: An Introduction**
*Editor: Susan Snow Wadley, Syracuse University*

**Social and Cultural Foundations in Global Studies**
*Editor: Eve Stoddard, John Collins*

# Social and Cultural Foundations in Global Studies

Eve Stoddard
John Collins

Routledge
Taylor & Francis Group

NEW YORK AND LONDON

Published 2017
by Routledge
711 Third Avenue, New York, NY 10017

and by Routledge
2 Park Square, Milton Park, Abingdon, Oxon, OX14 4RN

*Routledge is an imprint of the Taylor & Francis Group, an informa business*

*Library of Congress Cataloging-in-Publication Data*
Names: Stoddard, Eve Walsh, 1949– author. | Collins, John
    (John Martin), editor.
Title: Social and cultural foundations in global studies / Eve Stoddard,
    John Collins.
Description: New York, NY : Routledge, 2017. | Series: Foundations
    in global studies
Identifiers: LCCN 2016013537 | ISBN 9780765641250 (hardback) |
    ISBN 9780765641267 (pbk.) | ISBN 9781315717364 (ebook)
Subjects: LCSH: Globalization—Social aspects. | Globalization—
    Social aspects—Case studies.
Classification: LCC JZ1318 .S748 2017 | DDC 303.48/2—dc23
LC record available at https://lccn.loc.gov/2016013537

ISBN: 978-0-76-564125-0 (hbk)
ISBN: 978-0-76-564126-7 (pbk)
ISBN: 978-1-31-571736-4 (ebk)


Typeset in Times New Roman
by Apex CoVantage, LLC

# Contents

# About This Book and Series

*Social and Cultural Foundations of Global Studies* provides an innovative introductory examination of the concepts, processes, and manifestations of globalization, seen particularly through social and cultural lenses. Along with its companion, *Political and Economic Foundations of Global Studies*, the book is meant to expose students to ways of analyzing the globalizing forces shaping their world. As in the rest of Routledge's Global Studies series—including *The Regional Landscape* and *Issues in Global Studies*—the *Foundations* books employ a straightforward two-part strategy: conceptual and theoretical underpinnings explored in the first part are enlivened by case studies in the second part. The rationale is simple: explore theory and then see it in action.

## Outline of the Book

Part One: Background, Theories, and Contexts opens with a comprehensive investigation of the *field of global studies*, including its history as an interdisciplinary mode of inquiry and the distinct approaches used in the field to examine "the complex, dynamic realities of globalization." This is followed by an exploration of the *history of globalization*, weaving in pre-contemporary antecedents, along with different viewpoints to present a multifaceted picture of how cultural connections in today's world are historically rooted. The third chapter then focuses explicitly on the *globalization of culture*—from an examination of the term *culture* to aspects and contexts of global processes at work today, such as imperialism, diasporas, and creolization.

Throughout the chapters in Part One, the interrelationship among disciplines is emphasized, as is the fact that the social and cultural lenses used to examine global phenomena cannot be completely separated from the political and economic approaches—a caution also noted in the companion volume. Indeed the distribution of political and economic strength influences the development of cultural and social relations in ways hard to disentangle—and vice versa.

This intertwining is also emphasized in the case studies in Part Two. Just as they illustrate the conceptual underpinnings covered in the first three chapters, they take into account the multidisciplinary approach that global studies engages, and they emphasize the wide range of contemporary cultural and social phenomena that can be explored through these methodologies. The list of case studies, all high-interest topics that resonate with today's readers, includes such subjects as the hybrid nature of yoga as practiced in the United States, LGBT identities in a global context, and the emergence of Al Jazeera and TeleSUR. Taken as a whole, the case studies aim to "illustrate the complex interrelationships between local realities and global flows and forces," while also exploring "the ways specific local traditions or practices . . . can have a much broader impact."

## Special Features of This Innovative Series

Several tools are used throughout the book—and the series—that augment coverage:

- Text boxes are employed to expand and emphasize specific material: they are used to open up the coverage to related topics or to call attention to especially critical material, such as historical milestones or key vocabulary.
- Resource boxes, set in a grey background, offer links that point readers to sources— mostly online—on the topics discussed. The links, which are live in the ebook version, include connections to timely data, reports on recent events, official sites, local and country-based media, and visual material. Taken together, they establish a rich archive of additional material for readers to draw on. The URLs included are known to be current as of July 1, 2015, and in the case of expired URLs, enough information has been provided for the reader to locate the same, or similarly useful, resources.
- At the same time, back-of-chapter References and Further Research lists help students to trace the material used by authors or to follow more general leads relating to the topics covered in the chapters.
- Images highlight specific details of the case studies, helping to bring the subjects alive. The captions and source notes for the photos will also help readers seek additional resources on the case studies as their interests dictate.

These special features—along with the simple two-part strategy of employing case studies to explore concepts and theory—aim to chart an innovative path of high-interest and enhanced utility for readers. They are the cornerstones of the entire *Foundations in Global Studies* series.

# PART ONE

# Background, Theories, and Contexts

# 1

# What Is Global Studies?

*Scholars working in global studies are interested in America's war on terror and in the global marketing and fan base of Manchester United, in the theory and practice of human rights and in the discrepancies in the distribution of wealth and life-chances between North and South, in the democratizing possibility of global information and communication systems and in migration patterns, labour exchanges and friendship networks.*

(O'Byrne and Hensby 2011, 4)

In late 2012, the video for the Korean rapper Psy's "Gangnam Style," a song that provides ironic commentary on the lavish lifestyles associated with the South Korean elite, became the first video to receive one billion hits on YouTube. In the popular media, this quintessential twenty-first-century milestone was greeted with great fanfare for the way it showed not only the global popularity of the entire "Gangnam Style" phenomenon—the song, the original video, the dance moves contained in it, the memes, the hundreds of versions and parodies created by YouTube users—but also the remarkable power of social media itself. If CNN's live coverage of the 1991 Gulf War had served as a declaration of how twenty-four-hour cable news was taking over the news industry, the transnational success of Psy's video confirmed the remarkable ascendance of YouTube and other social media platforms, particularly their ability to act as distributors and multipliers of cultural content and cultural trends.

Two months before the video reached the one billion mark, Psy had followed in the footsteps of other global cultural icons such as Bono, the lead singer of the band U2, in meeting personally with the secretary-general of the United Nations. Further evidence of his global notoriety came in the form of invitations to speak at major universities, offer his opinions on hot-button political issues such as the tensions between North and South Korea, and perform on major television programs and at political rallies. Not surprisingly, given the amount of cultural and political translation involved in the spread of something like "Gangnam Style," the singer and his work quickly became enmeshed in a variety of controversies, particularly as others began to use the song and the video for purposes related to their own "local" political agendas and desires for cultural expression.

The interdisciplinary or transdisciplinary academic field known as global studies is uniquely positioned to make sense of this kind of cultural phenomenon by connecting its cultural aspects with a whole set of broader social, political, and economic processes. In this respect, while "Gangnam Style" may be an unusually popular and influential example, it is hardly a unique one. On the contrary, the same kinds of issues raised by studying it— issues having to do with the globalization of culture, the music industry, social media, the power of music videos, the rise of East Asia, class conflict, user-generated content, satire, celebrity, and so on—inevitably come to the fore as soon as we begin to apply global studies theories and methods to the study of any cultural or social phenomenon. So what exactly is global studies, and what makes it particularly well suited to study the complex social processes of our twenty-first-century world?

In many ways, global studies fits the general pattern established by other, earlier interdisciplinary fields. All such fields of study emerge out of a process of dissatisfaction with inherited academic divisions and categories. At the same time, no field is ever completely original. Even the most radical inventions are built upon a process of selectively incorporating elements of other fields, combining them in new ways (not unlike the way many people today enjoy "mashing up" sound, image, and video to create new cultural texts), and subjecting them to critical scrutiny in order to push beyond traditional boundaries. New fields also emerge in response to changes in the world, changes that require novel approaches to the pursuit of knowledge. A good example is the field of environmental studies, whose emergence was closely connected with the rise of the environmental movement and the growth of ecological awareness among scholars, activists, and ordinary citizens. Other fields, such as women's studies and various forms of ethnic studies, have similar histories, and all have shown the ability to evolve in response to changing conditions.

Global studies is the product of sustained efforts to understand the complex, dynamic realities of globalization, from changes in the structure and distribution of political and economic power to changes in the creation and circulation of cultural forms and social practices. The purpose of this introductory chapter is to offer an overview of how, when, and why global studies came into being as a distinct intellectual field; how it is connected with, but also different from, existing disciplinary and interdisciplinary fields (especially international relations, international studies, and area studies); and what distinguishes its particular approach to studying social and cultural processes often associated with globalization. The chapter addresses key elements of epistemology, methodology, and ethics, before concluding with a brief discussion of the educational benefits of global studies.

## The Emergence of Global Studies

The creation of global studies programs is the latest stage in a longer process through which colleges and universities have sought to "internationalize" their curricular offerings, student bodies, and campus cultures. The creation and promotion of off-campus study opportunities, the recruiting of international students, the introduction of initiatives to promote diversity and multiculturalism, the building of new courses and programs that expose students to non-Western perspectives (e.g., world literature and history, ethnic studies)—all of these are part of this broad effort to transform higher education. Programs labeled "Global Studies"—whether academic units offering majors and minors or offices designed to coordinate study abroad and international student recruitment—are an important marker of the ways in which many colleges and universities have gradually become more "international" or "global" in their outlook in recent decades.

As a field of academic research and teaching, global studies is also organically related to globalization, and both are famously difficult to define. Globalization is an emergent phenomenon, constantly changing as the world is woven together ever more tightly through a wide range of political, economic, cultural, social, and technological processes. In a similar way, global studies is an emergent academic field, always seeking to make sense of these changes and what they mean for people all over the world. Understanding global studies, therefore, requires that we take a look at globalization itself.

While there is significant disagreement among scholars about the origins of globalization—a topic covered in greater depth in Chapter 2 of this book—the work of Roland Robertson and others reveals a general consensus that the widespread awareness of globalization is a newer phenomenon than globalization itself. Awareness of globalization, however, is really just the latest phase of a much longer process through which humans have come to understand what it means to view the world as a single unit. This gradual process includes important milestones in astronomy (e.g., the Copernican Revolution), geography (e.g., the maps and travelogues created by the early Chinese, Arab, and European explorers), transport (e.g., the invention of the airplane), warfare (e.g., the invention of the atomic bomb and the threat of planetary annihilation), communication (e.g., the invention of the telegraph), religion (e.g., the global spread of Christianity), politics (e.g., the creation of the United Nations), economics (e.g., the development of the concept of the market), social movements (e.g., the emergence of a labor movement built upon global workers' solidarity), and even photography (e.g., NASA's famous "Blue Marble" image of the earth taken from outer space).

The term *globalization* really entered into popular discourse shortly after the end of the Cold War. As scholars, policymakers, business elites, activists, and journalists worked to make sense of post-1989 global realities, globalization quickly became a buzzword. While its exact meaning was (and is) contested, it often served as a shorthand way of describing all sorts of emerging transnational realities that didn't fall easily into old paradigms dominated by nation-states and the relations among them. Issues such as free and fair trade, the "McDonaldization" of culture, outsourcing, and the cultural and economic shifts associated with new waves of transnational migration became hot-button public issues and subjects of intense investigation by scholars during the 1990s. The attacks of September 11, 2001, and the subsequent declaration of a "global war on terrorism" by the United States inaugurated a new phase in the awareness of globalization and its many ripple effects.

Global studies is an intellectual and academic product of all of these post–World War II changes in the world and of our perception of them. In particular, one can point to several recent factors shaping the emergence of global studies, such as

- the continued extension of capitalism, along with the social relations associated with it, throughout the world;
- the growing role of financial markets and financial elites in shaping national and supranational economic policies in ways that tend to favor approaches associated with neoliberalism;
- the phenomenon of time/space compression, in which the world begins to feel increasingly small, thanks to the operation of new communications and transportation technologies that accelerate social and economic relations and the rhythm of social life in general;
- changes in global intellectual culture set in motion by the transnational migration of people from the Global South to the Global North during and after formal colonization; and
- the work of influential scholars who pinpointed globalization itself as an issue of general concern.

An important milestone in the development of global studies as an academic field was the creation of the Global Studies Association (GSA) by scholars in the United Kingdom in 2000. A North American branch of the GSA was founded two years later. Both organizations hold annual conferences, and both are affiliated with important global studies journals, including *Global Networks* and *Globalizations*. For more information, see the following websites:

Global Studies Association (https://globalstudiesassoc.wordpress.com)
Global Studies Association North America (http://www.net4dem.org/mayglobal/index.html)
*Global Networks* (http://onlinelibrary.wiley.com/journal/10.1111/(ISSN)1471—0374)
*Globalizations* (http://www.tandfonline.com/toc/rglo20/current#.UYfGJ7pXtIo)

Many well-established academic fields, both disciplinary and interdisciplinary, have long sought to investigate "global" issues and themes. These include anthropology, area studies, environmental studies, geography, history, international relations, political economy, and sociology. Global studies draws on many of these approaches while also seeking to chart a distinct intellectual course that enables scholars and students to "debate the processes and dynamics impacting upon all aspects of contemporary social life" (O'Byrne and Hensby 2011, 4). Such an agenda is obviously ambitious and necessarily broad, as the quote from O'Byrne and Hensby at the start of this chapter indicates.

An important part of a global studies approach is the recognition that all contemporary global processes have deep historical roots. So, for example, when looking at the growing global popularity of a company like Starbucks Coffee, a global studies scholar would find it necessary to explore this topic in light of various issues, including

- the global history of coffee production and its role in the expansion of European empires;
- the history of how coffee drinking in general emerged and spread throughout the world as a cultural habit associated with particular forms of work, social organization, taste formation, leisure, consumption, and so on;
- the more recent history of how the awareness and consumption of different forms of coffee has become a marker of personal identity, an object of intensive consumer marketing, and a way of distinguishing one's social class; and
- the longer history of "global brands" (e.g., Coca-Cola, Nike, Disney) and their interaction with and influence on local cultures throughout the world.

This brief example also illustrates why, for global studies scholars, social and cultural processes can never be separated fully from political and economic processes. For this reason, readers will find that many of the case studies in this book often include information about how political economy fits into the analysis.

---

**Political Economy: Definition and Scholars**

The term *political economy* refers to the social system that shapes the conditions governing the circulation, accumulation, and distribution of wealth, capital, and power. This system always includes a range of interlocking institutions, social relationships, and structures. Political economy also refers to the academic field focused on the study of these processes. Some of the most important classical and modern scholars of political economy are Adam Smith, Karl Marx, Samir Amin, Immanuel Wallerstein, Susan Strange, and David Harvey.

---

Useful resources on political economy may be found at these websites:

Centre for Global Political Economy (http://www.sussex.ac.uk/cgpe/)
Marxists Internet Archive (http://www.marxists.org/)
*New Political Economy* (http://www.tandfonline.com/action/aboutThisJournal?sho
   w=aimsScope&journalCode=cnpe#.Ua9H-rq0Ovc)
World-Systems Archive (http://wsarch.ucr.edu/)

With all of this in mind, how can we locate global studies in relation to the academic universe that gave birth to it and that continues to surround it? We know that global studies scholars seek to produce knowledge that is marked by a high level of integration. One school of thought characterizes global studies as an *interdisciplinary* field that creates intellectual integration by addition—that is, by combining elements of existing disciplines. There is also another school of thought, however, that seeks to create integration by deliberately questioning the value of dividing knowledge into disciplines in the first place. From this *transdisciplinary* perspective, which is addressed in more detail later, disciplines play a key role in supporting power and knowledge structures that tend to privilege certain perspectives, ways of knowing, and social groups over others.

A classic example is the creation of economics and political science as separate disciplines more than a century ago, a shift that broke apart the older, more integrated field of political economy. This split served not only the interest of the British and other European empires, but also the interests of elites in general by obscuring the political nature of wealth and capital accumulation. Political economy, in other words, was a more integrated way of studying how power works. A global studies scholar using an interdisciplinary approach to studying power might emphasize the need to supplement the analysis of political power with analysis of economic forces in order to achieve a more holistic understanding. A scholar using a transdisciplinary approach would question whether it is possible (even for analytical purposes) to identify "political" and "economic" as two separate spheres of social activity. The goal would instead be to go beyond disciplines, their categories, and their assumptions by making power itself the central focus of analysis. Taking such a step, many transdisciplinary scholars argue, is an important move toward social transformation because it pushes us to imagine alternative ways of organizing the world.

Both of these frameworks, the interdisciplinary and the transdisciplinary, continue to play a key role in the development of global studies. Regardless of which school of thought a particular scholar may prefer, it is important to emphasize that even as global studies scholars seek to maximize integration and breadth, they also make great efforts not to sacrifice depth (e.g., an in-depth understanding of a particular place, culture, or institution).

While global studies is still a young academic field, it seems likely that it will continue to be defined more by themes and questions than by a common set of methods and canonical texts. Nonetheless, it is important to understand how global studies can be distinguished from the academic fields that preceded it. Many people often wonder how global studies is different from international relations, international studies, or area studies. The following section explores these differences while recognizing that global studies remains organically related to all of these other fields.

## Distinguishing Global Studies

It is common to assume that global studies is really the same thing as *international relations* (IR). The latter, however, is actually a subfield of the larger discipline of political science, and it has a narrower mandate than global studies. Just as international political economy (another subfield of political science) focuses on the operation and interaction of national economies, IR primarily explores the diplomatic and security policies of nation-states. In both cases, the state is the primary unit of analysis, and there is a strong emphasis on the creation and analysis of state policy. To put it another way, these subfields of political science tend to be "top-down" in their angle of vision, looking mainly at how decisions are made at the state level and how they affect those below.

Global studies scholars, by contrast, tend to begin from a different set of assumptions, and also, as we will see later, from a more "bottom-up" angle of vision. Rather than starting with the state and building a model around that, global studies scholars start with global processes, a term that refers to processes that spill across traditional boundaries of community, nation-state, social class, and academic discipline. They then try to examine how those processes work at a variety of scales and spaces (local, regional, urban, rural, national, transnational, virtual, global/planetary, etc.) and how they create different kinds of social relationships across and between the various scales and spaces. The processes being studied are perhaps best described as *global-local interactions*, with the assumption that, in these interactions, effects are being generated in both directions. The result is a complex approach that might be characterized in terms of multiscaled relationality. To return to the contrast with IR, we can say that in global studies, states are still important but are seen as embedded in structures and processes that are both smaller and larger than the state. Finally, whereas cultural and social processes play a relatively marginal role in IR, in global studies they are given equal treatment and are typically integrated with the study of political and economic processes.

An example from one of the case studies covered in this book helps illustrate the basic differences between IR and global studies. The Zapatista movement that emerged in Chiapas, Mexico, in 1994 in response to the implementation of the North American Free Trade Agreement (NAFTA) articulated a range of grievances on behalf of the indigenous population of southern Mexico. From an IR perspective, such a movement would be of interest primarily insofar as it represents a challenge to the authority of the Mexican state, and perhaps, by extension, to the long-standing partnership between the political elites of the United States and Mexico. Yet while the Zapatistas clearly showed an awareness of these elements of international relations, they also presented their grievances in a way that highlighted their transnational nature. The movement's decision to announce itself on the day of NAFTA's official inauguration was a deliberate effort to focus attention on power structures (in this case, a global regime of free trade) that operate not only between states, but above and beyond them. Moreover, as an indigenous people's movement, the Zapatista rebellion also sought to help cultivate a global sense of indigenous consciousness and solidarity while challenging an entire set of historical and cultural narratives that give primacy to the formation, the worldviews, and the actions of nation-states. A global studies approach would seek to bring all of this together in order to understand not only what the Zapatista movement means for the U.S. and Mexican states, but also what it means for the people of Chiapas, for indigenous people elsewhere, for how we understand the impact of neoliberal economic policies, and for a variety of global audiences viewing the movement through the lenses provided by the media.

*International studies* is a second field that is often confused with global studies. Understanding how these two fields differ requires looking at their respective institutional contexts and histories. Many colleges and universities created interdisciplinary programs in international studies throughout the latter period of the Cold War as part of the wider internationalization efforts referred to earlier. Such programs were typically built by bringing together faculty and courses from a range of departments in the social sciences and humanities, often with interdisciplinary courses offered at the introductory and capstone level. Most international studies programs have been additive in their basic approach, operating on the basic assumption that combining geographic areas (e.g., Africa + Europe + Latin America + Asia) and disciplines or departments (e.g., sociology + history + economics + literary studies + anthropology) can help students pursue an education that is "international."

Global studies programs emerged somewhat later, in some cases as stand-alone departments with their own full-time teaching positions. The decision to choose a global studies identity over an international studies identity is a significant decision with important intellectual consequences. Whereas international studies programs often tend to assume that intellectual integration will happen as students compare and combine different disciplinary perspectives found in individual courses, global studies programs emphasize the idea that integration should be built into the courses themselves. As a result, many professors in global studies programs find that their disciplinary training becomes less and less important as the program becomes more transdisciplinary and more focused on themes and processes.

Finally, we can distinguish global studies from another interdisciplinary structure with which it has a close relationship: *area studies*. As many scholars have noted, the concept of area studies (e.g., African studies or Middle Eastern studies) emerged after World War II thanks to strong support from the U.S. government, which saw the training of geographic area experts as a key part of its global economic, diplomatic, and military strategy. While not identifying itself explicitly as an empire, the United States followed the example of the earlier British and French empires in putting significant resources into creating the academic structures necessary to produce knowledge about the cultures and societies in which it was becoming more closely involved. These structures included academic departments and programs, journals, professional associations, research and travel grants, and opportunities for foreign language training. One implication of this history of state support is that area studies scholars have regularly found themselves trying to strike an uneasy balance between putting their knowledge in the service of the state (e.g., by developing policy papers or advising the military) and maintaining a more independent, critical position.

Scholars trained as area experts became central players in the development of international studies and, later, global studies programs. Indeed, area studies and global studies have much in common, including the willingness to consider new ways of organizing knowledge other than via traditional academic disciplines and departments. Similarly, both fields share the desire to go beyond the nation-state as a privileged unit of analysis. While many area studies scholars were and are committed to their disciplines, others prioritize the transnational, interdisciplinary study of regions whose political boundaries were often determined arbitrarily by colonial powers. In many ways, global studies may be viewed as the logical next step: examining processes that cross not only national, but also regional, boundaries to become truly global processes. What this means in practice is that global studies research and teaching are often defined as much by themes (e.g., migration, violence, identity) as they are by geographic areas or disciplines.

A number of philanthropic foundations supported work on the linkages between area studies and global studies during the late 1990s and into the twenty-first century. One of the most influential initiatives was the "Regional Worlds" project hosted at the University of Chicago as part of its Globalization Project (1996–2002) funded by the MacArthur and Ford foundations. For more information on this program, see the project's website (http://regionalworlds.uchicago.edu/about.html), including its publications page (http://regionalworlds.uchicago.edu/pub.html).

To summarize, while the emerging field of global studies is directly shaped by preexisting academic fields, global studies also seeks to avoid some of the limitations imposed by traditional knowledge structures. At a time when globalization appears to be moving more quickly than our ability to grasp it intellectually, the work of creating flexible new categories, theories, and analytical tools is especially urgent. Inevitably, this means asking critical questions about the intellectual tools we have inherited. In asking such questions, global studies shows the influence of critical theory, cultural studies, post-structuralism, world-systems analysis, and other theoretical frameworks that include the analysis of knowledge structures in their broader critical analysis of society and culture. The value of such critiques goes far beyond their recognition of the arbitrary nature of academic categories. The most funda-mental insight that global studies draws from these frameworks has to do with how power produces, organizes, utilizes, and categorizes knowledge in ways that often (but not always) reinforce existing social boundaries and hierarchies.

Like the division of political economy into the separate disciplines of economics and politi-cal sciences (see earlier), the role of the U.S. government in the creation and support of area studies is an excellent example of this power–knowledge relationship. As we will see later, awareness of power–knowledge relationships also informs the work of scholars who are try-ing to dismantle the Eurocentric knowledge structures that accompanied the global spread of European empires. By developing this awareness and integrating it into their work, global studies scholars seek to contribute to what amounts to a new intellectual architecture for the twenty-first century—one that focuses more on integrated processes and relationships than on fixed categories and hierarchies. This work is closely connected with the continuing democratization of global debates about power, culture, and the future of humanity.

## The Integrated Study of Global Processes

As noted earlier, global studies scholars tend to put global processes at the center of their research and teaching. Examples of such processes include

- the transnational movement of people (e.g., labor migration, refugees, human traffick-ing, tourism);
- the circulation of cultural texts through news media, social media, advertising, film and television, peer-to-peer sharing, piracy, and so on;
- the global movement of capital and commodities;
- social movements that stretch across national borders;
- war, terrorism, and other forms of political violence; and
- the global circulation of information.

Under each of these broad categories one can imagine an infinite number of specific research topics, ranging from the cultural translation of "Gangnam Style" in user-generated parody videos, to the role of private security companies in the militarization of humanitarian aid in East Africa, to the cultural impact of European tourism in Southeast Asia.

Studying global processes through these kinds of examples can help reveal linkages that might otherwise remain unnoticed or de-emphasized. At times a single event can provide the opportunity for exploring such linkages and demonstrating why they matter. Consider the case of the horrific 2013 building collapse in Dhaka, Bangladesh, that killed over one thousand people, including many who had worked in garment factories contained in the building. Highlighting some of the global processes connected with this tragedy—the global demand for inexpensive clothing, the longer global history of industrial accidents affecting textile workers, the way the event was covered in the news media in different parts of the world, the impact it had on the large Bengali diaspora community—can be an important way not only to boost one's understanding of these processes, but also to make sure that the tragedy itself is not simply remembered (or forgotten) as a "local" event disconnected from the lives of others.

One key way in which global studies scholars try to shed light on global processes is by bringing together perspectives rooted in a wide range of social locations. This approach is built upon a belief in the importance of developing a deep and complex understanding of *positionality*, or an awareness of one's own social location (nationality, social class, gender, sexuality, race/ethnicity, religion, etc.), and of the particular life chances, forms of knowledge, identities, and responsibilities that derive from this location. Here global studies reflects the influence of many critical theorists who have explored the relationship between knowledge production and the operation of pervasive social hierarchies.

The feminist scholar Donna Haraway, for example, emphasizes that all knowledge is "situated" in the sense that it is the product of a particular cultural and social context that brings a whole set of limitations with it. Michel Foucault, one of the most influential philosophers of the twentieth century, calls our attention to the ways in which dominant social structures and their associated bodies of knowledge tend to ignore, dismiss, or actively suppress what he calls the "subjugated knowledges" produced by marginalized groups. These knowledges have played a key role in the work of Frantz Fanon, Paulo Freire, and other revolutionary thinkers associated with liberation movements in the Global South. Other contemporary scholars of postcolonialism and critical race theory such as bell hooks, Stuart Hall, Gayatri Spivak, and Edward Said have used these fundamental insights to develop their own critiques of how Western racism and imperialism function, in part, through claims to superior knowledge and efforts to denigrate people of color.

For a bibliography of Donna Haraway's work, including links to speeches and lectures, see her web site at the University of California, Santa Cruz ( https://people.ucsc. edu/~haraway/).

Recognition of these power-knowledge patterns leads to two additional commitments shaping global studies approaches to studying global processes. The first is the commitment to respecting cultural diversity as a basic fact of social life and a key element of constructing just societies and a more just world. The second, closely related to the first, is a commitment to a more democratic and cosmopolitan form of knowledge production, as opposed to knowledge production that is dominated by privileged elites concentrated in the Global North.

This integration of diverse perspectives is important for social justice, but it also helps generate better knowledge that can be more useful in addressing complex problems. Eve Stoddard and Grant Cornwell use the metaphor of a global positioning system (GPS) to explain how employing a global studies framework can help us become "geocitizens." A GPS device (e.g., on a phone or in a car) uses a satellite-aided process of triangulation to help the user get oriented and find her or his way; the more data points the device can combine, the more accurately it can pinpoint the user's location. Similarly, a GPS-type approach to global processes seeks to help individuals become more aware of their own position on issues by triangulating as many perspectives as possible. Having considered these perspectives, their social and intellectual roots, and their points of convergence and divergence, we can put ourselves in a better position to exercise the complex forms of ethical judgment that are needed in a globalized world. Being able to do this is especially important in a world where people are becoming increasingly aware of the existence of radically different worldviews.

To return to our earlier example, something like the Bangladesh building collapse can generate a wide range of responses and interpretations grounded in an equally wide range of social locations, political commitments, and intellectual paradigms. Some might interpret the event as illustrating a need for stronger state regulation of the construction industry, while others might emphasize the role of corruption in reducing the impact of existing regulations. International advocates might seize on the event as another chapter in the ongoing global struggle for worker safety, consumer awareness, or women's rights (as many of the workers killed and injured in the building collapse were women). Nationalist elites in Bangladesh or in the diaspora might seek to contest interpretations that place the country or its government in a negative light. Media analysts might point out how little coverage the event received in the Global North when compared with stories about sensationalized murder trials, the lives of celebrities, or the everyday remarks of prominent politicians. Making sense of all of these perspectives and using them to illuminate something about the global processes mentioned earlier would require an effort to understand positionality and its role in shaping knowledge. Global studies scholars, further, would make a special effort to ensure that the voices of ordinary people in Bangladesh are not drowned out by the voices of external analysts.

## Epistemology and Methodology

The kind of integration found in global studies is closely connected with *epistemology*, the study of issues related to the nature of knowledge itself. Global studies approaches to studying the world provide a challenge to the dominance of positivism, one of the foundational elements of the modern natural and social sciences. Within a positivist epistemology, knowledge generated through direct observation and the application of the scientific method is assumed to be more valid than other forms of knowledge because it reveals the operation of social "laws" that are analogous to the laws of nature studied in the natural sciences. Positivism, along with modified approaches often called post-positivism, does play a role in global studies, but these are not privileged over other approaches. Instead, global studies scholars recognize that there are many legitimate ways of producing knowledge—not only scientific experimentation and observation, but also intuition, textual interpretation, personal experience, artistic expression, dialogue, political action and engagement, and a host of other avenues. A good global studies researcher seeks to put multiple forms of knowledge and knowledge seeking into conversation with one another while also examining each of them critically.

An additional type of integration associated with global studies concerns research *methodology*, or the logic that informs the researcher's choice of research methods. Because global studies has always been an interdisciplinary (or transdisciplinary) field with a respect for epistemological diversity, its approach to seeking knowledge through research is also marked by methodological diversity. Rather than developing its own unique methodology, global studies generally seeks to borrow and combine a range of methodological tools from other fields in order to find the best way to approach a particular research question. The goal of this kind of methodological diversity is not to find the perfect methodology that will yield foolproof results; rather, the assumption is that the skilled researcher can generate interesting and meaningful knowledge through a variety of methodological approaches.

How might these commitments to epistemological and methodological diversity play themselves out in real research? Consider the hypothetical example of a global studies researcher who wants to investigate the relationship between punk music and economic crisis across multiple cultures. Taking a positivist approach to such a project (e.g., by measuring the amount of punk music being produced in a given culture at a given moment and trying to correlate it with statistics on unemployment, poverty, etc.) might yield some interesting results, but those results would be restricted by the limitations of positivism itself. A global studies approach would recognize that we can "know" punk as a sociocultural phenomenon in many different ways—by doing it, by reading about it, by listening to it, by talking about it, etc.—and that a more diverse methodological strategy might lead to richer results. The researcher might therefore choose a strategy that employs some combination of the following: surveys of musicians, ethnographic observation, content analysis (e.g., of song lyrics, fan blogs, or critics' reviews), photography, analysis of demographic data, direct musical participation, in-depth qualitative interviews, and comparative sociological analysis.

## Beyond Eurocentrism to Global Relationality

Just as global studies seeks to challenge the hegemonic epistemological position of positivism, it also seeks to challenge *Eurocentrism*—the systematic privileging of viewpoints, narratives, and categories derived from Europe. While positivism is associated primarily with the natural and social sciences, Eurocentrism extends into the humanities and arts and can be seen, for example, in the overrepresentation of white, European authors in the literary canon and the relative exclusion of authors from the non-European parts of the world. The epistemological dominance of Europe was so strong for so long that the very term "Eurocentrism" didn't even come into existence until the post–World War II wave of anticolonial movements forced a more critical examination of how Western imperialism had long been aided by forms of epistemological exclusion. In recent decades there has been a sustained (but still very much unfinished) effort throughout the academic world to "unthink" the patterns associated with Eurocentrism and foster a more egalitarian, multicultural outlook (in the work of Janet Abu-Lughod, Dipesh Chakrabarty, Renato Rosaldo, Ella Shohat, and Robert Stam, among many others). Global studies builds upon and contributes to this process by trying to make sure that voices from the Global South have an equal seat at the table whenever global processes are being studied.

So far, we have seen how global studies combines a commitment to cultural diversity with a commitment to epistemological and methodological diversity through its move beyond positivism and Eurocentrism. It is also important to recognize that in global studies, all of the various perspectives under consideration are viewed in relational terms rather than as separate or sequential. Too often, educational curricula treat human experience as inherently divisible by nation, continent, or culture—as if "African history" could really be contained within the boundaries of the African continent, for example. Similarly, there is a tendency to assume that cultural change unfolds in a sequential way, with some cultures located "behind" others in the process. In contrast, a relational approach highlights how all human experiences, actions, and ideas are shaped by their interaction with others and, indeed, cannot be fully understood without examining closely the nature of this interaction. In trying to conceptualize relationality, one can think of a spectrum of types of interaction, ranging from the most egalitarian (e.g., people of different cultural backgrounds working together in a nonhierarchical way for a common purpose) to the most unequal (e.g., the relationship between powerful governments and stateless people).

Edward Said's pioneering work on the concept of *Orientalism* illustrates how a relational approach can help correct some of the distortions caused by Eurocentric thinking. Said, one of the most influential voices in debates on the cultural aspects of imperialism and globalization, tells us that geographic categories such as West/Occident and East/Orient are not objective facts; instead, they are shaped by the existence of hierarchical relations among different cultures, nations, and peoples. Said reminds us that the relations between "West" and "East" have long been unequal relations conditioned by the expansion of empires (chiefly British, French, and American). Moreover, he insists, this Western imperial power has also included ideological power, through which the West claims to "know" the East through the work of prominent "Orientalists" who study it, generalize about it, speak for it, and categorize it. What is important for our purposes here is that, for Said, no matter how oppressive imperial power may be, empire remains a relationship that deeply shapes the identities, worldviews, and imaginative geographies of everyone involved.

What this means is that far from being separate processes, the histories of "East" and "West" are really part of the same history, unfolding together in a complex dynamic marked by dialogue, conflict, and mutual influence. Many people are unaware, for instance, that the thing often referred to as "Western culture" could not have emerged when and where it did without the central role of medieval Arab scholars who protected, developed, and transmitted new historical and scientific knowledge to the "West." Similarly, while it has become common to associate Christianity and Judaism with the West and Islam with the East, the reality is that all three monotheistic religions have grown and changed by crossing all sorts of geographical and cultural boundaries. During the past century, the discovery of oil in the Middle East has produced a complex set of cultural, social, and political relationships that provide another example of the intertwined histories of "East" and "West."

An additional implication of this framework is that if history and cultural change are relational, then so is identity. Here identity mirrors geography: just as "West" and "East" are only relative categories on a round planet—if you are standing on the coast of California, then Japan is "the West"—the identities associated with those categories are equally relational. As Said's work demonstrates, the imperial relations between West and East enable a process of mutual identity construction in which the Self only makes sense in relation to the Other. In our own time, particularly in the years since the September 11 attacks and the launch of the U.S.-led "war on terrorism," this process of mutual identity construction often takes place through the prism of gender. Many proud proclamations of "Western" and "Islamic" identities are regularly built upon an implied or openly stated contrast between how "we" treat "our" women and how "they" treat "theirs." Similar dynamics can be seen in the West's relationship with the nations and cultures of East Asia, such as when political and economic tensions (e.g., over the growing dominance of Japanese automobiles during the 1970s and 1980s, or Chinese-manufactured goods more recently) lead to strident defenses of cultural superiority on both sides of a divide and a general failure to recognize how each culture is profoundly influencing the other all the time.

Regardless of how one feels about any of these particular examples, Said's larger point about cultural relationality points us toward the intellectual value of stepping outside Eurocentric frameworks. This is another area where the global studies focus on integration enables scholars and students to avoid some of the epistemological, methodological, and political problems associated with more traditional academic paradigms.

## Angles of Vision and Ethical Commitments

As noted earlier, global studies differs from international relations by relying less on the kind of top-down approach that privileges the actions and perspectives of states and other elite institutions. In other words, these two academic fields tend to employ significantly different *angles of vision*. Identifying one's angle of vision requires answering two related questions: Where are you located, and in what direction are you looking? In other words, angle of vision is directly related to the issue of positionality, but also to the issue of *ethics*, the study of how to determine right action. It is important to recognize that all academic paradigms, whether they acknowledge it or not, contain within them a set of ethical assumptions and commitments. Analysts in global studies tend to approach the issue of ethics in ways that align closely with the field's interest in moving beyond positivism as a privileged epistemological position, promoting methodological diversity, and challenging the categories and narratives associated with Eurocentrism.

Because academia itself is an elite social institution, it is not surprising that most models of academic research tend to employ an angle of vision that is some combination of top-down (e.g., state-centered international relations research, elitist approaches to studying "high culture") and center-out (e.g., Eurocentric models of cultural diffusion or economic development). Ordinary people do appear in the field of vision to some extent, but only as relatively passive objects and recipients of policies and cultural processes that originate elsewhere. By contrast, global studies places a high value on what might be called a bottom-up angle of vision that is built on a more complex understanding of how ordinary people fit into the world. This alternative angle of vision is quite similar to the approaches employed in some varieties of cultural studies (particularly those that take a nonjudgmental approach to studying popular culture) as well as some branches of history (e.g., the influential work of Howard Zinn), anthropology, and sociology that put ordinary people front and center. A bottom-up angle of vision emphasizes that ordinary people play a central role in shaping the world every day through their labor, their cultural production, their participation in social movements, and so forth. Because it begins from a premise that is both more democratic and more hopeful, viewing the world in this way is an important step toward creating positive social change.

In addition to the ethical reasons, feminist scholars such as Sandra Harding argue that adopting a bottom-up angle of vision has real epistemological consequences and benefits. When structures and social relations are hierarchical, Harding notes, those on the top can develop a naïve and distorted view of how the system works, and often they are quite insulated from a detailed awareness of the injustices that are built into the system—yet through the operation of power, their perspective is typically naturalized as "common sense." Those on the bottom, by contrast, often have a very detailed knowledge of the system because such knowledge is essential to their survival. Yet once again, through the operation of power, their perspective is typically discounted or actively suppressed.

Understanding these power–knowledge dynamics is essential to developing research strategies that will actually help reveal the nature of the system along with the structures, processes, and relations that constitute it. When trying to understand whiteness and white privilege, for example, it makes little sense to prioritize the perspectives of white people who are, in many cases, either unaware of this privilege or unwilling to acknowledge its importance. It makes much more sense to prioritize the perspectives of the people of color who must be constantly aware of the dynamics of racism and racial hierarchies. The same goes for structures of inequality with respect to gender, sexuality, social class, and other markers of social difference.

From a global studies perspective, looking at the world from the point of view of those on the margins—women, workers, youth, minorities, refugees, people in the Global South, and others—can yield a different and better understanding of how powerful global elites think and act, how powerful global institutions operate, and how the world is shaped by ongoing processes of political struggle in which ordinary people are deeply implicated. We see this general approach in the work of authors addressing a variety of global studies themes, including global migration (e.g., Gloria Anzaldúa, Paul Gilroy), urbanization (e.g., Saskia Sassen, David Harvey), theories of cosmopolitanism (e.g., Kwame Anthony Appiah, Homi Bhabha), imperialism and anti-imperialism (e.g., Eduardo Galeano, Frantz Fanon), political economy (e.g., Amartya Sen, Naomi Klein), and social movements (e.g., Giovanni Arrighi, Jackie Smith). More generally, as the anthropologist George Marcus and many others have argued, a great strength of this approach is that it enables one to move back and forth between the local and the global in order to see how each is present in the other.

Online sources by most of these scholars are easily available online. Some are listed here.

Lectures of Saskia Sassen are available online at her website (http://www.saskiasassen.com/interviews.php#lectures).

Talks, lectures, and interviews by Kwame Anthony Appiah available online can be found at the press page on his website (http://appiah.net/press/audio/).

Interviews and speeches by Naomi Klein can be found at the video-audio link on her website (http://www.naomiklein.org/video-audio).

To summarize, for global studies scholars, foregrounding the perspectives and experiences of ordinary people is both an intellectual choice and a political/ethical choice. These choices are grounded in the belief that the pursuit of a more just world requires developing the best possible intellectual understanding of how global structures and processes actually work. This includes a complex, flexible understanding of how the impact of these structures and processes is distributed globally in ways that reflect people's varying social locations and life chances. The intellectual and political tasks are connected, and both require a bottom-up angle of vision in order to be able to see the world differently.

## Why Global Studies?

Among people who are learning about global studies for the first time, it is common to ask, "What can I do with a degree in global studies?" While the sense of uncertainty is normal with any emerging academic field, the evidence indicates that global studies is, in many ways, an ideal field of study for anyone who wants to be able to navigate a rapidly changing, multicultural, twenty-first-century world. Indeed, global studies programs were designed specifically with that world in mind. The learning goals of many such programs intersect in profound ways with the general goals for twenty-first-century liberal learning promoted by top educators. The growing number of graduate programs in global studies and related fields is another indication of how global studies has succeeded in identifying a range of questions, paradigms, and practical skills that are essential for promoting critical global citizenship. Consequently, global studies graduates who wish to pursue further study as a prelude to a career in research or teaching find that they can be competitive and successful in a broad array of academic fields, whether traditional disciplines (e.g., history, political science, geography) or emerging interdisciplinary programs (e.g., global governance, conservation, gender studies).

Given the way global studies stretches its analytical focus beyond state-level processes and perspectives, it is not surprising that many global studies graduates tend to find work in nongovernmental organizations (NGOs) and other locations in the nonprofit sector. The kinds of skills needed in this sector—research, grant writing, advocacy, a strong understanding of diversity issues, the ability to work in a range of global settings—dovetail very well with the learning outcomes of global studies programs. Students whose work in global studies coincides with a personal or political interest in specific issues and geographic areas find that they are very well equipped to do nonprofit work in areas such as human rights, community development, environmental justice, and grassroots empowerment.

Another common career path for global studies students is to pursue work in the broader field of international education. Many colleges and universities around the world are looking for individuals with the intellectual tools and the intercultural experience to help them build and administer study abroad programs, support international students, and "global-ize" their curricula. There is similar demand from companies and nonprofit organizations that organize study tours for high school students, international study programs for college students, and continuing education programs for older learners. Many global studies gradu-ates find that their own experience of learning a second language, learning about multicul-turalism, and studying in other cultural contexts enables them to make a seamless transition to helping others make the most of their own intercultural travel and study opportunities.

It should also be obvious that this sort of preparation lends itself well to work in the public sector. This includes policy work (e.g., helping to develop environmental policy that is sensitive to the needs of diverse global stakeholders), diplomacy (e.g., helping to resolve armed conflicts and reintegrate combatants into society), education (e.g., teaching global studies in a high school or public university), and hands-on work in global contexts (e.g., serving in the Peace Corps). The same goes for the field of international business, where companies of all sorts are constantly seeking to hire people who are able to adapt quickly to new challenges, make use of their detailed understanding of global processes, and work collaboratively with international partners.

For all of these career paths, as well as many others (e.g., law, public health, journalism, translation, publishing, public relations, urban planning), the key skills associated with a global studies education can be summarized as follows:

- Critical global thinking. Global studies helps students learn how to think for them-selves by evaluating information from multiple perspectives and social locations, think-ing beyond and between disciplines, and refusing to take conventional wisdom for granted.
- Engaged and experiential learning. Global studies helps students see and experience the connections between what they are learning in the classroom and what is happening in the real world. Its focus on global processes means that students are constantly con-fronted with issues that matter to the kinds of people students meet when they travel and study in intercultural contexts.
- Problem solving. Global studies helps students develop the ability to address complex problems that require integrated, creative strategies. In the twenty-first century, solving problems requires understanding that these problems have many interlocking aspects (social, political, economic, cultural, ethical, environmental, etc.) that cannot simply be addressed separately.
- Diversity and multiculturalism. Global studies helps students develop a deeper, more complex understanding of why diversity matters. While most colleges and universi-ties have programs designed to promote multicultural awareness, global studies is built upon an intellectual and ethical approach that demonstrates why diversity is central to the challenge of addressing the complex problems facing nations, institutions, commu-nities, and ordinary people every day.

For all of these reasons, students who choose to immerse themselves in the world of global studies find that their choice has intellectual benefits that will shape them both in their immediate education and in the rest of their lives and careers.

## References and Further Research

Abu-Lughod, Janet. 1991. *Before European Hegemony: The World System A.D. 1250–1350*. New York: Oxford University Press.

Amin, Samir. 1977. *Imperialism and Unequal Development*. New York: Monthly Review Press.

Anzaldúa, Gloria. 1987. *Borderlands: The New Mestiza = La Frontera*. San Francisco: Spinsters/Aunt Lute.

Appadurai, Arjun. 2000. "Grassroots Globalization and the Research Imagination." *Public Culture* 12, no. 1: 1–19.

Appiah, Anthony. 2006. *Cosmopolitanism: Ethics in a World of Strangers*. New York: W. W. Norton.

Arrighi, Giovanni. 2010. *The Long Twentieth Century: Money, Power, and the Origins of Our Times*. new and updated ed. New York: Verso.

Bhabha, Homi. 2001. "Unsatisfied: Notes on Vernacular Cosmopolitanism." In *Postcolonial Discourses: An Anthology*, edited by Gregory Castle, 38–52. Oxford: Blackwell.

Chakrabarty, Dipesh. 2000. *Provincializing Europe: Postcolonial Thought and Historical Difference*. Princeton, NJ: Princeton University Press.

Fanon, Frantz. 1967. *A Dying Colonialism*. Translated by Haakon Chevalier. New York: Grove Press.

Foucault, Michel. 2003. *Society Must Be Defended: Lectures at the Collège de France, 1975–76*. Edited by Mauro Bertani and Alessandro Fontana. Translated by David Macey. New York: Picador.

Freire, Paulo. 1974. *Pedagogy of the Oppressed*. Translated by Myra Bergman Ramos. New York: Seabury Press.

Galeano, Eduardo. 1973. *Open Veins of Latin America: Five Centuries of the Pillage of a Continent*. Translated by Cedric Belfrage. New York: Monthly Review Press.

Gilroy, Paul. 1993. *The Black Atlantic: Modernity and Double Consciousness*. Cambridge, MA: Harvard University Press.

Hall, Stuart, Dorothy Hobson, Andrew Lowe, and Paul Willis, eds. 1980. *Culture, Media, Language: Working Papers in Cultural Studies, 1972–79*. London: Hutchinson.

Haraway, Donna. 1988. "Situated Knowledges: The Science Question in Feminism and the Privilege of Partial Perspective." *Feminist Studies* 14, no. 3: 575–599.

Harding, Sandra. 2004. "How Standpoint Methodology Informs Philosophy of Social Science." In *Approaches to Qualitative Research*, edited by Sharlene Nagy Hesse-Biber and Patricia Leavy, 62–80. New York: Oxford University Press.

Harvey, David. 2005. *A Brief History of Neoliberalism*. New York: Oxford University Press.

Harvey, David. 2012. *Rebel Cities: From the Right to the City to the Urban Revolution*. London and New York: Verso.

hooks, bell. 1992. *Black Looks: Race and Representation*. Boston: South End Press.

Klein, Naomi. 2007. *The Shock Doctrine: The Rise of Disaster Capitalism*. New York: Metropolitan Books/Henry Holt.

Marcus, George. 1995. "Ethnography in/of the World System: The Emergence of Multi-Sited Ethnography." *Annual Review of Anthropology* 24: 95–117.

Marx, Karl. 1992. *Capital: Vol. 1, A Critique of Political Economy*. Reprint ed. Translated by Ben Fowkes. New York: Penguin Classics.

Nussbaum, Martha. 1997. *Cultivating Humanity: A Classical Defense of Reform in Liberal Education*. Cambridge, MA: Harvard University Press.

O'Byrne, Darren, and Alexander Hensby. 2011. *Theorizing Global Studies*. New York: Palgrave Macmillan.

Robertson, Roland. 1992. *Globalization: Social Theory and Global Culture*. London: SAGE.

Rosaldo, Renato. 1989. *Culture and Truth: The Remaking of Social Analysis*. Boston: Beacon.

Said, Edward. 1993. *Culture and Imperialism*. New York: Knopf.

Said, Edward. 1994. *Orientalism*. Rev. ed. New York: Vintage.

Sassen, Saskia. 1998. *Globalization and Its Discontents*. New York: New Press.

Sen, Amartya. 1999. *Development as Freedom*. New York: Knopf.

Shohat, Ella, and Robert Stam. 1994. *Unthinking Eurocentrism: Multiculturalism and the Media*. London and New York: Routledge.

Smith, Adam. 1976. *An Inquiry into the Nature and Causes of the Wealth of Nations*. Edited by R. H. Campbell and A. S. Skinner. Oxford: Oxford University Press.

Smith, Jackie. 2008. *Social Movements for Global Democracy*. Baltimore: Johns Hopkins University Press.

Spivak, Gayatri Chakravorty. 1987. *In Other Worlds: Essays in Cultural Politics*. New York: Methuen.

Stoddard, Eve Walsh, and Grant Cornwell. 2003. "Peripheral Visions: Towards a Geoethics of Citizenship." *Liberal Education* 89, no. 3: 44–51. https://www.aacu.org/publications-research/periodicals/peripheral-visions-towards-geoethics-citizenship.

Strange, Susan. 1988. *States and Markets*. London: Pinter.

Wallerstein, Immanuel. 2004. *World-Systems Analysis: An Introduction*. Durham, NC: Duke University Press.

Zinn, Howard. 1999. *A People's History of the United States: 1492–Present*. 20th anniversary ed. New York: HarperCollins.

# 2

# A History of Globalization

The field of global studies developed as a response to the proliferation of global processes known collectively as globalization. As explained in Part One, these processes are not confined to any one discipline, interconnecting and spanning as they do such disparate phenomena as climate change, outsourcing, migration, transnational corporations, social networks, antiwar movements, human rights, gender and sexuality issues, world musics, and more. Also noted in Part One is the fact that the word *globalization* entered into popular discourse long after the phenomena it describes began. The term itself has been transformed from a new and contested word to a commonplace, if ambiguous, buzzword. Its ambiguity derives from the fact that it functions as shorthand for a vast number of related concepts and phenomena.

While the focus of this volume is on the social and cultural aspects of globalization, they cannot be entirely separated from the political and economic aspects. Both are related to the weakening of state borders and the proliferation of transnational flows. The same Internet that facilitates the instantaneous transmission of money, product orders, and government surveillance also facilitates the transmission of consumer goods and YouTube videos. But before considering the historical and conceptual frameworks scholars use to analyze globalization, it is helpful to review the history and context of the term itself and how it has been understood and popularized since the early 1990s.

## Globalization as Part of the Post-1989 New World Order

One of the first scholars to define and emphasize the concept of globalization was Roland Robertson, a sociologist of religion. In 1992 Robertson published *Globalization: Social Theory and Global Culture*, defining globalization as "the compression of the world and the intensification of consciousness of the world as a whole" (8), focusing on the shift in human awareness and perception effected by the hyper-availability of knowledge about the world. Robertson also introduced the term *glocalization*, from Japanese usage, to capture the relationship between the local and the global—a classic example being McDonald's changing its menus from culture to culture. Robertson's definition of globalization emphasizes the subjective, mental impact of globalization, or the change in human consciousness brought about by an awareness of the entire world.

A few years later, several books attempted to describe the new world order of the 1990s for a more popular audience. One of the first was Benjamin Barber's *Jihad vs. McWorld*, published in 1995. Thomas Friedman, a columnist for the *New York Times* and author of many books, published *The Lexus and the Olive Tree: Understanding Globalization* in 1999; six years later he wrote one of the most popular accounts of globalization, *The World Is Flat*, which is discussed later. Both Barber and Friedman focus on the actions and reactions produced by greater connectivity in the world. Barber's book describes how the Americanization of local places—a process he calls "McWorld," invoking the plastic uniformity of McDonald's—produces a negative reaction against the West and all that it represents, a reaction he refers to as "jihad." Many people took exception to his technically inaccurate and potentially inflammatory use of the Arabic word *jihad* (which means a religious struggle that can be entirely within the individual or on behalf of the faith), but he captured the reality that many supposedly "traditional" practices are in fact a modern response to an incursion of Western ways. Barber also noted that the transnational power of both McDonaldization (economic and cultural globalization) and what he means by jihad—a violent backlash against the West and what it represents—undermines democracy. It's important to note that Barber's terms fuse the cultural with the political-economic aspects of globalization. The global presence of McDonald's restaurants is an economic phenomenon, but also a cultural one that promotes uniformity and fast food in cultures across the world. The concept of jihad is religious, but it has come to be associated with political insurgency.

Thomas Friedman's book *The Lexus and the Olive Tree* (1999) emphasizes the unanticipated consequences of distant actions and reactions in a world ever more tightly interconnected and economically integrated. It explores—mostly through anecdotes—the importance of speed in communications and the power of corporations in the new world order. The "Lexus" of the title represents capitalist consumer desire across cultures, while the "olive tree," parallel to Barber's "jihad," represents a desire for local culture and tradition. Although Friedman and Barber recognize similar tensions in their descriptions of globalization, Barber sees both globalization and the reaction against it as antidemocratic, while Friedman optimistically emphasizes the democratization wrought by the spread of computers and information and the opening of borders to global trade. Notably, these differing views are based on differing concepts of democracy. To Barber, democracy means the ability of a nation to exercise sovereignty over itself through self-determination, while Friedman refers to democratization on the individual level, as an opening of access to freedom of speech, inquiry, and entrepreneurship.

By the early years of the new millennium, many more books on globalization appeared. For example, in 2002 the Nobel Prize–winning economist Joseph Stiglitz published *Globalization and Its Discontents,* following it up five years later with *Making Globalization Work.* Around the same time, books like Jan Aart Scholte's *Globalisation: A Critical Introduction* (2000) and Manfred Steger's *Globalization: A Very Short Introduction* (2003) were published. A more scholarly book from that period is James H. Mittelman's *The Globalization Syndrome* (2000). Also in 2002, the *Stanford Encyclopedia of Philosophy* created its first entry on "Globalization," written by William Scheuerman, and in 2007 Routledge published the first *Encyclopedia of Globalization*, edited by Roland Robinson and Jan Aart Scholte.

Just as globalization is a huge and complex concept to unpack, it also carries a great deal of ideological baggage. It can be used simply to *describe* the multifaceted and interconnected processes of the world we live in, but more often, especially in popular discourse, it is invoked either with enthusiasm or scathing critique. Scholarly analyses tend to present both benefits and costs associated with the processes of globalization, often focusing on one dimension of it, such as economics or culture, health or environment. To understand the vocabulary and concepts associated with globalization today, some knowledge of key political-economic institutions and policies is necessary, precisely because so many global processes are interrelated. Advocates of free trade, and therefore of weak state boundaries, see a positive side to globalization, believing that breaking down national barriers will lead to a more productive and peaceful world. In the 1970s, for example, David Rockefeller, the prominent

American philanthropist and chairman of the Chase Manhattan Corporation for many years, declared that "broad human interests are being served best in economic terms where free market forces are able to transcend national boundaries" (quoted in Brecher and Costello 1998, 15).

---

### International Economic Institutions

#### World Bank and International Monetary Fund (IMF)

In July 1944, meetings were held in Bretton Woods, New Hampshire, to create two institutions for promoting global peace and prosperity: the World Bank (www.world bank.org) and the International Monetary Fund, or IMF (www.imf.org/). The World Bank provides technical support and guides development strategies in developing countries. The IMF's purpose is to stabilize the international monetary system. It lends money to states under economic stress, and sometimes, in return, it mandates specific economic policies, such as structural adjustment programs (SAPs). SAPs typically force countries to cut down public-sector employment and social welfare programs, open themselves to foreign investment, and dedicate their economies to increasing exports, often of single commodities such as monocrops or mineral resources. The purpose of these SAPs is to ensure that countries can make their debt payments to the IMF, but they usually lead to greater unemployment and poverty within debtor nations. The governing structure of the IMF and World Bank provides the United States with the largest percentage of votes, followed by Japan, Germany, France, and the United Kingdom, which have fairly equal shares of power.

#### World Trade Organization (WTO)

Established in 1995, the WTO's mission is to lower trade barriers among all countries: "A country should not discriminate between its trading partners and it should not discriminate between its own and foreign products, services or nationals" (www.wto. org). Implementing this mission, in effect, minimizes the sovereign authority of states to protect their own workforces or industries and privileges transnational corporations in their goals of maximizing profits by minimizing costs, whether for labor or tariffs. The workings of the WTO are largely secret, and it has the power to override democratically established policies within states.

---

## Neoliberalism, the Ideology Driving Globalization

One of the most important shapers of global capitalism was Milton Friedman (1912–2006), a Nobel Prize laureate and University of Chicago economist. As an ideologue, Friedman preached that free markets are the solution to all social and economic problems. He was relentlessly opposed to government intervention for, or even government support of, social needs, and he led the conservative war against taxes. While his ideas are now commonplace orthodoxy for many, they were not in the 1960s and 1970s. In fact, the principles of laissez-faire advocated by Friedman and implemented during the 1980s by Ronald Reagan and Margaret Thatcher were in fact a radical shift away from the dominant post-Depression policies of Milton Keynes, who advocated a mixture of capitalism regulated by governments and social welfare goals supported by governments. This shift to the current economic consensus is termed *neoliberalism*, which refers to a revival of eighteenth-century laissez-faire theories. The term can be confusing for Americans, because the word *liberal* is commonly used to describe left-of-center Democrats who believe that government should intervene to produce greater equality in society, while it is conservatives who support neoliberalism today. Policies such as using taxes to redistribute wealth; regulating industries and trade; or supporting the arts, higher education, housing, and health care are rejected by supporters of neoliberalism.

---

**Questioning Milton Friedman's Ideas**

A 2007 article about Milton Friedman's life's work in the *New York Review of Books* highlights the extent to which the worldview of many policymakers has moved closer to Friedman's perspective:

> By any measure—protectionism versus free trade; regulation versus deregulation; wages set by collective bargaining and government minimum wages versus wages set by the market—the world has moved a long way in Friedman's direction. And even more striking than his achievement in terms of actual policy changes has been the transformation of the conventional wisdom: most influential people have been so converted to the Friedman way of thinking that it is simply taken as a given that the change in economic policies he promoted has been a force for good. But has it?
>
> (Krugman 2007)

The essay distinguishes between Friedman's technical analyses as an economist and his ideological work in pushing laissez-faire policies, leaving individuals and markets alone to pursue their own self-interests.

---

Following Friedman's influence, the World Trade Organization states on its website that "the opening of national markets to international trade, with justifiable exceptions or with adequate flexibilities, will encourage and contribute to sustainable development, raise people's welfare, reduce poverty, and foster peace and stability" (World Trade Organization 2015). This statement makes clear that the WTO's goals are not strictly economic. Fostering sustainable development and increasing people's welfare are philosophical objectives that involve every aspect of human life, from the ways families are organized, to how they work, to what and how much they eat. For instance, the opening up of China's economy to free trade has led hundreds of thousands of young women to leave their villages to work in city factories. While there is an economic aspect to this, it also involves a huge social and cultural transformation, affecting families, gender roles, and daily life in rural villages and opening up a more cosmopolitan existence to factory workers, despite the often harsh conditions under which they live and work in China's cities. The same processes have led to an abundance of cheap goods in the United States—an economic effect that also changes American lifestyles by promoting overconsumption and waste.

In addition to advocating the deregulation and privatization of social enterprises, including media, pensions, and prisons, neoliberalism as a social theory takes the individual as the main unit of society, autonomous and responsible for her or his own successes and failures. For example, some neoliberals might argue that people should save on their own for retirement rather than relying on the government to provide old-age pensions or Social Security. Neoliberalism theorizes that private interests lead to public good. That is, if each individual seeks to maximize his or her wealth or happiness, the greatest sum total of wealth or happiness will be produced. This contrasts with the belief that the social collective or the state should regulate the production of wealth and social goods for the maximum benefit of society.

Thus, a major controversy over the impact of global capitalism centers on how increased wealth is distributed. Opening up a country like India or China to free trade increases the country's gross domestic product (GDP), but how widely is that growing wealth distributed? This is a question not just about income but about the way income affects quality of life and about the way class differences affect social life within a nation. If education is privatized, many people will not be able to afford it, and their life chances will be diminished. If government does not regulate television shows, the quality of programming will be affected. To give one example of the cultural impact of neoliberal policies, in postwar Britain before the 1980s, the state subsidized the arts heavily, according to Michael Billington (2013), and there was a thriving theater scene. Once subsidies were cut, ticket prices were increased to cover more of the production costs. As a result, less affluent people could no longer afford to go to the theater, and producers had to choose more commercially viable plays in order to attract tourists and affluent British people to their productions.

Debates over neoliberalism often revolve around the value of individual freedom. Within Western cultures freedom is highly valued, though not uniformly. In the United States, for example, the freedom to choose one's own doctor has been highly prized, along with the availability of high-tech medical treatments. However, these options are available only to the very wealthy who can pay for them, or to workers with good health benefits. This contrasts with a country like Cuba, where there is less freedom but excellent and widespread free medical care, with more doctors per resident than in any other country in the world, or England, where every resident is entitled to free health care but people often have to wait for long periods to see specialists or have elective surgery. Similarly, the United States prizes free speech highly, whereas a country like Canada balances the advantages of free speech against the harm of hate speech and has instituted laws against hate speech with strict penalties. The two countries are quite similar in many ways, but the former leans toward an almost absolute value on freedom, while the latter curtails freedom in order to protect certain values, as shown in the example of radio content next.

These examples illustrate the ways that neoliberal values and policies cut across economic, political, social, and cultural arenas of life. An example of how government regulation can positively affect culture while regulating free speech is the Canadian system of regulation over what kind of music is played on radio stations. This example of national protection, counter to the spirit of free trade, reflects the dual language traditions—French and English—that are a part of Canada's cultural landscape. Indeed, both French and English are important in preserving cultural production. There are seven different types of radio stations, and each is required to play a specific percentage of Canadian content. Commercial stations must play at least 35 percent Canadian content in popular music, whether French or English. The public station, CBC Radio, has to play at least 50 percent Canadian content. This promotion of national content erects a barrier against the domination of the airwaves by foreign music and shows the interconnections between politics, economics, and the arts. Because Canadian songwriters and performers have a much better chance of getting airtime on Canadian radio than they would in a globalized free-trade environment, they are encouraged to be creative and pursue their art. They are more likely to be commercially successful by selling records or giving concerts, and consequently the Canadian public is exposed to music by their fellow citizens.

A neoliberal might argue against the Canadian policy, stating that such protection keeps out exciting new music from the rest of the world, and perhaps keeps the costs higher by limiting competition. Social and cultural globalization involves many trade-offs. In the Canadian case, nation building and sovereignty are pitted against freedom of exchange and competition, while national identity is pitted against cosmopolitanism. Tight national borders can be used to promote cultural viewpoints, even to protect cultures from extinction, or they can stifle creativity through a lack of interchange. Many of the case studies in the second part of this book illustrate these kinds of trade-offs.

While other factors have played a major role in the spread of globalization, especially new technologies of communications and travel, the free-trade policies pushed by Friedman and his followers have made it difficult for less powerful states to control what happens within their borders. International financial institutions like the World Bank, the IMF, and the WTO forced these policies on many countries in the Global South just as they were finding their feet following postcolonial independence.

Stephanie Black's 2001 documentary *Life and Debt* uses the case of Jamaica to illustrate how indebtedness to the IMF along with direct military pressure from the United States kept Jamaica from developing independently. While the power exerted over Jamaica by the IMF's enforcement of structural adjustment plans (SAPs) appears to be a political-economic issue, affecting the ability of farmers to grow local crops and of men to get jobs, it also affected the social fabric of Jamaican life, including increasing violence in the society, as the film shows. See the film's website (http://www.lifeanddebt. org/) for further information.

Some critics see the economic and development policies of the IMF and World Bank as imperialist or neocolonial, with the two organizations moving into the vacuum created by European powers as they retreated from their colonies. Indeed, living under the dictates of a foreign power affects not just a nation's economy, but also its identity and quality of life, as shown by many anticolonial writers from Thomas Jefferson to Frantz Fanon to Jamaica Kincaid (Kincaid's text *A Small Place* is used by the narrator in the documentary film *Life and Debt*). Countries that became independent in the 1960s barely had a chance to establish their sovereignty before they became indebted to the IMF and subject to its policies; many were forced to shift resources into export-oriented production and away from growing food for their own people or investing in schools and hospitals. This shift often led to emigration and a fragmenting of families, and thus to new social problems. Moreover, the demise and collapse of the Soviet Union in the late 1980s and early 1990s discredited socialism and communism as alternatives to capitalism. This coincided with the consensus about market capitalism emerging from Friedman-influenced policymakers in the United States in the 1980s—referred to as the "Washington Consensus." Whereas previously the world's two "superpowers" vied with each other to control or support weaker countries, the collapse of the Soviet Union left the United States as the only superpower.

In this context of free trade and deregulation, the term *globalization* is often used as a catch-all by activists who believe that many of the problems in the world derive from the policies associated with it. The concerns of these activists range from environmental issues, including global climate change and degraded air and water quality, to economic concerns, such as the proliferation of sweatshops, job loss, and union breaking in the developed world. Activists also point to cultural issues, including the loss of traditional ways of life and languages in the developing world, as well as security concerns, including wars over natural resources, such as those in the Democratic Republic of the Congo. And many critics across the political spectrum point to growing economic deregulation coupled with the increasing transnational connections between banks as the cause of the economic recession of 2008, the worst economic crisis, according to many observers, since the Great Depression of the 1930s.

Websites relating to academic research on globalization and activism related to glo-balization include the following:

Global Research Council (http://www.globalresearchcouncil.org/)
Global Transformations (http://www.polity.co.uk/global/)
The Globalization Website (http://sociology.emory.edu/faculty/globalization/theories03.html)
International Forum on Globalization (http://www.ifg.org/)

## Historical and Conceptual Contexts for Globalization

While the word *globalization* became common in the mid-1990s to early 2000s, some of the concepts it signifies have had currency among scholars for much longer. The anthropologist Eric Wolf's book *Europe and the People Without History* (1982), for example, anticipated the development of global studies, as described in the first chapter of this book, by arguing that "populations construct their cultures in interaction with one another, and not in isolation" (ix). Thus, to study global interactions, it is necessary "to cross the lines of demarcation that separate the various human disciplines from one another, and to abrogate the boundaries between Western and non-Western history" (x). In this work, Wolf was challenging the prevalent focus in anthropology on separate, isolated "traditional" cultures, arguing that people of different cultures have been interacting with and influencing each other since the beginning of humanity. He was also challenging the European colonial view that countries of the Global South were timeless and undeveloped, "without history."

### A Timeline of Transnational Processes in the Modern Era*

1301–1922: Ottoman Empire, stretching from western Asia to Eastern Europe.

1400s–1500s: Beginning of European voyages of exploration and conquest.

1526–1857: Mughal Empire in Asia.

1600s–mid-1800s: African slave trade; accumulation of capital by Britain.

1600s–1900s: European colonization.

1800s: Industrial Revolution, including improvements in communication and transport.

1884–1885: Berlin Conference and the "Scramble for Africa."

1945: End of World War II; Bretton Woods Agreement, which establishes the World Bank and International Monetary Fund (IMF); UN Charter signed; decoloniza-tion and the Cold War set in motion.

1960: Over fifteen African countries gain independence from their European colonizers.

1989: Collapse of the Soviet Union; end of the Cold War; beginning of "new world order."

1989–1991: Creation of the World Wide Web.

1995: Founding of World Trade Organization (WTO).

1999: Anti-globalization protests at WTO meeting in Seattle.

2001: U.S. President George W. Bush begins what he calls the "war on terror."

\* If this timeline started before the modern era, it would include a number of non-Western empires from earlier periods.

The transatlantic encounters between European powers and the peoples of Africa and the Americas in the colonial era support Wolf's view. In the late fifteenth century, European empires initiated major contact among European, African, and indigenous American peoples, decimating Americans through disease and war and then transporting about twenty million kidnapped Africans to the Americas to serve as forced laborers. The ensuing transformations were vast and resulted in cataclysmic, often tragic, upheavals involving the organized movements of peoples; the mixing of cultures; creative adaptations to new environments; vast accumulation of capital; and technological innovations in transportation, discipline of workers, organization of labor, and industry—all elements of what we call globalization today. The sociologist Orlando Patterson, in fact, argues that these disruptions had profound ideological effects. In particular, he posits that slavery of Africans by Europeans actually led to the modern concept of freedom and to companion developments as well, including techniques of resistance and insurgency, powerful art forms, and other important philosophical concepts.

Since the eighteenth century, ideas such as cultural relativism (the concept that each culture has its own values that are good and right for it, but not necessarily for other cultures) and trade as a means to intercultural understanding have developed in dialogue with more exploitative relations of colonialism and conquest. Adam Smith's *Wealth of Nations* (1757) was the first full theorizing of the benefits of free trade. In 1795, following the ancient Stoics, the German philosopher Immanuel Kant wrote his *Essay on Perpetual Peace*, advocating cosmopolitanism, hospitality, and peace among nations and spelling out specific policies conducive to peace, such as having no standing armies and welcoming travelers from other countries. His work is considered a blueprint for the League of Nations, the precursor to the United Nations.

In the nineteenth century, Karl Marx's theory of capitalism and history arose as a reaction against the impact of laissez-faire and industrialization on society, and it became a major precursor to global theorizing. Marx analyzed the contradictions within capitalism, such as the idea that owners seek to maximize profits by paying workers as little as possible, which leads to a situation where the workers cannot buy the commodities the system produces. Today, that logic has led to outsourcing from Western industrialized countries, leaving workers there without manufacturing jobs. Marx argued that history was driven by class conflict caused by such contradictions. Marx also articulated a strong relationship between the economic mode of production and social and cultural values, formations, and practices. According to Marx and the scholars who have carried on his way of thinking, social phenomena can be divided into the "base" (economic mode of production) and the "superstructure" or ideology (beliefs, ideas, laws, politics, education, family). Various historical modes of economic organization and production, such as feudalism, capitalism, and socialism, have produced parallel sets of social ideas and institutions.

An example of the way Marxian analysis sees culture as a reflection of the economic mode of production is the transition from feudalism in medieval Europe to capitalism in the seventeenth through nineteenth centuries. Marx argued that the ruling ideas, or dominant ideology, in any society would reflect the interests of the ruling class. Under the feudal economic system, the aristocracy was the ruling class, while the serfs, who were agricultural laborers tied to specific places on the land, were the oppressed class. The urban craftspeople and merchants were the group from whom the next dominant class, the capitalist owners, would emerge. The Roman Catholic Church was the religious and moral basis of medieval society. Scholarly learning was controlled by the Church and reflected its hierarchies. Loyalty to authority was a key value in religion, just as it was in social life. All learned discourse was in Latin, and the serfs could not read Latin or the vernacular language, but instead had to trust the authority of the priests and the aristocracy.

Various changes led to the breakdown of feudal society and the emergence of capitalism as the dominant economic mode of production, reflected in and supported by capitalist ideology. One of the major changes that had to occur for the capitalist mode of production to succeed was the freeing of serfs and peasants from their attachment to specific estates. In Britain, where the Industrial Revolution and capitalism developed relatively early, in the eighteenth century, an ideology of freedom had also developed fairly early, as reflected in the thirteenth-century Magna Carta. Although the Magna Carta reflected a struggle between the nobility and the king, it was the beginning of a long process of limiting the power of the monarchy and introducing ideas of freedom that culminated in the Whig Revolution of 1688. Other developments that bolstered the development of capitalism and a wealthy middle class were the Protestant Reformation of the seventeenth century and the parallel Scientific Revolution, both of which broke down the Catholic Church's authority and encouraged the development of individualism. After the feudal system broke down and capitalism developed, the middle class—with values of individualism, competition, and freedom—gradually became the locus of power. Workers who had been attached to the land under feudalism ultimately, under capitalism, became free wage laborers, to be hired and fired by factories. No one was obligated to protect them, and they were free to improve their lot in life, to seek their own work, or to starve without it. In Britain these changes occurred gradually, with wealthy capitalists gaining titles and estates, blurring the boundaries between the capitalist class and the older aristocracy. In France, however, the revolution that began in 1789 signified a more violent and abrupt transition from feudalism to capitalism.

Marx's utopian *Communist Manifesto* presented socialism, and ultimately communism, as an alternative to global capitalism. In it he speculated that capitalist workers would unite to overthrow the owners of factories and other capital (the bourgeois) and take collective ownership of the means of production. While Marx's ideas helped to inspire the creation of the Soviet Union and Maoist China, many smaller movements and groups developed under Marx's ideology. His critique of capitalism and its associated values has been reinvigorated in today's debates over globalization, and most anti-globalization writing owes some debt to the Marxian tradition of thought.

## Major Conceptual Frameworks for Analyzing Globalization

Globalization today can be characterized by a range of features, including

- a weakening of national boundaries and states in the face of transnational movements of capital, people, products, ideas, illnesses, and so forth;
- considering the world as the unit of analysis as opposed to states (countries);

- increasing interconnectedness across national boundaries, especially of capital and corporations;
- increasing acceleration of communications, travel, production, and consumption; and
- increasing threats to the ecosystems of the planet caused by climate change and other environmental threats.

These are the phenomena, in varying configurations and points of view, that the following theories of globalization attempt to describe, critique, or explain. The fact that so many theories of globalization depend on metaphors reflects the difficulty scholars and other observers confront when examining the subject. Trying to grasp the world as a unit, along with its multiple layers of interconnectedness, is a complex analytical task. But while metaphors are useful, they can also be limiting, so it is helpful to think about what they illuminate, what they leave out, and what they share with each other.

## World-Systems Analysis

In the twentieth century, after Marx's theories had taken hold, a body of work considering the world as a unit of analysis developed, anticipating the post-1990 explosion of writing on globalization. World-systems theory, first formulated by Immanuel Wallerstein (b. 1930) in Volume I of *The Modern World System* (1974), analyzes global capitalism from its origins in the late fifteenth century in Europe. Although his primary field is sociology, Wallerstein anticipated global studies by arguing that knowledge about the world must be multi- or even nondisciplinary, emphasizing history. In many ways, world-systems analysis is a set of epistemological (knowledge-related) claims, methods of knowing, and guidelines for research that are well suited to an understanding of globalization. Wallerstein argues that the world must be considered as a whole, but he notes that within the world there are many institutions. In his words,

> states and the inter-state system, productive firms, households, classes, identity groups of all sorts . . . form a matrix which permits the system to operate but at the same time stimulates both the conflicts and the contradictions which permeate the system.
>
> (Wallerstein 2004, x)

He divides the labor (populations) of the world-system into the core (wealthy, developed nations), periphery (underdeveloped nations), and semiperiphery (positioned between the two, having some features of each). However, there are peripheries within cores, such as Native American reservations within the United States. Wealth, largely through raw materials, is shifted from periphery to core.

The origin of the current world-system, according to this line of thinking, is the period of European exploration and colonization, beginning with Spain and Portugal in the fifteenth century, followed by the Netherlands and then Britain as the leading powers. During the eighteenth and nineteenth centuries, capitalists became the dominant group within nation-states and were able to use state power to bolster their interests. The industrialized core was able to obtain raw materials and labor at low prices from the periphery and to develop an export market between itself and the semiperiphery and the periphery—and sometimes a market within the core itself. Thus, within the sugar and slavery economy of the late sixteenth to the mid-nineteenth centuries, Britain and France imported slave labor—virtually free, except for cost of transport and minimal sustenance—from Africa to the Caribbean to produce raw sugar, which was then transported to Europe for industrial refining. It was then consumed as white sugar both in Europe and in the colonies.

While Wallerstein's school of thought is original, it developed out of Marxist analyses of capitalism, dependency theory, and the Annales school of history, among other influences. The Marxian emphasis on contradictions within the structure of capitalism and the influence of class conflict on changing structures of dominance is important in Wallerstein's thought, while the idea of long cycles of history (the *longue durée*) and ecological regions as units of analysis derive from the Annales school. Dependency theory, a model of development from the social sciences, suggests that resources flow from underdeveloped nations to developed ones, using the terms *periphery* and *core* to categorize the nations. However, some critics of Wallerstein argue that world economies preceded the development of the European-centered capitalist economy, notably with the Mongol Empire. Others argue that Wallerstein pays too little attention to local struggles and to culture.

## Time-Space Compression

While he did not focus on the term itself, one of the earliest and most important theorists of globalization is the geographer David Harvey, whose 1989 book *The Condition of Post-modernity* introduced the concept of *time-space compression* to describe globalization. It refers, in simple terms, to the acceleration of change and the accumulation of knowledge brought about by high-speed communications and travel. For example, in the eighteenth century, when travel was dependent on sailing ships, and hence on weather and currents, the trip from New York to London took about three weeks, barring storms or calm waters. Today, a flight from New York to London takes between five and six hours. In this time-space compression, decreased travel time makes the distance feel much shorter. Whereas ship travel allows for the perception of the space being covered, airplane travel seems to erase distance; the air traveler perceives a time lapse rather than a spatial journey. An even more dramatic acceleration of time results from the electronic technology that sends ideas, commands, texts, and images over the Internet. A friend in London, for instance, can receive news from you instantaneously, while parents on the other side of town may not hear it for hours. This acceleration of information has been developing from the time of sailing ships to the invention of the telegraph (including the transatlantic cable laid in 1866), the telephone, and the fax machine. As technology has sped up the time information takes to travel, the costs for doing so have steadily decreased. In the 1980s a transatlantic phone call was quite costly. Now Skype or e-mail allows virtually free communication. In this sense, both time and space are compressed.

There is more to Harvey's theory, however. Using the acceleration of communications and travel, corporations developed "regimes of flexible accumulation," which were also made possible by the IMF's 1973 decision to float world currencies rather than keeping them at fixed exchange rates. The IMF's move allowed corporations to shift production sites in search of ever-cheaper labor costs and to move capital around quickly to more advantageous locations. For example, a can of apple juice that you purchase could have been packaged in a number of different locations, depending on local labor and currency conditions, and the can does not list the exact location where the apples were grown, but rather a set of possible countries.

Harvey points out that the speeding up of production has also reduced continuity in the lives of workers. If workers try to organize for improved benefits, the manufacturer can move production to another country. Harvey notes that "the active production of places with special qualities becomes an important stake in spatial competition between localities, cities, regions, and nations" (1989, 295). Local authorities can manipulate the characteristics of their locale to appeal to transnational corporations, including a docile workforce, low taxes, and good air transport. Thus Walmart has been able to negotiate with the Chinese government for favorable labor conditions in its effort to move into the retail space in China. Moreover, computer systems now organize last-minute workers' shifts at retailers such as Walmart, Jamba Juice, Pier One, and Aeropostale so that there are not too many or too few staff at any given time. This highly limits the predictability in workers' lives—they cannot schedule taking classes or child care in advance, for instance.

Harvey notes that consumption has also sped up. Companies like H&M and Target pioneered the fast production of cheap fashionable clothes so as not to keep them in stores for very long. Traditionally, winter clothes and summer clothes might stay in stock for four or five months. Now, however, there might be monthly shifts in fashion stocks. This contrasts with the much longer durability of goods produced domestically under the Fordist system of manufacture, which revolutionized manufacturing at the beginning of the twentieth century. Harvey foresaw the future when he observed that "ephemerality and instantaneous communicability over space then become virtues to be explored and appropriated by capitalists for their own purposes" (1989, 288). The ephemerality he refers to can be thought of as the consumption of services that are fleeting, such as massages.

---

**Fordist Production**

"Fordist production" refers to the industrial methods perfected by Henry Ford at the beginning of the twentieth century in the production of cars. In this model of production, goods are produced through a division of labor using assembly lines. Such products are fairly identical and produced for a mass market of consumers. Inventory is kept for months, and products last for years. The organization is hierarchical, and most employees stay at their jobs for decades, if not for a lifetime. Fordist production contrasts with outsourcing and globalized, flexible, just-in-time, networked production.

---

Harvey, as a critic in the Marxist tradition, sees a relationship between the mode of production and cultural behaviors and values. He links modernism (meaning, in this analysis, a belief in universal humanity, industrialization, and development and the ability of the state to protect the welfare of society) with the Fordist method of production, and postmodernism with flexible accumulation and time-space compression of globalization. Harvey believes that postmodernism is, in effect, a crisis within modernism. Some of the features of postmodernism include an emphasis on identities defined through differences, as in multiculturalism. In postmodernism, spatial relations supplant the depth of history and personal introspection. Attempts to unify understanding and experience are replaced by fragmentation and anachronistic conjunctions—like tweeting that you are part of a letter-writing club on campus, or people using cell phones in regions that lack electricity and running water. The focus is on images and image management, so that surfaces rather than deep meanings become more important. For example, Facebook and Twitter can be used to construct images of people's lives, and people can have thousands of "friends," whereas writing letters to maintain relationships with distant friends or keeping a detailed diary of one's life in book form were ways of constructing social and personal meaning before time-space compression became important.

## The Network Society

Manuel Castells (b. 1942) is an influential Spanish sociologist whose body of work, including *The Rise of the Network Society* (1996; revised 2000), among other books and articles, captures another prominent metaphor or model for globalization, one that connects the realm of culture and ideas with those of power and finance in important ways. In *The Informational City: Information Technology, Economic Restructuring, and the Urban Regional Process* (1989), he coined the term "space of flows," a key concept in this model of globalization. "Space of flows" refers to the networking of key locations around the world through both electronic communications and high-speed transportation. At the same time, Castells believes that local spaces experienced in more traditional ways—through our bodies and our emotions, or the places we walk our dogs and shop for groceries—are made less real and less important.

Castells defines globalization as the process of being able to work as a unit on a planetary scale—a process that requires technological, institutional, and organizational capacity (2010, 261–262). Institutional capacity has been created in part through neoliberal policies of deregulation and privatization. Those excluded from globalized networks are marginalized, and in response they cling to their local identities. An example of this can be seen in the case study on indigenous peoples presented later in the book.

Like world-systems analysis, Castells's "network society" articulates a research method and a set of questions for researchers to answer using that method. Telecommunications networks are Castells's model for power, production, and culture in the globalized world. In his "Network Theories of Power" lecture, Castells claims there are two main kinds of power in the network society: "power in networks" and "network-making power." The first has to do with who is in the network and who is excluded. For example, the Internet excludes millions of people in the world who do not have access to computers or regional connectivity to Internet infrastructure. Further, within networks, some people have much more power than others; they establish the protocols, set the rules, and control the terms of discourse. However a network can't be unified without central power: networks are dispersed and have to connect with each other. Castells gives the example of world-class research universities that have great power to control disciplinary discourses and to exclude the ideas of those outside their networks. For example, MIT, Castells argues, is uniquely positioned to connect with the U.S. Defense Department, and thus bring an academic network of scientific and technological knowledge together with a military network.

For further information about Castells' ideas, see the following Internet links:

- Manuel Castells's website (http://www.manuelcastells.info/en/)
- Manuel Castells's "Network Theories of Power" lecture (http://www.youtube.com/watch?v=skcUYhRaEas)

However, discourses (an important concept discussed throughout Part One) are generated in the world of ideas, through cultures, before being part of a technological network's discourses. Therefore, the second form of network power—network-making power—is more important for Castells. In a computer network, this function would be *programming*. It sets the agenda. On the level of politics, Castells cites the Bretton Woods institutions and the WTO as examples of network-making power. Certain concerns are made prominent in these agencies, and some are excluded. For instance, the WTO does not concern itself with questions such as "How can I protect my country's culture from being overwhelmed by outside influences?" or "How can I protect my country's foodways and traditions from fast food restaurants?" In fact, its mission—to break down barriers to the free flow of trade—refuses to recognize such concerns and allow them into the discourse it creates and controls.

Besides programming or setting the agenda, the other key form of network-making power is *switching*. Switches connect different networks, just as MIT connects certain kinds of knowledge with military networks. Networks are interconnected but without central control. However, disruptions in one can spread to others, which is how resistance through social action occurs. Castells's concept of *counterpower* works off the power structure of networks, in some cases subverting it. Indeed, protests organized over social networks use the media to *counter* the state's media messages and what they exclude. Castells believes that those who are excluded from network power can find meaning in their lives by disrupting the networks through political actions, such as joining the Occupy Movement.

## Clash of Cultures

Samuel Huntington (1927–2008), a controversial yet highly influential political scientist, introduced another model of globalization in his 1993 article for *Foreign Affairs* titled "The Clash of Civilizations?" Huntington spent most of his academic career at Harvard, but also co-edited the journal *Foreign Policy*. He also served as consultant to the U.S. government during the Vietnam War and as coordinator of security planning for the National Security Council during the Carter administration. In his 1993 *Foreign Affairs* article, he was responding to the demise of the Soviet Union and the end of the Cold War, and he expanded his ideas in 1996 into the book *The Clash of Civilizations and the Remaking of World Order*. His thesis is captured in the title: differences in culture would replace the ideological or economically driven conflict between capitalism and communism that had dominated the post–World War II period. Huntington was not alone in identifying cultural and identity issues as a chief driver of conflict in the post–Cold War period, as the former Yugoslavia fell apart into genocidal interethnic war (1991; 1992–1995) and Rwanda (1994) underwent an ethnicity-driven genocidal conflict during this period as well.

Virtually all theorists of globalization who are not strictly economic in their analyses note the centrality of cultural and ethnic identities as part of the reaction against globalization, including Castells, Barber, and Friedman (discussed at great length in the next section of this chapter). What makes the "clash of civilizations" metaphor relevant to theories of globalization is the emphasis on transnational culture and religion as opposed to state actors. When cultures cross state boundaries, resulting in multicultural entities, ethnic conflict can occur, as in Rwanda and Bosnia. But cultures that cross boundaries can also create regional blocs of countries with similar identities, as in Western Europe and North Africa. Thus, the major "civilizations" Huntington identifies are Western, Latin American, Islamic, Sinic (Chinese), Hindu, Orthodox, Japanese, and African. But the boundaries between them are not so clear. For example, Latin America can be considered its own space, or it can be considered part of the West. Furthermore many nations are "cleft countries," to continue with Huntington's terminology, because their populations are divided. Therefore, the whole system, as is often the case with simplified models, is not as clear as it might seem to be.

Prior to the 1989 collapse of the Soviet Union, political scientists did not typically use culture as an analytical construct. However, in the wake of the terrorist attacks of September 11, 2001, many people saw Huntington's work as prophetic, especially since, although Huntington listed many civilizations, he in fact zeroed in on clashes between Islamic societies and non-Islamic ones. He recognized that the West's drive toward universal values, such as democracy, provokes resistance in Muslims, who come from a proselytizing religious tradition. Huntington believed that cultural differences are more resistant to change than are political ones, though political, cultural, and economic differences are often intertwined. In the end, Huntington's predicted clash is a binary one—either between the West and everyone else, or between the West and Islam. His thesis has been harshly criticized on a number of bases, among them the idea that there should be a dialogue among civilizations (proposed, in fact, by President Mohammad Khatami of Iran prior to September 11, 2001) and that societies are not and should not be homogeneous but should value diversity.

Huntington argued that if the West is to maintain its dominance then it must strengthen itself culturally. The U.S. application of this can be seen in his 2004 book *Who Are We?: The Challenges to America's National Identity.* In this book he considers Latino immigration a threat to American identity, bringing as it does a second language and different culture into prominence in the United States. It is interesting to note that his theory of global realities, like Thomas Friedman's, led him to worry about a threat to American hegemony.

## A Flat World

Thomas Friedman (b. 1953), mentioned earlier, is a prolific, three-time Pulitzer Prize–winning writer; foreign affairs columnist for the *New York Times* since 1995; and popularizer of economic and political topics. Friedman has had a long-standing interest in the Middle East, having studied abroad in Egypt and Jerusalem, and having begun his journalism career as a reporter in Beirut from 1979 to 1981. Influenced by time he spent in India, he wrote *The World Is Flat: A Brief History of the Twenty-First Century* (2005), a best-selling book on globalization. He followed it in 2008 with *Hot, Flat, and Crowded: Why We Need a Green Revolution—and How It Can Renew America.* This book argues that the United States has lost its way and that the key to revitalization is innovative technologies to address climate change and other environmental issues. Written anecdotally, Friedman's books on globalization cannot really be compared with those of scholars like Wallerstein, Harvey, and Castells, but the metaphor of the flat world has been influential in popular discourse, and in many ways Friedman represents the pro-globalization perspective of the United States and the global elite.

Friedman's metaphor for the globalized world—flatness—was inspired by the comment of an Indian businessman who told him that the playing field of the world is being leveled. The metaphor of flatness is an ironic twist on the story of Christopher Columbus's "discovery" of the New World, which he mistook for India—a misrecognition that led to the global rise of Europe and North America. In Friedman's flat world, electronic communications are far more important than ship travel, so the physical shape of the planet is much less important than it was in 1492. Friedman emphasizes the compression of space in the Internet age that has enabled outsourcing and global supply chains. These global production methods enable corporations to cut costs in a difficult economic climate, and they bring jobs to developing countries, but Friedman worries about the future of American workers in light of the competitive, cheap labor provided by India and China.

Friedman's metaphor of the world's flatness is not just about geography, but also about ethics. Leveling the playing field involves justice, which requires the removal of the unfair advantages and privileges of the powerful. People in the United States, as an example, will have to relinquish some of their privileges if the playing field is indeed to be leveled. Friedman also acknowledges that the world is not flat for everyone, because millions of people still live in poverty with no access to the Internet or to the kind of education that fosters global entrepreneurship.

## The Race to the Bottom

This "race to the bottom" metaphor for globalization derives from what is called a different "angle of vision" in Chapter One. An ironic play on the promise of economic neoliberalism, the model describes circumstances that are often reproduced across the globe as free trade encourages competition between producers of goods: such open-market deregulation lowers wages, reduces the quality of life of workers, and threatens the welfare of a society. It represents the viewpoint of those opposed to globalization; those who participate in social movements against various manifestations of globalization; and those who desire local control over the food they grow and eat, the cultural performances they produce and enjoy, and the jobs available to them.

The "race to the bottom" metaphor for globalization challenges the supposed benefits of free trade and of the transfer of local and national power to transnational corporations and global institutions like the WTO. The 1999 Seattle protests against the WTO catalyzed alliances among very different interest groups, including women's organizations, environmentalists, and people of color, on the basis of a shared belief that big, especially multinational, corporations have a destructive impact on quality of life in multiple ways.

The metaphor of a "race to the bottom" comes from a guide to anti-globalization activism called *Global Village or Global Pillage: Economic Reconstruction from the Bottom Up* (1998) by Jeremy Brecher and Tim Costello. Social movements in the age of globalization, many taking a lead from Brecher and Costello, have achieved rapid interconnection, facilitated by cell phone and social networking technologies. Protests against the WTO, policies of the Group of 8 (or G8, a group of the wealthiest countries in the world), and the 2003 war in Iraq, along with Vandana Shiva's "March Against Monsanto" and Greenpeace campaigns against genetically modified organisms (GMOs), are a few examples of anti-globalization social movements. A popular 2000 guide to anti-globalization activism, *Globalize This*, called for global grassroots revolution to take back democratic control from corporate power. Immediately after the Seattle WTO protests of December 1999, Naomi Klein published *No Logo: Taking Aim at the Brand Bullies*. The World Social Forum is an annual meeting of nongovernmental organizations (NGOs) opposed to globalization; their first meeting was at Porto Alegre in Brazil in 2001.

As applied to contemporary globalization, the "race to the bottom" describes the consequences of competition among different locations to provide cheaper labor, lower taxes, and fewer regulations in order to attract businesses and, on the consumer side, sell products and services at the lowest prices. The phrase represents a popular critique of the economic policies of neoliberalism, deregulation, and privatization that have led to a shift away from manufacturing in developed areas like the United States and Europe. The costs of production in the postwar West became relatively high because trade unions were able to bargain for good wages and benefits, while governments created regulations to protect the health and safety of workers and curb pollution of the natural environment.

At the same time technological developments in transportation and communications made it feasible to locate different segments of production in various countries. This led to free-trade agreements like the North American Free Trade Agreement (NAFTA) in 1994 and the creation of the WTO in 1995. The dismantling of trade barriers in the 1980s and 1990s facilitated the movements of raw materials and products. Thus, for example, automobiles went from being produced in specific countries, notably the United States, Japan, and several Western European countries, to being *assembled* in those countries out of parts produced all over the world. Factory production became highly mobile and flexible, going where the cost of labor was cheap, workers were docile, and taxes were low or nonexistent.

The outsourcing of manufacturing or services such as call centers is touted as beneficial to all because new jobs are created in developing countries, while consumers in the Global North are able to buy large quantities of inexpensive consumer goods, such as clothing. Stores such as Walmart, Target, H&M, and Primark sell clothes at prices that would have been unimaginable in the 1970s, enabling consumers to buy new clothes frequently, often updating their wardrobes every season. But this abundance of cheap goods affects workers around the world, while also creating the conditions for environmental degradation.

Indeed, the underside of this explosion in cheap goods is the inhumane conditions under which the factory workers in developing countries toil. As mentioned in Part One, the May 2013 collapse of a Bangladesh facility, the Rana Plaza factory complex, where the Irish firm Primark's clothes were made, illustrates the consequences of the "race to the bottom." When the poorly built building collapsed, 1,127 people were killed. The owner and the factory boss had refused to let the workers leave when cracks were noticed in the building a few days earlier. After the collapse, which followed a notorious fire in November 2012 in another Bangladesh factory where Gap clothes were made, a number of clothing companies—including H&M, Marks & Spencer, Tesco, Primark, Zara's parent company Inditex, Mango, Benetton, and PVH (owner of Calvin Klein and Tommy Hilfiger)—signed an agreement to improve factory safety in Bangladesh, but Gap refused. Western clothing manufacturers have been drawn to Bangladesh because it is the country with the lowest minimum wage in the world ($38 a month). In fact, 80 percent of Bangladesh's exports are in the clothing sector.

> Information about the Accord on Fire and Building Safety in Bangladesh, calls to action, and personal testimonies are available at the UNI Global Union website (http://www.unibangladeshaccord.org/?lang=en). An up-to-date list of the companies that have signed the accord can be found on the "Signatories" page (http://www.unibangladeshaccord.org/?page_id=139).

The "race to the bottom" affects all the countries in the world. For example, within the U.S. working class, people in the Rust Belt and other areas have lost good manufacturing jobs with pensions and benefits as their work has been outsourced beyond U.S. borders. This high-quality employment has been replaced with part-time, low-paying jobs without benefits. In hopes of attracting manufacturing back, local workforces are typically pressured to take lower pay and stay non-unionized. Further, localities offer corporations tax incentives and access to government services, such as free water. This in turn reduces the tax base, setting in motion a classic "race to the bottom": cutbacks in government services likely result in the loss of jobs in the public sector, which affects the quality of schools; loss of tax revenue likely results in reduced policing and street cleaning, making the area less attractive to live in. And the cycle goes on.

Walmart illustrates the way globalization cuts across national borders, resulting in an increasing gap between the wealthy and the poor, as well as the way transnational corporations are able to circumvent democratic processes. Walmart employs more people in the United States than any other private company, meaning it holds a tremendous power in the labor market. In 2012, despite the fact that its revenues were 444 billion dollars, the majority of its employees with children were living below the poverty line. As the largest importer of goods from China, it is able to negotiate directly with the Chinese government for favorable terms; in fact, Walmart acts and is received abroad more like a state than a company. Consumers want the cheap products Walmart offers, states want the jobs, and Walmart has the power to silence opposition, despite many lawsuits by employees.

---

For more information on Walmart and activism against it, see the following articles:

"How Walmart Is Changing China," *The Atlantic* (http://www.theatlantic.com/magazine/archive/2011/12/how-walmart-is-changing-china/308709/)
"Suing Wal-Mart: Bad Business Practices Lead to Litigation," *Washington Times* (http://www.washingtontimes.com/news/2014/dec/31/suing-wal-mart-bad-business-practices-lead-litigat/?page=all)
"Walmart Outlines Own Bangladesh Safety Plans," BBC News (http://www.bbc.co.uk/news/business-22535653)

---

## Global Destruction

Another negative view of globalization focuses on its potentially devastating environmental effects, including the damage being done to the planet and its climate by excessive consumption of energy and cheap goods, particularly in more developed countries, and the possibility of irreversible and unknown ecological effects of GMOs, a development relating to the urgent question of food security for a rapidly expanding global population. Two case studies in Part Two of this book relate to environmental destruction: "Climate Change and Changing Global Imaginaries" and "Indigenous Peoples and Intellectual Property Rights." As the climate-change case study illustrates, ecologists and environmentalists have come up with a variety of ways to imagine both a healthy Earth and a damaged one, and the environmental slogan, "Think globally, act locally," so appropriate to global studies, has been on bumper stickers since the 1970s. The Gaia hypothesis, discussed in the case study, is also a way to imagine taking the world as a unit of analysis, with all its parts working together as a whole. The indigenous people case study shows how food security and the rights of indigenous peoples to their own agricultural patrimony are wrapped up in the actions and politics of multinational corporations.

There are multiple aspects of global environmental degradation, including pollution of water and air, global warming, desertification, and loss of species diversity, many of which are interconnected issues resulting from human processes of production and consumption. Food security (related to weather, land ownership, and trade relations) and global climate change produced by the emissions of greenhouse gases are two of the biggest issues facing the global population today. People in wealthy nations consume more and more cheap goods made elsewhere, and people in developing countries, exposed to Western-style consumption (through participating in export manufactures or consuming Hollywood films and television shows), have increased their consumption levels as well. As discussed in the section earlier on the "race to the bottom" view of globalization, a disincentive for developing countries to impose environmental regulations exists, in that a more robust regulatory environment will make them less attractive to transnational corporations seeking cheap production facilities and labor.

Global environmental issues can be explored in the following online resources:

"Doha Climate Gateway," UN Framework Convention on Climate Change (http://
unfccc.int/key_steps/doha_climate_gateway/items/7389.php)
Farmer-to-Consumer Legal Defense Fund (http://www.farmtoconsumer.org/
news_wp/?p=1752)
Friends of the Earth Europe (http://www.foeeurope.org/gmos)
GMO-Free Europe (http://www.gmo-free-regions.org/)
Greenpeace (http://www.greenpeace.org/international/en)
Info Center about Genetically Modified Organisms (http://www.infomg.ro/web/en/
GMOs_in_Europe/)
"Kyoto Protocol," UN Framework Convention on Climate Change (http://unfccc.
int/kyoto_protocol/items/2830.php)
Seed Freedom (http://seedfreedom.in/)
350.org (http://350.org/en/mission)
"Wangari Maathai," The Green Belt Movement (http://www.greenbeltmovement.
org/wangari-maathai)

Both local and global social movements have sprung up to counter the global processes of environmental degradation, such as Wangari Maathai's Green Belt Movement in Kenya and the Chipko movement in India, which fights deforestation. Global climate change, however, is by its nature everywhere at once, and it must therefore be fought through global movements. The Kyoto Protocol, adopted under the auspices of the United Nations in 1997 and put into effect in 2005, was the first global recognition of the seriousness of greenhouse gas emissions. It committed Kyoto signatories to reducing emissions to specific levels by 2012. The United States, however, which was the largest contributor of such emissions until the early 2010s (when China overtook it), did not ratify the protocol, a shortfall that seriously weakened the accord. Nonetheless, the United States has, by many accounts, met what would have been its target to reduce carbon dioxide ($CO_2$) emissions, though the reduction came from a slowdown in the economy and an increase in the use of natural gas for energy. As with many environmental issues, trade-offs come into play: while natural gas produces considerably less greenhouse gas emissions, it is itself a source of considerable environmental concern due to its method of extraction—hydraulic fracturing, commonly called "fracking."

An amendment was made to the Kyoto Protocol in 2012, called the Doha Amendment. It extends and expands the goals of the Kyoto Treaty in light of the greater acceptance today of the reality of climate change. It was followed up in December 2015 with the "Paris Agreement," which will go into effect in 2020 if it is ultimately ratified by enough states. However, some activists fear that will be too late. For example, the environmental writer and activist Bill McKibben, who published *The End of Nature* in 1989, founded the global campaign 350.org to stop global warming. The name stands for the safe level of $CO_2$ in the earth's atmosphere (350 parts per million), according to McKibben, a measurement that now is at 392 parts per million. Allied with 350.org is a worldwide network of young people called Global Power Shift that uses new methods of organizing and training to halt climate change. In June 2013 a summit was held in Istanbul, from which the five hundred representatives returned to their home countries to spread their activism across the world. On September 13, 2014, the largest climate march ever, organized by McKibben and his followers, took place in New York City.

Climate change and food production are interconnected. Wealthy populations consume a great deal of beef, requiring vast amounts of grain to be grown for cattle, not people. But cattle are one of the main causes of global warming. According to a 2006 UN report, 30 percent of the Earth's surface is used for pasturage of livestock and for the production of grain for their consumption:

> When emissions from land use and land use change are included, the livestock sector accounts for 9 per cent of $CO_2$ deriving from human-related activities, but produces a much larger share of even more harmful greenhouse gases. It generates 65 per cent of human-related nitrous oxide, which has 296 times the Global Warming Potential (GWP) of $CO_2$. Most of this comes from manure. And it accounts for respectively 37 per cent of all human-induced methane (23 times as warming as $CO_2$), which is largely produced by the digestive system of ruminants, and 64 per cent of ammonia, which contributes significantly to acid rain.
>
> (United Nations 2006)

One of the ethical problems facing the global community is the inequitable consumption of goods and energy. In particular, as China, with a population approaching one and a half billion of the world's seven billion, continues to develop economically and increases aggregate consumption, its environmental footprint will expand as well. Many commentators and policymakers in the developed nations, however, seem to suggest that China should curb its own growth while not reducing their own. In an ideal world new green technologies would solve the problem transnationally, but such technological solutions are a long way off.

---

**Getting Involved Globally**

The social movements around environmental issues and consumer choices are a prime opportunity for young people to become involved and have a voice in change. Local movements such as farmers' markets, small organic farms, and community-supported agriculture (CSA) can be networked with global movements like Global Power Shift and 350.org. The same is true of campus-based environmental awareness campaigns and organizations to support greener methods of transportation. College students have also made important changes with other kinds of organizations related to globalization, such as the United Students Against Sweatshops. Social media and blogs offer unprecedented possibilities for networking with others around the world, posting videos and pictures documenting abuses, and learning from what others are doing. Student-based global movements include the following:

Global Power Shift (http://globalpowershift.org/)
United Students Against Sweatshops (http://usas.org/)
United Students for Fair Trade (https://maizepages.umich.edu/organization/usft/about)

---

Also related to food security are concerns about genetically modified organisms and farmers' livelihoods in the face of multinational agribusiness. Vandana Shiva's movement, Seed Freedom, based in India, is a leader in efforts to protect farmers' rights to save and use their own seeds, a seemingly simple and straightforward issue. Traditionally, farmers saved the seeds for the next and future years' harvests from their most well-adapted plants, those that had naturally adjusted to local conditions of soil, insects, water, and climate. Over the past century, various technological efforts have been made to "improve" crops by making them resistant to pests or to produce fruit that could be shipped long distances. One of the most recent technological developments is that of GMOs, which are controversial not only due to their unknown health and environmental effects, but also because of the way corporations that develop them use their outsized marketplace power to deploy them. As discussed in the case study on indigenous peoples, primarily in relation to South America, Shiva's activism—known worldwide—focuses on India, where farmers are compelled to register their seeds and pay for them when contamination from seeds patented by transnational corporations such as Monsanto occurs. This ethically questionable policy leads both to a loss of biodiversity (as corporate seed control promotes the use of specifically modified varieties) and to indebtedness for farmers, many of whom have killed themselves as a result.

While the United States grows 50 percent of the world's GMO crops, there is much hostility toward GMOs in Europe. Some countries, such as Germany, ban them, and the European Union (EU) requires that food products containing GMOs be labeled as such. In 2006 the United States, along with Canada and Argentina, brought suit through the WTO against the EU's moratorium on GMOs in a textbook example of economic globalization at work, showing how globalized institutions can override laws passed by other entities to protect their citizens. However, although the EU lifted its ban, it allows individual countries to pass their own restrictions. And even though the United States supported the WTO suit against the EU and doesn't require labeling of GMO products, internal pressure is rising against GMOs. There is a movement to ban them from infant formula, since much formula contains soy protein, and soybeans are one of the common GMO crops in the United States. Anti-GMO activity is happening at the state level also. In July 2014, Vermont became the first state to require GMO labeling, but the state is being threatened with lawsuits from the agriculture industry, and pressure is mounting in Congress to void the ability of states to pass such individual laws. Many other states are considering such regulations, however, and there is evidence that food manufacturers, despite the difficulties involved in complying with individual state regulations, are quietly getting ready for eventual labeling requirements on a national scale.

In the end, GMOs are a way in which multinational corporate capital can gain control over agriculture. Many seeds are specifically adapted to withstand large amounts of herbicide and pesticide. The companies engaged in developing GMOs—which stand to profit from them—no doubt believe they are promoting stronger plants that will be more efficient to produce, but the long-term consequences are unknown. In the eyes of activists, the GMO controversy is one more way in which cavalier attitudes about global environmental processes and interconnectedness—and the reluctance and inability to institute effective worldwide regulation—may threaten global destruction.

## References and Further Research

Anderson, Sarah, John Cavanagh, and Thea Lee. 2005. *The Field Guide to the Global Economy*. Rev. ed. New York: New Press.

Appadurai, Arjun. 1996. "Disjuncture and Difference in the Global Cultural Economy." In *Modernity at Large: Cultural Dimensions of Globalization*, 27–43. Minneapolis: University of Minnesota Press.

Barber, Benjamin R. 1995. *Jihad vs. McWorld*. New York: Times Books.

Billington, Michael. 2013. "Margaret Thatcher Casts a Long Shadow over Theatre and the Arts." *The Guardian*, April 8. http://www.theguardian.com/stage/2013/apr/08/margaret-thatcher-long-shadow-theatre.

Blackwell, Richard. 2012. "Ontario loses WTO Ruling on Green Energy Policies." *Toronto Globe and Mail*, October 15, n.p.

Brecher, Jeremy, and Tim Costello. 1998. *Global Village or Global Pillage: Economic Reconstruction from the Bottom Up*. 2nd ed. Boston: South End Press.

Castells, Manuel. 1989. *The Informational City: Information Technology, Economic Restructuring, and the Urban-Regional Process*. Oxford: Blackwell.

———. 1996. *The Rise of Network Society*. Malden, MA: Blackwell.

———. 2001a. "Epilogue: Informationalism and the Network Society." In *The Hacker Ethic and the Spirit of the Information Age*, edited by Pekka Himanen, 155–178. New York: Random House.

———. 2001b. "The Network Society and Organizational Change." Interview with Manuel Castells, by Harry Kreisler. http://globetrotter.berkeley.edu/people/Castells/castells-con4.html.

———. 2004. *The Power of Identity: Vol. 2 of The Information Age: Economy, Society and Culture*. Malden, MA: Blackwell.

———. 2010. "The New Public Sphere: Global Civil Society, Communication Networks, and Global Governance." In Globalization: The Greatest Hits, *a* Global Studies Reader, edited by Manfred B. Steger, 259–276. Boulder, CO: Paradigm.

Central Intelligence Agency. 2013. "Field Listing: Sex Ratios." In *The World Factbook*. https://www.cia.gov/library/publications/the-world-factbook/fields/2018.html.

Danaher, Kevin, and Roger Burbach, eds. 2000. *Globalize This! The Battle Against the World Trade Organization and Corporate Rule*. Monroe, ME: Common Courage Press.

Falk, Richard. 1999. *Predatory Globalization: A Critique*. Cambridge, UK: Polity Press.

Friedman, Thomas. 1999. *The Lexus and the Olive Tree: Understanding Globalization*. New York: Farrar, Straus and Giroux.

———. 2005. *The World Is Flat: A Brief History of the Twenty-First Century*. New York: Farrar, Straus and Giroux.

———. 2008. *Hot, Flat, and Crowded: Why We Need a Green Revolution—and How It Can Renew America*. New York: Farrar, Straus and Giroux.

Habermas, Jürgen. 2001. *The Postnational Constellation: Political Essays*. Cambridge, MA: MIT Press.

Harvey, David. 1989. *The Condition of Postmodernity: An Enquiry Into the Origins of Cultural Change*. Oxford: Blackwell.

Held, David. 1995. *Democracy and the Global Order: From the Modern State to Cosmopolitan Governance*. Stanford, CA: Stanford University Press.

Held, David, Anthony McGrew, David Goldblatt, and Jonathan Perraton. 1999. *Global Transformations: Politics, Economics and Culture*. Stanford, CA: Stanford University Press.

Huntington, Samuel. 1996. *The Clash of Civilizations and the Remaking of World Order*. New York: Simon & Schuster.

———. "Samuel Huntington on the 'Clash of Civilizations'." Interview by Charlie Rose. http://www.youtube.com/watch?v=3SNicJRcUqs.

Jones, Charles. 1999. *Global Justice: Defending Cosmopolitanism*. Oxford: Oxford University Press.

Kant, Immanuel. 1795. *An Essay on Perpetual Peace*. Available online from Internet Archive, at http://www.archive.org/stream/perpetualpeaceph00kantuoft/perpetualpeaceph00kantuoft_djvu.txt.

Klein, Naomi. 2000. *No Logo: Taking Aim at the Brand Bullies*. New York: Picador.

Krugman, Paul. 2007. "Who Was Milton Friedman?" *New York Review of Books*, February 15. http://www.nybooks.com/articles/archives/2007/feb/15/who-was-milton-friedman/.

Kymlicka, Will. 1999. "Citizenship in an Era of Globalization: Commentary on Held." In *Democracy's Edges*, edited by Ian Shapiro and Casiano Hacker-Cordon, 127–133. Cambridge: Cambridge University Press.

Lovelock, James E., and Lynn Margulis. 1974. "Atmospheric Homeostasis by and for the Biosphere: The Gaia Hypothesis." *Tellus* 26, no. 1–2: 2–10.

McKibben, Bill. 1989. *The End of Nature*. New York: Random House.

McMichael, Philip. 2008. *Development and Social Change: A Global Perspective*. 4th ed. Thousand Oaks, CA: Pine Forge Press.

Mittelman, James H. 2000. *The Globalization Syndrome: Transformation and Resistance*. Princeton, NJ: Princeton University Press.

Nest, Michael. 2011. *Coltan*. Cambridge, UK: Polity Press.

Nike, Inc. 2013. "Manufacturing." http://nikeinc.com/pages/manufacturing.

Organisation for Economic Co-operation and Development. 2006. "International Migrant Remittances and Their Role in Development." In *International Migration Outlook: Annual Report 2006*. Paris: Organisation for Economic Co-operation and Development. https://www.oecd.org/els/mig/38840502.pdf.

Peled, Micha X., dir. 2001. "Store Wars: When Wal-Mart Comes to Town." In *Independent Lens*, PBS. http://www.pbs.org/itvs/storewars/stores3.html.

Robertson, Roland. 1992. *Globalization: Social Theory and Global Culture*. London: SAGE.

Sassen, Saskia. 1991. *The Global City: New York, London, and Tokyo*. Princeton: Princeton University Press.

Schaeffer, Robert K. 2003. *Understanding Globalization: The Social Consequences of Political, Economic, and Environmental Change*. 2nd ed. Lanham, MD: Rowman and Littlefield.

Scheuerman, William. 2014. "Globalization." In *The Stanford Encyclopedia of Philosophy*, edited by Edward N. Zalta. http://plato.stanford.edu/entries/globalization/.

Scholte, Jan Aart. 1996. "Beyond the Buzzword: Towards a Critical Theory of Globalization." In *Globalization: Theory and Practice*, edited by Eleonore Kofman and Gillians Young, 43–57. London: Pinter.

———. 2000. *Globalization: A Critical Introduction*. New York: St. Martin's.

Schell, Orville. 2011."How Walmart Is Changing China." *The Atlantic*, December. http://www.theatlantic.com/magazine/archive/2011/12/how-walmart-is-changing-china/308709/.

So, Alvin Y. 1990. *Social Change and Development: Modernization, Dependency, and World-Systems Theories*. Newbury Park, CA: SAGE.

Steger, Manfred B. 2003. *Globalization: A Very Short Introduction*. Oxford: Oxford University Press.

Stiglitz, Joseph. 2002. *Globalization and Its Discontents*. New York: W. W. Norton.

———. 2007. *Making Globalization Work*. New York: W. W. Norton.

Tomlinson, John. 1999. *Globalization and Culture*. Chicago: University of Chicago Press.

UNI Global Union. "The Accord on Fire and Building Safety in Bangladesh." http://www.uniglobalunion.org.

United Nations. 2006. "Rearing Cattle Produces More Greenhouse Gases than Driving Cars, UN Report Warns." *UN News Center*, November 29. http://www.un.org/apps/news/story.asp?newsID=20772#.V9GzJxTCSOo.

Virilio, Paul. 1977. *Speed and Politics*. Los Angeles: Semiotext[e], 1986.

Wallerstein, Immanuel. 2004. *World Systems Analysis: An Introduction*. Durham, NC: Duke University Press.

Wolf, Eric R. 1982. *Europe and the People Without History*. Berkeley: University of California Press.

World Trade Organization. 2015. "What Is the WTO: Overview." https://www.wto.org/english/thewto_e/whatis_e/whatis_e.htm.

Zolo, Danilo. 1997. *Cosmopolis: Prospects for World Government*. Cambridge, UK: Polity Press.

# 3

# Key Concepts and Processes in the Globalization of Culture

Because the processes of globalization are so complex and their effects so widely dispersed, they have required new multidisciplinary concepts to analyze them. In the realm of culture, an increased pace of cross-cultural encounter and transnational exposure to foreign media, styles, and ideas has raised many questions about the impact of globalizing or Westernizing forces on local, or "traditional," societies. These forces include a wide range of phenomena, from the increasing dominance of the English language as the language of air traffic control, the Internet, and much transnational business to the global popularity of Latin American telenovelas and the spread of McDonald's and Thai food around the world.

Understanding these debates and the theoretical lenses used to analyze them requires an understanding of the complex term *culture*, including how it has been defined in different academic disciplines. The borders of these disciplines need to be crossed to engage with the processes of cultural globalization. Moreover, each discipline has developed analytical tools to deal with cultural phenomena, and in global studies these tools can be combined. The following are three different uses of the concept of *culture* that have historically been studied in different disciplines:

- First, there is "high" culture, which includes various forms of classical music, dance, literature, theater, and fine arts. Many societies have had their own specific forms of high culture, such as Indian classical dance, Persian poetry, and Japanese Noh theater, as well as the familiar European artistic "masterpieces." These have been studied academically in the disciplines of the arts and literature.
- Second, there is the culture of everyday life as studied by anthropologists, including what a particular society believes, how it organizes its families and its work, what kinds of symbols and rituals are practiced around major life events, and so forth.
- Third, there is the arena of mass or popular culture, mostly manufactured or mass-produced, such as comics, radio and television shows, films, posters, popular music, and so on. These were traditionally the province of sociology or communications studies.

Despite these three different meanings of culture, the realities of new communications media and travel, increased transnational migration, and the cultural revolutions from the 1960s to the 1980s led to a blurring of the boundaries between these arenas and to a new interdisciplinary approach called *cultural studies*, which used the analytical tools of literary and artistic analysis to study mass and popular culture. Simultaneously, the discipline of anthropology went through a revolution in which it started to draw on literary analysis, self-critique, and a focus on Western societies, thus breaking down some of the differences between it and the other two arenas of cultural study. Another field, *postcolonial studies*, emerged as scholars from newly independent nations talked back to the Eurocentric preoccupations of their former colonizers. Scholars and texts from the Global South—from African, Caribbean, Latin American, Indian, and other societies outside the West—shifted the subject matter and perspectives used to analyze culture.

Part of cultural globalization is the recognition that there are minority cultures within societies. *Multiculturalism* is the label given to the cultural and political differences that exist within most societies to varying degrees due to migration and conquest. These groups have altered the way culture is studied, not just through academic interventions in the curriculum, but also through social movements, such as the Black Power movement, AIM (American Indian Movement), and Chicano movements in the United States, or the protests of the North African populations in France and the Québéquois population in Canada. The demand for recognition by such diverse groups within many societies is a major phenomenon of the post–Cold War period.

Thus, both transnationally and within nations, cultures and languages have intermingled and mixed, and as a result of the processes of globalization and new media since the mid-1980s, most have changed, and some are close to disappearing. While cultures are always evolving in response to new ideas and influences, both dominant elite cultures and less powerful cultures have been affected at an accelerated pace. This is part of what has been labeled the *postmodern* condition, a world with fragmented and incoherent differences arrayed across spaces with different temporalities and alternative modernities. Traditionally, in Western cultures, there has been a linear sense of progress and development, an "imaginary" of modernity, in which societies progress along a line from sustainable agriculture to urbanization and industrialization. In today's world that line is fragmented and disrupted: you can visit a family in rural Kenya that does not have electricity or indoor plumbing, but does own a television running off a car battery and a cell phone operating via satellite. You can go to Cuba with its state-of-the-art medicine and see oxen being used to plow the land and 1957 U.S. cars next to 1980s Soviet cars and contemporary buses from China. You can see an Indian Muslim procession in Trinidad performed in its nineteenth-century form, though it has disappeared from modern India. You can have a friend in college in the United States who goes home on vacation to a village in Nepal that is a five-day trek up a mountain from the end of the nearest road.

Another aspect of the contemporary postmodern condition is the way digital "reality" sometimes seems more real than actual reality and actual reality can be distanced to a sense of unreality by digital media. Young people text friends sitting next to them at a bar rather than talking to them face to face. You remember it's your sister's birthday when you see it on Facebook. When you travel to visit the Grand Canyon or the Statue of Liberty or the Eiffel Tower, your reaction is that it looks just like what you have seen repeatedly in the movies, reversing the relations of "original" and "copy," or real and simulacrum, a phenomenon noted by the French sociologist Jean Baudrillard. "Reality" television shows confuse the boundaries between fiction and reality. And war can be confused with war games, as in the Iraq War, when some soldiers expressed the sensation that dropping bombs felt like playing a video game.

New theoretical questions, concepts, and approaches have been developed to analyze these disjunctive phenomena. Key concepts and processes are introduced later, and the case studies in this book will examine in depth a set of selected issues raised by social and cultural globalization.

## Cultural Imperialism

*Cultural imperialism* is the claim that Western, particularly American, culture is invading and dominating societies everywhere and homogenizing global cultures. During the earlier period of European colonization, specific colonies were pressured to adopt aspects of the colonizer's culture, such as religion and language, but these power imbalances resulted from specific one-on-one relationships—between Senegal and France, for example, or between Barbados and England. Under that form of colonization, profoundly destructive psychological effects resulted from instilling a sense of the colonizer's superiority into the colonized through education and discipline. The Kenyan author Ngũgĩ wa Thiong'o's book *Decolonising the Mind* (1986) describes these harmful effects, as do the works of many other postcolonial writers. Under contemporary globalization, however, U.S. cultural dominance across the world is the main concern. This phenomenon is indeed distinct from the European colonial period, for it does not necessarily follow specific relations with a specific nation, nor does the United States have to instill its superiority overtly. Rather, through media images from television, Hollywood films, and the Internet (as well as travel), the U.S. way of life, especially its consumerism and apparent freedom, appears attractive to many people, even though they can also see what is lost by it. The seductiveness of the imagined Western form of modernity, with its plentiful consumer goods, serves the needs of capitalism for constant growth.

The global predominance of the English language is a link between older European colonization and contemporary cultural globalization. In the nineteenth century, Britain was the dominant colonial power, and its former colonies—from the United States and Anglophone Canada to Australia, much of the Caribbean, Ireland, Kenya, Nigeria, Ghana, India, Hong Kong, and many other countries—share the legacy of the English language. Since World War II, as the United States has become the dominant world power, American English has become the language of the Internet, of air traffic control towers, and of Hollywood films. And like media images, language carries culture with it. As middle-class Indians and Nigerians and others increasingly raise their children to speak English, trying to give them an edge in global competitiveness, the concepts and values encoded in their native languages are lost from their consciousness.

Cultural forms and practices are transmitted through media and the Internet, as well as directly through transnational capitalism. One example is the spread of fast food chains like McDonald's, Kentucky Fried Chicken, and Pizza Hut, along with global beverage brands such as Coca-Cola and Pepsi. As of June 2013, for instance, only countries in the world did not sell Coca-Cola, and one of them, Myanmar (Burma), had just allowed it in. The other countries are Cuba and North Korea, against whom the United States has trade embargoes. In the case of Myanmar, the Coca-Cola marketing team seeks to wean the people of the country from the sugar water and "imitation" Coke they drink. And since Coke is seen as an elite product there, the relatively high price—thirty-three cents—is printed on the label.

A report on the National Public Radio program *Planet Money* concerning the selling of Coca-Cola in Myanmar, "How to Sell Coke to People Who Have Never Had a Sip" (http://www.npr.org/sections/money/2013/06/07/189184092/how-to-sell-coke-to-people-who-have-never-had-a-sip), speaks volumes about the preponderance of the global brand. It is portrayed as an imperative for the people of the country, so that accepting Coke as their destiny goes hand in hand with achieving democracy.

The economic dimension of this invasion is important, but the cultural aspect is critical as well. A fast-paced way of life goes along with fast food, as does a sense of uniformity and connection to the U.S. way of life. In many societies, from France to Nepal, families prize sitting down together for a leisurely meal that has been prepared at home. The methods of preparation of food, of serving it, and the way it is eaten—whether with chopsticks, hands, or fork and knife—are all part of a particular culture. There is a fear in many places that local cultural practices around eating will be lost to American-style fast food. Similarly, the spread of Hollywood films and television shows inundate people around the world with images of what they believe to be American life, with lots of guns, affluent homes, open sexuality, and other markers of a consumer-driven society, on the one hand, and stereotyped urban black people, on the other. Many people outside the United States believe that every American has a gun and lives in a large sprawling home, and most know about racism against black people. Another sign of spreading U.S. cultural influence can be seen in clothing and style. Across the world, boys and men dress in baseball caps and jeans—iconic American clothes—and the excessive thinness of Western fashion models and actresses is influencing women in some cultures that once prized curviness. In fact, some women in East Asia get plastic surgery to make their eyes look more Western.

This export of Western culture occurs through various channels—some driven by corporate media, and some through piracy. U.S. television networks dump their shows in small countries like Trinidad and Tobago, selling them so cheaply that local production can't possibly compete. What is being sold is the American way of life, from material goods to individualism, thus paving the way to American political influence. Chains of movie theaters control the distribution of films. In 2012, a Chinese company, Dalian Wanda, took over the U.S. movie theater chain AMC, creating the largest theater chain in the world. AMC has over five thousand screens in the United States, but part of the deal will bring more Hollywood films to China. Other U.S. film companies, such as Walt Disney and DreamWorks, are merging with Chinese companies as well. Policy changes in Beijing are encouraging this trend—China agreed to increase the cut that foreign companies can take from box office receipts to 25 percent, for example.

The big question about cultural imperialism revolves around the threat to local cultures: Are they being obliterated or absorbed by the incursions of Western pop music, dress, ideas, images, and fast food, or does something different happen when cultures interact on this scale? Eric Wolf, the anthropologist mentioned in Part One, argues that cultural interactions and cross-fertilization have existed since the beginning of human history. Humans like to get new ideas from each other—to take what they like from others and keep what they prefer of their own. In fact, the pirating of music and films is a huge business around the world, illustrating the fact that foreign cultures are not always spread through domination, but also through the agency of local entrepreneurs. Some societies are more conservative and traditional than others, and some are outward looking. Is it even possible to keep a culture pure and unchanged? Would that be healthy or would it be making a way of life into a museum exhibit?

But even if we embrace cultural interactions and appropriations, the question of cultural imperialism is one of balance and power. Are the influences all in one direction, from the powerful United States to the less powerful, or are they in multiple directions? Is the United States marketing a sense of its own cultural superiority, or is it embracing difference as much as other societies are influenced by American culture? Scholars and cultural activists debate these issues strenuously and arrive at different answers, depending on the specific arenas of culture and the specific locations under consideration. Part of the postmodern condition is that seemingly contradictory cultural symbols and behaviors can coexist side by side. For example, Saudi Arabia is a culturally conservative Muslim country where women must cover all but their eyes and mouth when they are among men outside their families and where they are not allowed to drive. At the same time, however, McDonald's is extremely popular, and as part of its local adaptation, it delivers to make its food available to women.

While McDonald's is the icon of Americanization of culture, it has adapted itself to local customs, such as selling wine in France. This is not necessarily out of respect for other cultures; it may just be good business. The popular culture critic John Fiske argued decades ago that viewers actively take what they want from television shows rather than being shaped passively by them. This is one view of how cultures interact. But is it the only view? This question can be answered by examining how life appears in various locations—even within the United States, but especially outside it. While it is possible to seek out the familiar when one travels, how familiar is it really? Does Pizza Hut or Kentucky Fried Chicken have the same meaning in another country as it does in small-town America? Do local people interact with it in the same way Americans do?

## Scapes and Flows

One of the most influential articles published on cultural globalization is Arjun Appadurai's 1996 "Disjuncture and Difference in the Global Cultural Economy." The article argues against the idea that cultural imperialism produces a common global culture as a consequence of the economic relations of global capitalism. Instead Appadurai claims that economic relations and cultural processes do not necessarily flow along the same routes. The global cultural economy is marked by ruptures and discontinuities, with various global processes flowing along different paths and in different directions. This is a postmodern view of global cultures. Appadurai believes that when images or ideas travel to new locations, they take on new meanings because of the differences in contexts. He uses two metaphors to describe contemporary global cultures: *scapes* and *flows*. "Scapes" is a metaphor based on the idea of landscapes. Appadurai postulates five different scapes that can be used as the basis for researching global cultures: ethnoscapes, mediascapes, ideoscapes, technoscapes, and financescapes. These are different "flows," or vectors of movement, that have been "deterritorialized," or disconnected from specific places. People, media images, ideas, technologies, and capital all flow from one place to another, like the wind or the Gulf Stream.

Migrants move around the world, creating new ethnoscapes, new multicultural mixes of people and identity. Ethnoscapes also describe the relationship between "nations" (large groups of people who believe they share a common heritage or identity) and "states" (bounded political places recognized by the international community of states). Thus, Tibetans are a nation within the state of China, which they do not identify with, and many live in exile in other states, such as India and Nepal. Palestinians are a nation without a state. Ireland is an island with two states on it, but a large portion of those who live in Northern Ireland, part of the United Kingdom, identify as Irish and hold citizenship and passports from the Republic of Ireland. They imagine an Ireland that comprises a "complete" thirty-two counties, rather than twenty-six in the Republic and six in the United Kingdom.

Media images also flow across national boundaries, but not necessarily in the same direction as mass movements of people. When people encounter these mediascapes, they create new meanings out of them, based on their own social contexts—making these flows complex and multidirectional. For example, Bollywood films may be mapped onto the Indian diaspora around the world, but Hollywood films are produced to appeal to Asian audiences as well. Latin American telenovelas are popular among African audiences as well as in the Americas. The U.S. television show *Ugly Betty* was an adaptation of a telenovela from Colombia that was made into at least eighteen other versions in countries around the world. These examples illustrate the multiple directions in which media images flow.

Ideoscapes are related to the other scapes, but in one of the most prominent applications of the concept, they are ideas that once had some coherence in the West, produced during the eighteenth-century Enlightenment and the French and American revolutions—ideas of individualism, rights, freedom, and democracy that have been disconnected from their origins and appropriated in various ways around the world. In Europe and North America they arose in relationship to capitalism, but they are now disjoined from it, and from each other. They are translated into different political and cultural contexts in new ways.

Technoscapes represent the spread of different technologies around the world, which saturate different places at different speeds. Thus people in some African countries had access to satellite mobile phones before people in North America, but those people in Africa might never have had landlines. Financescapes refers to the flows of capital and profits that drive the global capitalist economy. Appadurai's most important point is that these flows of ideas, images, technologies, people, and money do not parallel each other, but instead mark disjunctures. He is departing from the tradition of Marxist cultural theory that sees ideology, including law, religion, value systems, and so forth, as determined by or reflective of the dominant mode of production. Appadurai argues that under the present conditions of globalization, flows go in multiple, different directions. There is no single controlling unitary center, such as the United States. Instead local scapes are created by different flows and different local contexts. Global cultures are therefore not becoming homogeneous, as the cultural imperialism model would claim.

## Diasporas

Another way to talk about Appadurai's "ethnoscapes" is through diasporas. The term *diaspora* designates the movement of people from their homeland to different locations in the world. The term originated in the Hebrew scriptures, referring to the time the temple in Jerusalem was destroyed and the Jews were cast into exile. It has come to be applied to other nations of people who are living outside their imagined homelands, including Africans, Irish, Chinese, Indians, and many others. Members of a diaspora have a common identity even while they live in widely scattered lands. In some cases they aspire to return to their homelands, as is the case with Zionists, who imagined and supported the return of Jews to Israel and now defend Israel's cultural nationalism. In other cases, however, members of a diaspora have lost knowledge of their ancestors' precise locations.

The African diaspora is an informative point of analysis, illustrating as it does a complex ethnoscape with multiple flows and layers. While not true for all, descendants of the first wave of the African diaspora—people captured for the slave trade and put into slavery in the Americas—have largely been so disconnected from the specific ethnic group and homeland of their ancestors that they are considered part of an *African* diaspora rather than that of a specific people, such as Yoruban or Congolese. Thus, there have been social movements emphasizing pan-African identity and urging Americans and West Indians of African descent to return home to Africa. The Jamaican Marcus Garvey's back-to-Africa movement in the early twentieth century was transnational in its scope. The concept of diasporic identity would create a common identity for all people of African descent. However, this picture is complicated by the more recent migrants from African nations, who are able to travel home and to stay in contact with their places of origin and who do not necessarily identify themselves as African American or Afro-Caribbean. Nonetheless, applying the concept of an African diaspora to these groups foregrounds cultural legacies held to some degree in common across different populations, especially in the areas of music, oral tradition, and religion. Many Afro-Caribbean people are doubly diasporic, in fact, living as immigrants from the Caribbean in places like Toronto, London, and New York.

The Irish diaspora may be unique in its disproportion to the size of the actual population in Ireland. A steady flow of emigrants since the early 1800s accelerated with the Great

Famine of 1845–1847 and has never really stopped. Thus about thirty-five million Americans trace their ancestry to Ireland, while seventy million people worldwide do. In contrast, the population of both the Republic of Ireland and Northern Ireland combined is about 6.5 million. Since the 1990s, the Irish government has tried to capitalize on this diaspora for economic purposes, and it declared 2013 the year of The Gathering, encouraging people of Irish descent to visit "home." As with the African diaspora, differences exist between actual contemporary migrants and members of the diaspora whose families left Ireland in the nineteenth century. The availability of air travel and the Internet today make it easy to stay connected to the land one has left, whereas earlier migrants often left never to see their families or country again, and were thus determined to make a new start in their new home.

Today's migrants are important and valued sources of foreign exchange in their home countries, sending what are called "emigrant remittances" back to their families. Western Union plays an important role in enabling migrants to send money quickly and easily all over the world, though some remittances make their way through either intermediaries or the migrants themselves hand-carrying them. In 2002 migrants sent back about 150 billion dollars to their home countries. In 2012 the amount had grown to over 500 billion dollars. In some poorer countries these remittances are the main form of foreign currency coming into the country. These flows of money in 2012 were three times the amount of foreign aid sent to developing countries by wealthy ones. In some countries they were about 25 to 41 percent of the GDP, and in many they were 10 to 15 percent. India and China both received over fourteen billion dollars. These transfers of money have important economic effects in developing countries, leading a number of countries, like Ireland, to pay more attention to their diasporic populations. Another sign of the economic importance of the diaspora is India's Ministry of Overseas Indian Affairs.

The flows of people and money, signified in Appadurai's ethnoscapes and financescapes, make bridges among different cultures. The migrants who have left home may turn the eyes of their younger relatives toward migration, and in addition to the cash remittances they send, they may send gifts back home that symbolize North American, European, or Australian ways of life. The migrants may create enclaves in their new location, or they may be forced to assimilate into the dominant society, but either way new cultural contacts are made.

For examples of the growing importance of diasporic communities to their home countries, see these web pages:

"Diaspora Engagement," Ministry of Overseas Indian Affairs (http://www.mea. gov.in/diaspora-engagement.htm)
"Remittance Flows," by Roxana Torre (http://www.torre.nl/remittances/)

Migrants relate to their new locations in various ways. They might seek to cling to their home culture and join groups of similar people, or they might seek citizenship in the new location, desiring to adapt to the host society. They are often marginalized or stigmatized by the natives of their new home. In this process, identities can be destabilized. For example, in New York City, people from Honduras, Brazil, Mexico, and Cuba will be grouped together as Latino. Migrants from China, Vietnam, and India become "Asians." Migrants from the Dominican Republic, who are considered white at home, may be categorized by Americans as black. Women from strict societies where marriages are arranged may start dating, but they may still want an arranged marriage. These changes can be confusing or freeing. In postcolonial studies, the concepts of *creolization* and *hybridity* are used to talk about these changes in identity and culture.

## Creolization and Hybridity

Nineteenth-century biological racism, used to legitimate American slavery and European imperialism, was built on ideals of racial and cultural purity and hierarchy; that is, the idea different racial and ethnic groups should have strict boundaries and members of these groups should maintain their separation from each other. The caste system in India and apartheid in South Africa also required their members to practice *endogamy*, or to marry within their particular ethnic group, caste, or religion, as was the de facto case under slavery and European imperialism. Some populations were more open to mixing than others, but unity and purity were commonly held ideas among religious and cultural groups as well. Laws against miscegenation (marriage across racial lines) were in place in twenty-nine U.S. states in the mid-twentieth century. The U.S. Supreme Court, in the *Loving v. Virginia* case, overthrew all these laws as unconstitutional in 1967. However, the flows associated with globalization have thrown people of different identities, nationalities, and ethnicities together in schools, neighborhoods, and work, leading to interculturation on many levels around the world. These flows of migrants are creating what Avtar Brah calls "diaspora spaces" and what Homi Bhabha calls "third spaces," or "cultures in-between." The term *third spaces* indicates that they are neither one thing nor the other, but something created from hybridity, a metaphor drawn from interbreeding plants. This contrasts with the logic of racism or endogamy, of policing boundaries to protect purity. A mixed union creates a hybrid child, sometimes viewed as a bastard or a mongrel. This hybridity also results from the mixing of cultures, as in the creation of Asian tacos, world musics, or Catholics practicing Buddhist meditation. Whereas some groups and individuals want to maintain their cultural purity or single identity, Bhabha celebrates the rich potential of cultural hybridity, whether it is within one person's identity or the fusion of cultural practices. The societies of the Americas have long histories of cultural and reproductive mixing: the European colonization of indigenous peoples and, later, the transport of Africans and Indians to serve as plantation labor led to populations who were largely multicultural as well as ancestrally rooted outside the Americas.

Latin American societies have many terms for different kinds of hybridity, or racial mixes; the term *mestizaje* refers to the mixing of indigenous and European cultures and bodies. In Mexico, for example, this is the dominant national identity. From the perspective of people of Spanish descent, the term implies a symbolic embrace of the indigenous cultures conquered by the Spanish, whereas from the indigenous perspective it means adopting the Spanish language and Catholic religion. The term *mulatto*, considered acceptable usage in some countries but not in the United States, refers to a person of mixed black and white ancestry. The term comes from the Spanish for "mule," or the sterile offspring of a horse and donkey. Its use thus implied that blacks and whites were two distinct species and that interbreeding between them would result in a defective creature. Despite the negative connotation of the term, however, in popular culture, mulatto women were often considered to be especially beautiful.

In the Anglophone world, the acceptance and embrace of cultural mixing are fairly new. The United States long had a completely binary racial classification system: white versus nonwhite, or black. The "law" of hypodescent, popularly known as the "one-drop rule," placed anyone with any amount of African ancestry into the nonwhite category. In 2000, Americans were able to check more than one race on the national census form for the first time. Racial categories on the census have changed over the decades, sometimes including "Mulatto," other times not. To Americans, the one-drop rule seems somewhat natural, yet in other countries most of the people Americans consider "black" would belong to a range of other categories. The Dominican Republic follows almost the exact opposite way of thinking. Anyone not very dark skinned is considered "white," yet there is a range of names for different skin tones.

The term *creole* is another way of thinking about cultural mixing and adaptation. The word originated in the Americas, in the societies comprising primarily European colonizers and enslaved Africans. These societies were extremely unusual in that almost their entire populations came from far-flung parts of the world. Both groups had to find ways to adapt to a new climate and environment and to their brutally unequal relationship with each other. The Spanish colonizers used the term *criollo* to refer to the white colonizers who were born in the Americas. The British adopted the term *creole* for any kind of organism born in the Americas but not indigenous to the Americas. This included horses, enslaved people of African parents, and white colonizers. So *creolization* means being adapted to an environment beyond one's ancestral roots.

In French colonies like Haiti, Louisiana, and Martinique, the word *Creole* was also applied to the mixed languages that evolved in the new settings. Because Haiti became independent in 1804, Haitian Creole became a well-developed written as well as oral language. In other colonies, various creoles, or patois, existed alongside a more formal version of French, Dutch, or English, and the creoles remained primarily oral. Under colonialism these languages were regarded as a debased form of the European languages, a kind of pidgin used by the enslaved and their masters to communicate across their social differences. In the wake of independence and the reevaluations it has allowed, linguists now recognize that these creolized languages took West African syntax and plugged in English, French, or Dutch vocabulary. Indeed, there are many grammatical similarities across the different versions of Creole. Thus, these mixed or hybrid languages have become a metaphor for how whole cultures have developed and adapted to the particular environment to which people have been transplanted. A group of Martinican writers has produced a manifesto, *Eloge de la créolité [In Praise of Creoleness]* (Bernabé, Chamoiseau, and Confiant 1989), proclaiming it a prophetic response to globalization, a unique adaptation to the Caribbean environment and the unequal mixing of cultures that has occurred in the region. Just as Homi Bhabha celebrates hybridity and Gloria Anzaldua proclaims herself "the new *Mestiza*," some cultural critics embrace creoleness or creolization as the best way to think about cultural globalization, a process of migratory flows of people and ongoing interactions between cultures.

## Postcolonial Studies, Orientalism, and Subaltern Studies

As mentioned earlier, postcolonial studies comprises a set of approaches that foreground the conditions surrounding colonialism and decolonization, as well as postcolonialism, or independence, and neocolonialism. The work of Frantz Fanon, a psychiatrist of African descent from Martinique who practiced in Algeria during its war of independence from France, is an important precursor to postcolonial studies. Fanon analyzed the colonizers by day and the rebels by night, and in the process gained tremendous insight into the psychological damage produced by racism and oppression. Among his books, *Black Skin, White Masks* (1952) is especially valuable for its insights into racism. *A Dying Colonialism* (1965) and *The Wretched of the Earth* (1963) are insightful early analyses of the workings of colonialism, especially their impact on the colonized people. One way colonizers try to control the thought process of the colonized is through suppressing their native languages. Education in the colonizers' language, history, and literature causes children to internalize the view that they themselves are inferior. They are inculcated with an outsider's view of themselves, their skin color, and their way of life. Thus, language is an important topic of discussion among postcolonial writers and theorists. Ngũgĩ wa Thiong'o, mentioned earlier, switched from writing in English to using his Kikuyu (one of forty-plus ethnic groups in Kenya) mother tongue, arguing that it was the only authentic expression of his experience. The late Nigerian novelist Chinua Achebe, on the other hand, argued that it was more important to use English and to be able to reach a world audience.

Other postcolonial writers try to incorporate a sense of hybrid language into their writing. For example, Gloria Anzaldua, who writes about her border identity growing up in a part of Texas that had been part of Mexico, mixes English with Spanish and indigenous words and phrases. This is a writerly reflection of what is actually happening throughout the world. *Spanglish* is spoken on the streets of New York by first- and second-generation people from the Dominican Republic and Puerto Rico. *Sheng* is a mixture of Swahili and English spoken in the streets of Nairobi. Similarly *Hinglish* is the hybrid of English and Hindi spoken on the streets of India. According to Scott Baldauf, writing in the *Christian Science Monitor,* American fast food companies in India have appropriated this hybrid language for their ads:

> Pepsi, for instance, has given its global "Ask for more" campaign a local Hinglish flavor: "Yeh Dil Maange More" (the heart wants more). Not to be outdone, Coke has its own Hinglish slogan: "Life ho to aisi" (Life should be like this).
>
> (Baldauf 2004)

These are examples of creole languages in the making, just as English itself was originally a Germanic dialect infused with upper-class French and some Latin.

Postcolonial studies seeks to recapture history and literature from the perspective of the formerly colonized, even though much of official history is based solely on the views of the European colonizers. An offshoot, called *subaltern studies*, emerged from a group of historians in India who were trying to rewrite the history of various insurgencies from the perspective of the "subalterns," the colonized who were voiceless, who left no documentary evidence about their goals and strategies. An important postcolonial critic, Gayatri Chakravorty Spivak, in an article called "Can the Subaltern Speak?"(1988) argues that it is impossible to recover the subaltern voices from the colonizers' bureaucratic documents, because to do so is to adopt the colonizers' language and point of view. Another key theorist, the late Edward Said, wrote an influential book called *Orientalism* (1978) that explicates how the West's knowledge of the "Orient" (the region from the Middle East to China and Japan) is a particular kind of construction, a discursive formation that never lets the "East" be anything but the object of Western desire, knowledge, and control. Those in the "East" never get to talk back or present their own view of themselves. Moreover, the same sets of images and ideas of the "East" are always present, whether a nineteenth-century British politician is writing about India, or Walt Disney is making a movie about *Aladdin* or *Mulan,* or CNN is reporting on Saddam Hussein as the tyrant of Iraq.

The reason for this sameness, according to the Orientalist model, is that the Orient is always constituted by what the West is not. If the West is democratic, then the East is autocratic. If the West is puritanical about sex and luxury, then the East is sensuous and exotic and luxurious. If the West believes in monogamy and the nuclear family, then the Orient has harems. One of the most interesting features of Orientalism is that there is a great deal of admiration and desire in the West's gaze at the Orient. The materials written by Westerners about the Orient are a mixture of deep scholarly study and fantasy, of romance and fear. One of the ways Europeans, particularly the British, legitimated their colonial occupation of places like India was by claiming to rescue local women from the barbaric customs of their culture. This theme continues today in Western views of women in Islam (oppressed), Southeast Asia (sex trafficking), and Africa (female genital mutilation). As in earlier forms of Orientalism, the "facts" of the case are not necessarily false; the problem lies in the relationship between Western knower and agent versus Oriental object or victim. Escaping from this kind of objectification of the Other requires creating mutual and specific relationships where everyone has agency.

## Global Citizenship and Cosmopolitanism

To be cosmopolitan is to be a citizen of the world. This concept dates back at least to the Greek Stoics. It was revived during the eighteenth-century European Enlightenment and then brought into contemporary discourse by Martha Nussbaum's controversial 1996 publication *For Love of Country: Debating the Limits of Patriotism*. As a philosopher specializing in the classics, Nussbaum drew on the teachings of the Greek Stoics in order to critique patriotism and ethnocentrism. Historically, the majority of Americans have been inward looking, disregarding the study of geography and foreign languages, expecting others to speak English, and believing the American way is the best way. By contrast, the ancient Stoics believed one had to detach from over-regard for home in order to feel at home everywhere. Prior to the contemporary period of globalization, the term *cosmopolitan* referred to people who were well traveled and worldly, comfortable in any circumstances. Often, it was applied to the elite, diplomats, international business executives, journalists, and world travelers and to people who spoke multiple languages. Today, the idea of being a world citizen is more applicable to ordinary people, and perhaps especially to the migrants and refugees who leave, or are forced out of, their homelands and struggle to survive and adapt in alien circumstances. Given the multicultural environment of the United States and the intercultural workplaces around the world, many American colleges and universities have made educating global citizens part of their mission statements. What does this mean?

Nussbaum argues that a belief in the equality of all humankind entails treating all people as equally deserving of our regard and care. Thus, her approach to cosmopolitanism is primarily an ethical one. This has become important in the globalized world because we know so much more about what is happening to people everywhere, and we should know about our relationship to what is happening in various regions and to people across the globe. Actions and choices in one location ripple out along various flows, having an impact in many different places. For instance, if I am wearing clothes sold by Primark, the Irish-based clothing store popular throughout Europe, and the Primark factory collapses and kills over a thousand people, what is my ethical responsibility? If I buy new cell phones every two years, in another important example, what is my responsibility for the war in the Democratic Republic of the Congo that is raging over natural resources, in particular the metal coltan used in in the production of electronic communications devices?

### The Problem with Coltan

Coltan is a metallic ore from which the mineral tantalum is derived. Capacitors used in most electronics, not just cell phones, are made of tantalum, making it one of the most valuable economic commodities in the world. Nonetheless, coltan is unregulated, unlike other mining products such as copper, tin, and gold, and there are human rights and environmental abuses associated with its mining in multiple countries. If everyone were to slow down their consumption of electronics and to recycle the parts, an impact on these abuses would be felt. Coltan, to be sure, would be less valuable if it were less in demand. Further, people could advocate for the regulation of coltan mining.

For more information on conflicts surrounding natural resources and activism to achieve greater social justice, see the following websites:

Breaking the Silence (http://www.congoweek.org/component/content/article/41-homepage/91-student-activist-focuses-on-congo.html)
Global Witness (www.globalwitness.org)
Grassroots Global Justice Alliance (http://ggjalliance.org)
Social Movements and Culture (http://culturalpolitics.net/social_movements/environment)

Critics of Nussbaum's argument say it is unrealistic to expect people to have the same concern for strangers in other countries as they do for relatives or compatriots. Anthony Appiah, a Ghanaian philosopher who teaches in the United States, wrote a response called "Rooted Cosmopolitanism," which he followed up with a book, *Cosmopolitanism: Ethics in a World of Strangers* (2006). Appiah balances the needs for a universal ethic against particular ethical relationships and commitments to specific groups of people, using the phrase "universality plus difference" to refer to this approach.

Advocates of cosmopolitanism and global citizenship stand with the United Nations and especially the ideals enshrined in its Universal Declaration of Human Rights and subsequent conventions like the Convention on the Elimination of All Forms of Discrimination against Women (CEDAW). Some critics of cosmopolitanism, however, worry that the world lacks the global governmental institutions needed to support cosmopolitanism. For example, the WTO, discussed in Chapter 1, does not represent the interests of individuals or their rights. In fact, the UN embodies the ideals of cosmopolitanism, but the veto power of the world's most powerful nations who sit in the Security Council—the Russian Federation, China, the United States, the United Kingdom, and France as permanent members, plus ten other countries with rotating memberships—means that smaller or less influential nations often lack power.

Many in the world view the relatively new International Criminal Court (ICC) as a major achievement in global governance—with its mission to try individuals responsible for serious crimes of international concern, such as genocide. Independent of the United Nations and distinct from the UN's International Court of Justice (or World Court), the ICC was created by 122 state signatories in 1998 by the Treaty of Rome and was then ratified by 60 countries, coming into operation in 2002. At the time of this publication, it has been ratified by 122 countries. The United States has signed onto it but not ratified it. All but three countries in the Americas and all the countries in Europe have ratified it. While, in theory, the court has a broad mandate, it is limited in practice. For instance, an indictment for war crimes can be issued through the ICC's due process procedures, but forcing a sitting—or even former—head of state to trial is not easy.

For links to situations in the world that the ICC is investigating or concerned about, see its home page (https://www.icc-cpi.int).

Another aspect of cosmopolitanism is the role that transnational nongovernmental organizations (NGOs) play in global civil society and whether they provide a better solution to global governance than actual governmental organizations do. The World Social Forum, an annual meeting of groups and individuals concerned with social justice and human well-being across the world, is an example of this direction of grassroots global governance. Other examples are the NGO Working Group on Food and Hunger, which works for a more just and sustainable worldwide food system and is made up of NGOs active at the United Nations in New York; Doctors Without Borders and the Red Cross/Red Crescent, which bring humanitarian aid to crisis-torn areas; Amnesty International and Human Rights Watch, which bring pressure on states to improve human rights concerns; and Greenpeace and the World Wildlife Fund in the environmental arena. These are just a few of the larger NGOs working both with and against state governments in the cause of human rights, environmental justice, and human health and well-being.

### Cosmopolitanism in Action

- Information about the World Social Forum can be found at the Open FSM website (http://openfsm.net//).
- Two major organizations campaigning for human rights are Amnesty International (www.amnesty.org) and Human Rights Watch (www.hrw.org/).
- Two major organizations of global governance are the United Nations (www.un.org/en/) and the World Health Organization (http://www.who.int/en/).

### Becoming a Global Citizen

From an educational perspective, becoming a global citizen means learning to see the world from multiple perspectives and developing intercultural relationships and skills. It means knowing something about geography, history, and current events and making the effort to gather information from sources outside the mainstream corporate ones. Learning to speak languages other than one's own is also important in acquiring multiple perspectives, as is the opportunity to live outside one's native country for a period of time. All this does not mean that one will give up love of country; rather, the aim is to learn to balance multiple and alternative perspectives in playing the role of citizen, both nationally and globally.

## Global Gender Perspectives

In the late 1970s, the United Nations organized the drafting of a comprehensive supplement to the 1948 Universal Declaration on Human Rights (UDHR). Called the Convention on the Elimination of All Forms of Discrimination against Women (CEDAW), it was adopted by the General Assembly in 1979 and went into effect in 1981. The UN Commission on the Status of Women monitors the treatment of women around the world through country reports, and through UN Women (United Nations Entity for Gender Equality and the Empowerment of Women), it maintains linkages with NGOs dedicated to women's issues. Despite the votes in favor of CEDAW, many countries registered reservations about its provisions, reservations that undermine the notion of nondiscrimination.

Provisions for women's equality often run counter to states' and religions' models of marriage, family, and divorce. For example, at the time CEDAW passed, divorce was illegal in Ireland (it became legal in 1996), and in many Muslim societies today, a man can simply declare he wants a divorce, while a woman has to go through a Sharia judge (a judge interpreting Islamic religious law). CEDAW recognizes that culture, religion, and tradition play an especially strong role in restricting the equality of women. The various forms of fundamentalism—whether Christian, Muslim, or Hindu—that have strengthened in the past thirty years have made women the bearers of so-called tradition, leaving men free to participate in the global economy. An extreme version of this was the strictures against women in Afghanistan enforced by the Taliban when they were in power, whereby women could not go to school past the age of eight, could not be out in public without a male relative, and could not work, as well as the continued restrictions against women voting, which were at least partially lifted in 2014. Similarly, in Saudi Arabia a law of guardianship puts a male family member in charge of each woman so that she must ask permission to travel, work, or get medical treatment; other restrictions on women in the Saudi kingdom are slowly being liberalized.

---

The following websites and web pages are useful sources on global women's issues:

"Gender Equality Data and Statistics," The World Bank (http://datatopics.worldbank.org/gender/)

"Progress of the World's Women," UN Women (http://progress.unwomen.org/)

"Sex Ratio," CIA World Factbook (https://www.cia.gov/library/publications/the-world-factbook/fields/2018.html)

"The Status of Women: A Reality Check," (https://www.scribd.com/document/66039511/Swayam-Gi-Leaflet-31mar)

"Women in National Parliaments," Inter-Parliamentary Union (http://www.ipu.org/wmn-e/classif.htm)

Women Watch (http://www.un.org/womenwatch/directory/statistics_and_indicators_60.htm)

---

In her 1988 article "Under Western Eyes: Feminist Scholarship and Colonial Discourses," Chandra Talpade Mohanty made the important point that no universal condition of womanhood is shared by women in all times and places; rather, the idea of womanhood is heterogeneous, comprising many women whose lives reflect distinct concrete sociohistorical circumstances. Within a particular society there are wealthy women, poor women, ethnic minority women, women of different religions, and women with and without children. It is therefore difficult to make generalizations about what would empower all women universally. Moreover, when women in the West look at women's lives in a distant country, the chief problems they see may be very different from what the women within that society believe. This has been one of a number of critiques made by women from the Global South against well-meaning Western feminists who want to help women across the globe. According to Mohanty, these efforts might be considered neocolonial, because despite their good intentions, they maintain and legitimate the idea that the West is culturally and ethically superior to the rest of the world and that the enlightened West should teach the Global South how to behave and leave behind its barbaric ways.

One of the biggest transnational women's issues today, for instance, is the trafficking of women and children to serve in domestic work and the sex industry. This is a real issue of legitimate concern, especially when viewed within the "cosmopolitan" model of globalization discussed earlier, but often the people in the Global North who become involved in efforts to halt sex trafficking emphasize the otherness of the trade in women. These activists often see themselves as standing on the high ground of Western civilization, although people in their own countries are themselves guilty of trade in human beings—though perhaps of trafficking domestic workers or farm laborers rather than sex workers. Issues like rape and domestic abuse, as well as childhood poverty, are endemic in the United States as well as overseas. Sometimes it is easier to advocate for the exotic Other than to face issues at home.

Statistics show that women face inequality in many areas of life, from educational levels and nutrition to legal protection and representation in governments. However, these common issues manifest themselves in specific, concrete ways in different societies, and examining the specific context, without preconceived notions, is critical. Take, for example, two indicators of women's equality: representation in government and life expectancy. In terms of the former, the United States ranks seventy-eighth in the world, while Rwanda ranks first—likely a surprising comparison to many. Further, Canada and Australia are tied for forty-sixth, and Senegal, South Africa, and Nicaragua are in the top ten. However, life expectancy for women is another matter altogether: for Rwanda, it is fifty-six; for Senegal, sixty; Nicaragua, seventy-seven; the United States, eighty-one; and Canada and Australia, over eighty-three. This illustrates the unevenness of various criteria of equality and well-being for women in different contexts.

The ratio of girls to boys in a given society is another important measure of equality. Normally, more boys than girls will be born, but more males than females die over their life span, leading to a majority of women in the sixth decade of life. A "normal" ratio at birth would be about 1.05 boys to girls. In India it is estimated at 1.12, and in China at 1.13. Girls may be viewed as an economic liability in societies where families must pay a dowry to marry them off, and where once they are married, girls become responsible for their husband's parents, not their own. This has been the case in many parts of India, but specific strategies have been devised to combat these practices. India, China, and South Korea have all made abortion as a tool of sex selection illegal. Nonetheless the sex ratio of girls to boys is getting worse in India, where the 1994 Pre-conception and Pre-natal Diagnostic Techniques (PCPNDT) Act seems to be ineffectual: in 2011 the ratio was 914 girls under six to 1,000 boys. In the past, families might have continued to have more children until a son was born, but now, if a girl is born first, they tend to use abortion to prevent having more daughters. China also has a strong preference for boys; from 1979 until the beginning of 2016, when it was phased out, the government's one-child policy led to the aborting of many female fetuses. Today, a shortage of young women is making it difficult for men to find wives.

One major issue facing women transnationally is violence and sexual assault. Six hundred and three million women live under governments where domestic violence is legal. States often use the argument that their culture, religion, or tradition mandates specific forms of inequality for women. However, the point of human rights conventions is to empower the individual to be able to challenge the laws or actions of the state if they are in violation of human rights. In the spring 2013 meeting of the Commission on the Status of Women at the United Nations, an agreement was discussed by which states would protect women against violence, not accept religion and culture as a rationale for violence or rape, and guarantee women bodily integrity. According to Jill Filipovic (2013), the Vatican, Iran, and Russia were among those who would not agree to override culture and religion to rule out violence against women. The Egyptian Muslim Brotherhood said ruling out violence against women would bring about the disintegration of society.

The United States is not immune from the problem of gender violence. In 2000 in the United States, 1,247 women and 440 men were killed by an intimate partner. In recent years, 33 percent of female murder victims and 4 percent of male murder victims were killed by an intimate partner. These trends are so pressing that California has passed legislation to allow convicted felons to appeal their sentences based on the role of abuse leading up to the crime of murder. New York is considering similar legislation. Studies in New York have shown that the vast majority of women prisoners are survivors of abuse. In 2005, 75 percent of women convicted of murdering a person they knew well had been abused by the victim of their murder. Thus, when we think about issues facing women around the world, it is important to evaluate the full scope of issues and to consider the ways that the unequal treatment of women manifests itself in the West as well as other regions of the world. Within a particular society, some women may have near equality with men, while others are extremely oppressed based on class, caste, rural versus urban locations, religion, or race and ethnicity. Likewise, different aspects of the status of women may be highly variable from one society to another. In working for transnational social change, seeking multiple sources of information and forming organizations in which all participants are agents in a mutually respectful coalition are critical.

## Identities and Difference

One of the most salient features in the era of postmodernism and globalization—and one important to concepts such as diaspora and hybridity covered in this section—is the increased emphasis on various forms of identity-as-difference. From the eighteenth-century European Enlightenment until the 1960s, the ideals embodied in modernity envisioned a world of universal human beings moving at different rates along the same path of progress toward values of democratic freedom and equality, scientific rationality, technological development, material well-being, and health. The communist and capitalist worlds were not as far apart as they seemed on many of these values. The world wars were disruptions in this progress, but the formation of the United Nations and the Bretton Woods institutions were seen as strategies to forestall another such breakdown. However, the decolonizing movements that took place from the late 1940s to 1980s, the various separation movements within states such as the Quebecois in Canada and the Basques in Spain, and the civil rights and identity-based movements within states such as the United States all shifted the discourse of social justice from universal integration and sameness to recognition of difference. As the civil rights movement turned into the Black Power movement in the United States, for example, the agenda shifted from integration or assimilation to acknowledgment of uniqueness—to "black is beautiful." A similar trajectory happened with the Women's Movement as white middle-class women went from seeking equality within the status quo to transforming society to recognize gender and sexual differences.

Issues surrounding immigrants in the developed world also illustrated these trends, and at the same time, ethnic differences throughout the world came to the forefront of global consciousness. When the Hutus slaughtered Tutsis in 1994 in Rwanda over ideas associated with putative ethnic differences instilled and reinforced by European colonizers, ethnicity took center stage in international policy and in academic circles. Race, in particular, experienced a resurgence of interest as a scholarly topic. The anti-apartheid struggle in South Africa helped keep race in the public eye, and in 2001 the United Nations held a World Conference against Racism in Durban, South Africa. The topic continued its legacy of passionate controversy and denial as the United States and Israel withdrew from the conference over a draft suggestion that Zionism was equivalent to slavery. An extremely controversial issue was reparations for slavery. The question of reparations for historical exploitation continues to vex relations between the former colonists and their colonies. In June 2013, the United Kingdom broke new ground by apologizing for its crimes during Kenya's Mau Mau movement for independence in the 1950s. Britain is paying twenty million pounds to the torture survivors. This may set a precedent for future kinds of reparations based on racial, ethnic, or national identities.

Throughout the exploration of the concepts covered in this section, it is clear that a philosophical challenge for the postmodern age is balancing common humanity against the recognition of differences and finding common ground without enforcing cultural assimilation. The discourses of hybridity and cosmopolitanism, including human rights, are avenues in this direction. Emphasizing the fluidity and intersectionality (the idea that each person is the nexus of many different identities, some of them marginal and some dominant) of identities rather than their polar differences is another avenue. The technologies of the Internet, mobile phones, and social media are tools that have the potential to facilitate transnational alliances, but only if their users choose that direction. Grassroots alliances that seek to strengthen democracy from below, to resist the unbridled power of corporations and the endless desire for consumer goods, are another avenue toward social justice within and across nations.

## References and Further Research

Appadurai, Arjun. 1996. "Disjuncture and Difference in the Global Cultural Economy." In *Modernity at Large: Cultural Dimensions of Globalization,* 27–43. Minneapolis: University of Minnesota Press.

Appiah, Anthony. 2006. *Cosmopolitanism: Ethics in a World of Strangers.* New York: W. W. Norton.

Appiah, Kwame Anthony, and Henry Louis Gates Jr., eds. 1995. *Identities.* Chicago: University of Chicago Press.

Baldauf, Scott. 2004. "A Hindi-English Jumble, Spoken by 350 Million." *Christian Science Monitor,* November 23. http://www.csmonitor.com/2004/1123/p01s03-wosc.html.

Baudrillard, Jean. 1994. *Simulacra and Simulations.* Translated by Sheila Faria Glaser. Ann Arbor: University of Michigan Press.

Bernabé, Jean, Patrick Chamoiseau, and Raphael Confiant. 1989. *Eloge de la créolité/In Praise of Creoleness.* English translation by M. B. Taleb-Khar. Paris: Éditions Gallimard.

Bhabha, Homi. 1994. *The Location of Culture.* London: Routledge.

Brah, Avtar. 1996. *Cartographies of Diaspora: Contesting Identities.* London: Routledge.

Castle, Gregory, ed. 2001. *Postcolonial Discourses: An Anthology.* Oxford: Blackwell.

Fanon, Frantz. 1963. *The Wretched of the Earth.* Translated by Constance Farrington. New York: Grove Weidenfeld.

———. 1965. *A Dying Colonialism.* Translated by Haakon Chavalier. New York: Grove Press.

———. 1967 [1952]. *Black Skin, White Masks.* Translated by Charles Lam Markmann. New York: Grove Press.

Filipovic, Jill. 2013. "The UN Commission on the Status of Women Unmasks Equality's Enemies." *The Guardian,* March 18. http://www.theguardian.com/commentisfree/2013/mar/18/un-commission-status-women-enemies-equality.

Mohanty, Chandra Talpady. 1988. "Under Western Eyes: Feminist Scholarship and Colonial Discourses." *Feminist Review* 30: 61–88.

Nussbaum, Martha C., with Respondents. 1996. *For Love of Country: Debating the Limits of Patriotism.* Boston: Beacon Press.

Putnal, Olivia. 2010. "11 Global McDonald's Menu Items." *Woman's Day,* March 24. http://www.womansday.com/food-recipes/11-global-mcdonalds-menu-items-104999.

Rajchman, John, ed. 1995. *The Identity in Question.* New York: Routledge.

Rothenberg, Paula S. 2006. *Beyond Borders: Thinking Critically about Global Issues.* New York: Worth.

Said, Edward. 1978. *Orientalism.* London: Penguin.

Spivak, Gayatri Chakravorty. 1988. "Can the Subaltern Speak?" In *Marxism and the Interpretation of Culture,* edited by Cary Nelson and Lawrence Grossberg, 271–313. Basingstoke, UK: Macmillan Education.

Thiong'o, Ngũgĩ wa. 1986. *Decolonising the Mind: The Politics of Language in African Literature.* London: Heinemann.

# PART TWO

# Case Studies

# 4

# Introduction to the Case Studies

The case studies that follow are meant to illustrate the complex interrelationships between local realities and global flows and forces, as well as the ways specific local traditions or practices can themselves, as we say colloquially, "go viral" and have a much broader impact. While this text focuses primarily on cultural and social phenomena and methods of analysis, the case studies also show the ways that political and economic processes are interwoven with and affected by sociocultural phenomena. Each case study describes global or transnational movements and flows through the lens of theories and questions raised in the first part of the text.

## Global News Media: From the BBC and CNN to Al Jazeera and TeleSUR

An examination of the changing global news media sector provides an opportunity to study not only how patterns in news coverage are shaped by existing geopolitical hierarchies, but also how these patterns can be challenged. For most of the past century, news outlets based in the Global North have dominated the airwaves and exerted considerable influence on how global issues are framed. In recent years, however, the "politics of representation" supported by this arrangement have come under increasing scrutiny with the entry of additional outlets into the news market. This case study focuses on two of these outlets: Qatar-based Al Jazeera and Venezuela-based TeleSUR.

## Indigenous Peoples and Intellectual Property Rights

This case study examines the paradoxical status of indigeneity in a world characterized by flows of migration. Part of the paradox is the fact that small groups of people who understand themselves as rooted to a particular place and perhaps opposed to certain forms of modernization have had to employ social and mass media as well as the United Nations in order to bring their threatened status to world attention. As people who value a close relationship to a particular ecosystem, indigenous groups often have knowledge of the properties of plants that can be used for both food and healing. In recent decades global corporations have begun to see the value in these plants and seek to patent them under global intellectual property laws. Thus through "biopiracy," corporations gain private ownership of natural resources held in common by indigenous groups and often prevent those people from free access to their own plants and seeds.

## NGOs, Humanitarianism, and the Cultural Construction of Global Hierarchy

Globalization facilitates many types of human interaction, including the diverse forms of transnational assistance carried out under the umbrella of what is often called "humanitarianism." The social relations of global charity are deeply shaped by patterns that date back to the age of formal imperialism and the construction of racial, gendered, and other cultural hierarchies through ideas such as the "white man's burden." With this history in mind, this case study explores the contemporary cultural politics of humanitarianism in an age marked by the expanding role of nongovernmental organizations (NGOs) in providing social services previously provided by governments, the growing use of social media, and the widespread involvement of celebrities in humanitarian campaigns. Examples such as the Half the Sky project, the Save Darfur movement, and the #BringBackOurGirls campaign demonstrate the continuing power of what some critics have called a "white savior industrial complex" while pointing toward the need for alternative, less hierarchical forms of transnational assistance.

## Climate Change and Changing Global Imaginaries

While climate change is widely recognized as a scientific reality and a formidable political dilemma, it also has important social and cultural ramifications. This case study addresses the challenges that the growing awareness of climate change poses to our habitual ways of seeing the world. With their deep historical roots, these cultural "imaginaries" interact in far-reaching ways with our ethical frameworks, conceptions of identity and social responsibility, and ideas about the relationship between humans and the natural world. Discussions at the Table of Free Voices (a global dialogue event held in Germany in 2006) revealed a range of "imaginaries" representing a diversity of emerging perspectives on the meaning of climate change and its implications for humanity. Everyone, however, is confronted with the fact that climate change often feels too big to conceptualize and that its effects can be hard to visualize for those who are not on the front lines of its most dramatic manifestations. Consequently, artists and environmental activists continue to develop creative strategies for increasing the visibility of climate change.

## Transnational LGBT Identities: Liberation or Westernization?

Across the globe, ideas of individual choice have accompanied neoliberalism and global capitalism. One symbol of such freedom is the phenomenon of gay pride parades, which are now performed in many countries across the globe, including places such as Nepal and South Korea. However these belie the fact that homosexuality is still a crime in at least seventy-six countries. In addition, Western individualist celebrations of gay and lesbian identities can mask the imposition of Western binary gender definitions onto societies that formerly had more fluid understandings of gender. As transgender identity becomes more prominent in the West, it raises comparisons with other cultures' forms of gender that undermine that male–female opposition. This case study highlights the Western individualist notion of identity as it travels with the politics of sexual liberation.

## The Islamic Veil and the Global Politics of Gender

This case study explores the wide variety of meanings and practices associated with the wearing of head coverings by Muslim women. The chapter looks at both predominantly Islamic countries such as Turkey and Iran and at European nations where the practice of veiling among immigrant populations has clashed with ideas about national identity and equality for the genders. Especially in France, the wearing of the hijab, or veil, has brought about a crisis in national self-understanding. Most importantly the case study shows how wearing the hijab can signify pride in one's cultural identity under some circumstances and obedience to authority in others and that the twentieth century saw multiple changes in attitudes about women's clothing in a number of Islamic countries. These changes have been linked with nationalist reactions to Western influence in the Middle East.

## "Keeping It Real": State, Corporate, or Underground Voices in Global Hip-Hop

This case study maps the circulation and recirculation of popular and critical music forms from West Africa to the Americas and back again, focusing on hip-hop as a genre that exemplifies both the powerful commodifying forces of global capital and the counterforces of African traditions of resistance through rhythm and words. Hip-hop is thus the latest example of pan-African resistance and creativity and an extraordinarily successful form of world music. In Tanzania and Ghana hip-hop's rise among youth has been partly supported by freedoms and money accompanying neoliberalism. At the same time neoliberalism has undermined the politics and philosophies that undergirded the postcolonial formation of these states.

## Yoga in America: Competitive Sport or Spiritual Quest?

This chapter traces the evolution and shifts in the meaning of yoga as it has traveled from ancient India to the West in the twentieth and twenty-first centuries. While some in the West are attracted to yoga as a spiritual discipline that offers an alternative to the Judeo-Christian cosmology, many today practice ashtanga and power yoga simply as a form of exercise, one that has brought with it various forms of commodification, both of the practice itself and of clothing, mats, and other accoutrements. The Western adaptations of age-old Hindu practices are in turn spreading out to other parts of the world, including India itself. The case study asks whether such adaptations are creative offshoots of globalization or signifiers of a global capitalism that commodifies everything in its path.

## Global Solidarity Movements: Palestine, Tibet, and Beyond

Increases in global connectivity across national borders can enable new forms of conflict and violence, but they can also assist people in building new bridges in search of social justice. Global solidarity movements, in which people from many parts of the world come to identify with and participate in the struggle of marginalized or disenfranchised groups in other places, are a growing part of what has been called "grassroots globalization." Using Arjun Appadurai's concept of "scapes," this case study explores some of the key social and cultural elements of contemporary movements organized in solidarity with struggles in places such as Palestine, Chiapas (Mexico), South Africa, and Tibet. In the process, it connects with numerous concepts and processes, including diasporas, racialization, nonviolent direct action, social media, cultural translation, and the global impact of settler colonialism.

# 5

# Global News Media: From the BBC and CNN to Al Jazeera and TeleSUR

The two wars waged by the United States in Iraq since 1990 provide an excellent opportunity to understand the rapidly changing global news media environment. The first war, in 1991, was a kind of coming-out party for the Cable News Network (CNN), which had emerged in the previous decade as a dominant force in the growing market for twenty-four-hour news coverage. Many viewers recall the urgent eyewitness reports filed by CNN anchor Bernard Shaw from a Baghdad hotel room as U.S. forces began bombing the city. When the United States invaded Iraq again in 2003, however, CNN's coverage had changed dramatically. Viewers who tuned into CNN often saw images of the Baghdad night sky provided not by CNN's own cameras, but by a relative newcomer to the media world: Al Jazeera, the Qatar-based Arab satellite news channel, which had many of its own journalists on the ground in Iraq at a time when U.S. outlets were reluctant to do so.

CNN's use of Al Jazeera's live feeds, whether from Iraq or Afghanistan, revealed something important about how practices of outsourcing and subcontracting extend into the media sector, but it also revealed deeper patterns having to with what cultural studies scholars call the "politics of representation," or the struggles connected with the impact of existing social hierarchies that shape how reality can and should be represented, by whom, and for what purposes. In the documentary film *Independent Media in a Time of War*, award-winning independent journalist Amy Goodman points out that CNN was not willing to share with its American viewers the much more dramatic Al Jazeera footage showing the raw reality of military and civilian casualties (Hudson Mohawk Independent Media Center 2003). She also notes, however, that the network did share some of these images with its viewers outside the United States via its CNN International network. For their part, many American journalists, politicians, and commentators singled out Al Jazeera and other global news outlets for criticism for using "graphic" and "tasteless" images of the war. In response, many around the world criticized CNN and other U.S.-based outlets for "sanitizing" the war, romanticizing the role of American troops, and generally failing to give American viewers a full and complex understanding of what was happening in Iraq.

This example illustrates what is at stake in debates over how war and other major global news stories should be covered. Such debates point toward some of the deeper cultural and social effects of media globalization, particularly in the post-9/11 era. In general, recent processes of globalizing media have resulted in a market-oriented system dominated by transnational firms based in the Global North. As dominant Euro-American media giants such as CNN and the British Broadcasting Corporation (BBC) are challenged by newcomers based in the Global South, however, there is also the potential for altering the politics of representation that have long characterized social relations both within and among cultures throughout the world.

## Approaches to Understanding the News Media

While it is common to refer to "the media" as if they were a single, monolithic entity, it is important to remember that "media" is actually the plural of the word "medium." For at least a century, the media have been some of the most powerful institutions and social forces in the world. As the term indicates, the primary function of all media, including news media, is to mediate—to stand between us and the world and to represent aspects of the world to us. As such, they play a primary role in the *social construction of reality*, the process through which communication and interaction among human beings produce a collective sense of what is "real." Through repetition and the operation of power, dominant representations of "reality" come to take on a life of their own and appear as "natural."

These basic insights from theories of social construction lead to some of the key questions asked by media studies scholars: How should we conceptualize the process of mediation? What kind of mediators are the mass media (that is, those that are designed to reach large, diverse audiences), and how do they differ from other kinds of media? What kind of world are they presenting to us? Who is in control of this mediation, and what are its social effects? In exploring these questions, it is essential to recognize that the media are both *products* and *producers*. On the one hand, media are products of human action: they exist because people invent them, invest in them, work for them, and so forth. At the same time, media are also constantly producing all sorts of things: profits, programs, films, reports, attitudes, world-views, and identities. Grossberg, Wartella, and Whitney (1998) introduce the concept of "mediamaking" to summarize the complex relationship between people and media: we make media, but media also "make" us. Indeed, in today's hypermediated world, it is almost impossible to imagine any person whose identity has not been shaped profoundly by interactions with media.

There are a number of influential frameworks for understanding the social and cultural role of the news media, whose job is to investigate and present information about current events. Many scholars invoke Jürgen Habermas's (1989) concept of the "public sphere," a space where members of a community can come together to engage in rational discussion and debate about the issues facing them. Yet today's global media rarely, if ever, function in a way that facilitates the existence of an idealized public sphere. For many prominent critics, such as the late sociologist Herbert Schiller, the problem lies in private ownership and the drive for profit. The need to please shareholders, they argue, inevitably wins out over the need to make serving the public good a top priority. It is worth emphasizing that the media themselves constitute a significant sector of the economy, with major media firms such as Disney rivaling in size and profitability some of the dominant firms in the energy and pharmaceutical industries. As such, privately owned media producers have a strong interest in promoting not only their own products, but also the broader ideologies and cultural practices associated with consumerism and capitalism itself. In summarizing this line of analysis, Edward Herman and Robert McChesney describe the global media as "a necessary component of global capitalism and one of its defining features" (1997, 10).

An additional piece of the media's cultural role concerns the issue of political and social control. In one of the most provocative and influential contributions to the literature on news media, Herman and Noam Chomsky (1988) argue that even in "democratic" societies, news media can still serve a propaganda function. In particular, they contend, the role of news media in such cases is to promote the dominant "ideological system" that naturalizes and justifies policies driven by elite interests. Borrowing a phrase from Walter Lippmann, they refer to this process as "manufacturing consent," suggesting that the "democratic" consent of ordinary people is not freely given, but rather produced through ideological manipulation that is facilitated by compliant news media outlets. Finally, another influential tradition analyzes the role of media in supporting the construction and spread of a culture based on spectacle. This tradition emphasizes how media have assisted in blurring the lines between real social relations and their representation. In such a world, they argue, participation in social life increasingly takes the form of consuming highly mediated representations of reality.

As an influential piece of the larger media landscape, news media play a key role in all of these cultural and social processes. Importantly, however, news media can act as incubators of practices that provide alternatives to the dominant modes of representation. Independent news media outlets funded directly by reader/viewer support, community media projects such as low-power radio, and state-funded or NGO-based efforts at promoting "development journalism" are all good examples of such alternatives.

## News Media and the Politics of Representation

News organizations are constantly making choices about what to cover and what not to cover, how to present particular stories, and which voices and perspectives to prioritize. "The media do not simply and transparently report events which are 'naturally' newsworthy *in themselves*" (original emphasis), note the authors of one influential study from the 1970s. "'News' is the end-product of a complex process which begins with a systematic sorting and selecting of events and topics according to a socially constructed set of categories" (Hall et al. 1978, 53). Jaap van Ginneken uses the term "selective articulation" to describe how this "sorting" process is shaped by a range of cultural and political assumptions (1998, 16), starting with assumptions grounded in basic concepts of "self" and "other." There are always an infinite number of things happening in the world, as well as millions of people who might have an opinion on each of them. When a newspaper, television news program, or website presents the world's "news" on a given day, therefore, what they are really doing is articulating, wittingly or not, a particular vision of the world—a vision in which some stories, processes, and voices are implicitly assumed to be more important than others.

---

### Ethnocentrism and News Coverage

News produced in a given society will inevitably reflect the particular "local" concerns of that society. In other words, relatively benign forms of ethnocentrism are visible in most news coverage. It is often difficult, however, to separate these from the more prejudicial attitudes regarding the relative value of human lives according to race, ethnicity, nationality, and so forth.

One useful tool for viewing how all of these factors shape news coverage is Newsmap (http://newsmap.jp/), a website that uses the Google News aggregator to provide a real-time visual snapshot of which stories are getting the most attention in which parts of the world at a given moment. Visitors to the site can quickly see how news coverage originating in a particular country will tend to prioritize issues perceived to be of national importance there. At the same time, the "map" also reveals transnational hierarchies. Major news coming out of Washington, for example, is more likely to be "news" for everyone regardless of their location.

Critical analysis of global news, therefore, usually takes the form of identifying the patterns present in the coverage and then identifying what these patterns reveal about the underlying political, economic, cultural, and ideological structures that helped produce them. Key questions typically asked in critical news analysis include: Who is speaking and who is being spoken about? Who is speaking for whom? Who is being silenced? Who is deciding what to cover? How are the issues being framed, and from whose perspective? How does the coverage both reflect and shape popular attitudes? What kinds of assumptions are being made regarding the "newsworthiness" of events?

Examining patterns in news coverage can be an excellent way to explore the operation of social and cultural hierarchies grounded in gender, sexuality, social class, race, religion, nationality, and other markers of social identity. On the geopolitical level, for example, powerful news organizations have helped construct and perpetuate global hierarchies by offering stereotypical portrayals of non-Western people, presenting the worldviews of Global North elites as if they were natural or universal, or denying marginalized groups the right to narrate their own history and their own perspectives on an equal footing with others. Many social movements, particularly in the Global South, have sought to challenge these patterns by taking control of (or at least making use of) the media. Frantz Fanon's discussion of the role of radio in the Algerian revolution is a classic example; more recent examples can be found in everything from indigenous media production in the Americas or Australia to the use of social media by protesters in Egypt or Thailand.

Another pattern that appears consistently throughout the world in coverage of international issues is the uncritical reproduction of a cultural system of gender hierarchy, with dominant forms of masculinity at the top. This basic hierarchy is reflected at the global level, with dominant nations routinely constructed as masculine and "strong" and subordinate nations constructed as feminine and "weak." Not only have most news stories traditionally been written by men, but most also rely on sources whose place in the hierarchy makes them more "authoritative"—namely, men in general, men in positions of social power in particular, and male-dominated institutions. For feminist communications scholars like Sue Curry Jansen, these patterns amount to a "gender-based news blackout" that systematically marginalizes the perspectives and concerns of women (2002, 219).

Scholars working in cultural studies in the 1970s and 1980s, including a research team led by Stuart Hall, pioneered approaches to critical media analysis that identified similar patterns concerning race and class in British media coverage, where excessive coverage of street crime helped produce a "social panic" that played on public fears about the changing nature of British society due to economic restructuring, imperial decline, immigration from former British colonies (e.g., in South Asia and the Caribbean), and other processes. In van Ginneken's terms, the British media "articulated" social reality in a way that was highly "selective." Other examples from recent decades, such as media-aided panics over AIDS, drugs, and terrorism, demonstrate that these patterns in news coverage typically involve a process of exaggerating the threat posed by socially marginalized groups (e.g., immigrants, people of color, the poor) while legitimizing measures of social control taken by dominant groups. Equally important, the excessive attention given to these issues also means that attention is being deflected from other kinds of issues, particularly those that might paint dominant groups in a negative light.

## A Brief History of Global News Media

In the early period of the global news system, most content was disseminated to the far corners of the world from a small number of metropolitan centers. The emergence of wire services such as the AP, Reuters, and UPI is the clearest example of this pattern, as news outlets in many countries came to rely on the raw material produced by these companies.

An important implication of this core–periphery structure is that the content itself was inevitably colored by the cultural and political worldviews that dominated in the core. Whether viewed as cultural imperialism or as a more neutral process of cultural exchange facilitated by expanding empires, this system ensured that as news content traveled globally, it would be clothed in other layers of cultural meaning.

---

### Empire and Global Media

The story of global news media—that is, media that seek to reach sizable audiences in all parts of the world—is closely connected with the rise of modern imperialism. Agence France-Press, the world's first news agency, was founded in 1835, just five years after France launched its second colonial empire by invading and eventually subjugating Algeria. By the end of World War II, just over a century later, many other major news agencies and broadcasters (both private and state-owned) had emerged, including:

- Associated Press (USA, 1846)
- Reuters (UK, 1851)
- ITAR-TASS (Russia, 1902)
- United Press International (USA, 1907)
- Red China News Agency (China, 1931), now the Xinhua News Agency
- BBC Empire Service (UK, 1932), now the BBC World Service
- Canadian Radio Broadcasting Commission (Canada, 1932)
- Australian Broadcasting Corporation (Australia, 1932)
- South African Broadcasting Corporation (South Africa, 1936)
- Voice of America (USA, 1942)

The creation and growth of these global news providers went hand in hand with the spread of major world languages (English, French, Russian, Chinese), technologies of communication, models of journalism, and, of course, the regional and global empires themselves. The BBC, undoubtedly the most influential of the imperial broadcasters, combined all of these elements, providing tangible cultural evidence in support of the famous slogan that "the sun never sets on the British Empire."

---

The global wave of decolonization following World War II did not revolutionize this system immediately. The BBC, for example, remained a major global player, although it did acknowledge new geopolitical realities by changing its name from the BBC Empire Service to the BBC World Service in 1962. The emergence of the Cold War, however, did set in motion a series of changes that continue to unfold today. First, the major news outlets located in the United States (for example, CBS and other radio/television networks and the *New York Times* and other newspapers) grew into powerful global media forces with their own overseas bureaus.

---

### Trends in U.S. International News Coverage

Many observers have charted the U.S. news media's changing levels of commitment to covering international news. Most agree that the highest levels of coverage came at the height of the Vietnam War, when newspapers and television networks devoted considerable resources to informing their audiences about what was happening over-seas. During the 1980s, and especially after the end of the Cold War with the collapse of the Soviet Union in 1991, however, such coverage declined precipitously as industry deregulation, media consolidation, and a perceived change in audience interest drove owners to divert resources to other areas of operation. In 1998 a report in the *American Journalism Review* noted ominously that "international news coverage in most of America's mainstream papers has almost reached the vanishing point" (Arnett 1998). In a follow-up report thirteen years later, the journal revealed that the trend had accelerated through the turn of the century, with many major newspapers and chains having "shuttered every one of their overseas bureaus" (Enda 2010–2011). In response to the loss of coverage, some U.S. outlets have actually increased their over-seas presence and many others have increased their reliance on freelancers, "mobile journalists," and local reporters. It is worth noting that these trends have coincided with a dramatic increase in violent attacks on journalists worldwide: the Committee to Protect Journalists reports that over 1,100 journalists were killed from 1992 to March 2015, including over 166 in Iraq alone.

---

Information on trends in U.S. media coverage of international news can be found in the following reports in the archives of the *American Journalism Review*:

"State of the American Newspaper: Goodbye, World," by Peter Arnett, 1998 (http://ajrarchive.org/Article.asp?id=3288)

"Retreating from the World," by Jodi Enda, 2010–2011 (http://ajrarchive.org/article.asp?id=4985)

Up-to-date information on deaths of journalists worldwide can be found on a dedicated Committee to Protect Journalists web page (https://www.cpj.org/killed/), which offers regular detailed updates.

---

Second, new outlets emerged in other global centers, including India (Press Trust of India, 1949) and West Germany (Deutsche Welle, 1962), at a time when many nations, particularly in the Global South, were seeking to chart a relatively independent path between the capital-ist and socialist blocs. The creation of the Non-Aligned Movement in 1961, building on momentum from the 1955 Bandung Conference, gave expression to this alternative geopo-litical vision. Finally, the launch of the first geosynchronous communication satellite in 1963 pointed the way toward a new stage in global news broadcasting, one in which satellite technology would enable powerful news outlets to engage in round-the-clock news gathering and distribution. Here again, changes in the media sector are organically connected with broader aspects of globalization. The ability of news organizations to increase the speed of their operations while also extending their geographical reach to the limits of the planet exemplified the more general phenomenon of time-space compression, which is widely viewed as one of the central characteristics of globalization itself. Whether understood as heralding the creation of a "global village" (a term coined by the Canadian media theorist Marshall McLuhan in the 1960s) or the creation of a more claustrophobic world marked by real-time media and information overload, the enveloping of the world by satellites changed the news media world decisively.

The year 1980 stands out as a symbolic turning point, as a number of events in that year revealed ongoing tensions in the global news media system, and in the global information system more broadly. On the one hand, the launch of CNN revealed the ability of U.S. firms to dominate the emergent market in twenty-four-hour satellite news broadcasting. The global influence of CNN soon reached the point that scholars coined the phrase "CNN effect" to describe what they saw as CNN's direct role in shaping state policy and public opinion. In subsequent years CNN was followed by other major Global North satellite channels, such as Sky News and Euronews.

On the other hand, 1980 also saw the publication by UNESCO of the MacBride Report (officially titled *Many Voices, One World*), which strongly criticized the systematic inequalities in global information flows and called for a New World Information and Communications Order (NWICO) that would promote more democratic control of and access to information. For supporters of the NWICO idea, including many members of the Non-Aligned Movement, the existing information system represented a form of neocolonialism that preserved the dominance of the Global North. The NWICO initiative was ultimately marginalized through strong counter-pressure from the United States and United Kingdom, including transnational media firms based in those countries, and Robert Hackett and Zhao Yuezhi note that the UN responded by replacing "NWICO's potentially radical media-democratization project" with "a narrowly defined developmentalist project emphasizing the provision of Western-based technologies and professional training for Third World journalists" (2005, 5). Nonetheless, the debate over NWICO showed that Global South voices were becoming increasingly aware of the political and cultural importance of media issues—and increasingly willing to articulate alternative visions.

Arguably the most far-reaching development for global media during this period, however, was the wave of global deregulation spearheaded by U.S. President Ronald Reagan and U.K. Prime Minister Margaret Thatcher. Part of a broader process of neoliberal restructuring and privatization of state industries, deregulation radically changed the face of the media sector. When combined with the breakdown of the socialist bloc and the emergence of new digital technologies, the shift toward neoliberal restructuring "unleashed the force of capital and paved the way for the formation of a market-driven communication system on a global scale" (Hackett and Zhao 2005, 6). This shift enabled a sharp rise in mergers and acquisitions in the media sector.

The former *Washington Post* editor Ben Bagdikian warned of the dangers of media consolidation in his influential 1983 book *The Media Monopoly*, noting that deregulation had already enabled a few dozen firms to control the vast majority of media content, including everything from news and entertainment programing to book publishing, filmmaking, and music production. Since that time, the number of major players in the industry has dwindled further. While supporters of deregulation promised that more open competition would lead to a greater diversity of media content, critics of these policies argue that consolidation has done precisely the opposite, promoting a homogenization of content that bears the political and cultural stamp of conservative elites.

Information about the six major Global North media conglomerates may be found at the following links:

The Walt Disney Company (http://thewaltdisneycompany.com/)
Time Warner Cable (http://www.timewarnercable.com/en/about-us/company-overview.html)
News Corp (http://newscorp.com/about/) and 21st Century Fox (http://www.21cf.com/)

Bertelsmann (http://www.bertelsmann.com/company/company-profile/)
CBS Corporation (http://www.cbscorporation.com/)
Vivendi SA (http://www.vivendi.com)

Information about large regional media conglomerates in the Global South may be found at the following links:

Grupo Televisa (http://www.televisa.com/us/)
Organizações Globo (http://redeglobo.globo.com/)
IPP Media (www.ippmedia.com/)
Naspers (http://www.naspers.com/)
Network 18 (http://www.network18online.com/)
Shanghai Media & Entertainment Group (http://www.smg.cn/english_index.shtml)

The impact of these structural changes on the quality of mainstream news media coverage in particular has been the subject of much critical analysis. Equally important, however, the global news media status quo has been disrupted during the past two decades by three main factors, each of which in its own way challenges preexisting geographical and cultural patterns. The first is the emergence of Global South satellite broadcasters (such as Al Jazeera and TeleSUR, discussed in more detail later), a process that fits within broader processes of regionalization and South-South cooperation.

---

### The World Social Forum and the "Right to Communication"

Beginning in 2001, the World Social Forum (WSF) emerged as a focal point for the efforts of global social justice activists, particularly those located in the Global South. Whereas telecommunications issues tend to be relatively ignored in public discourse in the Global North, the WSF has sought to include these issues as part of a larger critique of global power structures and their impact on cultures and people's lives. A March 2013 declaration issued in Tunisia as part of a WSF-affiliated gathering notes that "information and knowledge are common goods" and argues that "the right to communication is a fundamental and inalienable right." The concept of a right to communication—relatively new in global public discourse—is connected with a wide range of interrelated issues, including privatization of the media sector, democratic access to information, the "digital divide" between those who have easy access to Internet technology and those who do not, and the role of media and communication in enabling meaningful citizen participation in public life. For many local and transnational activists, addressing other social justice issues will be impossible without significant attention to media and communication.

For another perspective on the WSF, see Hilde C. Stephanson's article "Media Activism in the World Social Forum," available from openDemocracy (http://www.opendemocracy.net/hilde-c-stephansen/media-activism-in-world-social-forum).

---

The second factor is the growth of powerful online firms such as Google, Yahoo!, Twitter, YouTube, and Facebook and their extension into the realm of circulating and even producing news content. While these firms are generally based in the Global North, they nonetheless represent interesting challenges to the kinds of traditional media firms that have dominated the market since the dawn of the broadcast age. The third factor, also rendered possible by Internet technology, is the explosion of new forms of noncorporate journalism, including citizen journalism, independent investigative journalism, and radical interventions such as WikiLeaks and the work of whistleblowers who either cooperate with major news outlets or bypass them altogether.

Information about key examples of alternative, noncorporate, and citizen journalism may be found at the following links:

NAM News Network (www.namnewsnetwork.org)
WikiLeaks (https://wikileaks.org/)
Independent Media Center (http://www.indymedia.org/or/index.shtml)
Institute for War & Peace Reporting (http://iwpr.net/)
Ohmy News (http://www.ohmynews.com/)
NCA Africa News Update (http://www.afrika.no)

Media scholars such as Natalie Fenton (2010) are quick to point out that belief in the ability of new technologies to produce more liberating social arrangements must always be balanced against the knowledge that those who already benefit from existing technologies and dominate existing institutions are almost inevitably able to leverage new technologies for their own benefit. As cultural studies scholars such as Raymond Williams (1973) have long argued, dominant cultures (in this case, the capitalist culture headquartered in the Global North) always respond to emergent cultural forms through strategies of selective incorporation, seeking to retain their dominance while allowing themselves to be influenced by alternative voices. How the various challenges discussed here will ultimately shape the nearly two-hundred-year-old global media system, and how this dynamic will influence the larger cultural politics of globalization itself, remains to be seen.

## Al Jazeera

Al Jazeera, which in Arabic means "the island" or "the peninsula," understood to refer to the Arabian Peninsula, was founded in 1996, with initial funding provided by the emir of Qatar, where the network is headquartered. While hundreds of Arabic-language satellite news channels now exist, Al Jazeera is by far the most influential, both within and beyond the region. Its twenty-four-hour Arabic-language news programming is widely available throughout the Middle East, where most people receive television via satellite dishes. It began producing programming in English in 2003 at the start of the Iraq War, launched an English-language channel (Al Jazeera International) in 2006, and drew widespread admiration for its comprehensive, on-the-ground coverage of the Egyptian revolution in 2011 and the wider events associated with the so-called Arab Spring protests. In early 2013, Al Jazeera launched a new twenty-four-hour news channel, Al Jazeera America, specifically aimed at a U.S. audience and designed to compete with dominant cable news providers CNN, Fox News, and MSNBC, but low ratings ultimately led the parent company to scrap the channel in early 2016.

This photo is taken from a balcony overlooking the main Al Jazeera English television studio in Doha, Qatar, where Al Jazeera has had its headquarters since it was founded in 1996.

*Source:* Liam Wyatt/Wikimedia Commons. https://commons.wikimedia.org/wiki/File:Al_Jazeera_English_Newsroom.jpg

---

### Al Jazeera on the Web

Al Jazeera content may be accessed online via the following websites:

http://www.aljazeera.net (official Arabic-language site)
http://www.aljazeera.com/ (Al Jazeera English)
http://america.aljazeera.com/ (Al Jazeera America)
http://balkans.aljazeera.com/ (Al Jazeera Balkans)
http://aljazeera.com.tr/ (Al Jazeera Turk)
https://www.youtube.com/user/aljazeerachannel (Arabic-language video)
https://www.youtube.com/user/AlJazeeraEnglish (English-language video)

---

Three major events in the region during Al Jazeera's first decade—the second Palestinian intifada (uprising) in 2000, the U.S. invasion of Afghanistan following the September 11, 2001, attacks, and the Iraq War in 2003—provided strong evidence of Al Jazeera's ability to disseminate news coverage and to shape public opinion among Arab viewers, whether located in the Middle East or in diasporic communities throughout the world. Mohammed El-Nawawy and Adel Iskander, the authors of one book on Al Jazeera's growing influence, use the example of an Arab-Canadian family in Halifax, Nova Scotia. The entrance of Al Jazeera into their world of news media options provoked lively debates not only about the content (e.g., the whereabouts of Osama bin Laden in late 2001) but also about the coverage (e.g., comparing Al Jazeera with CNN on the issue of showing pictures of civilian casualties in war). "For the first time, table talk revolves around politics, instead of what new music CD is selling, what the kids will do that evening, school reports, and phone bills," they write. "These days, Al-Jazeera sets the agenda . . . . Since the beginning of the second Palestinian Intifada, the network has been the preferred source of news for the family" (El-Nawawy and Iskander 2002, 2–3).

The founders of Al Jazeera set out to approach the process of news gathering and broadcasting through a philosophy of providing, according to the network's motto, "the opinion, and the other opinion." In doing so, they were conscious of the channel's potential impact both regionally and globally. At the regional level, the network sought to break a longstanding pattern of state-controlled news media in the Arab world and to create a space that would allow for open discussion and debate regarding issues affecting people in the region. In the 2004 documentary film *Control Room*, Samir Khader, a senior producer at Al Jazeera, expresses his own interpretation of the network's mission in relation to the people of the region:

> My own feeling is that the message of Al Jazeera is, first of all, education: to educate the Arab masses on something called democracy, respect of the other opinion, the free debate, and to try, while using all these things, to shake up these rigid societies, to awaken them, to tell them, "Wake up! Wake up! There is a world around you! Something is happening in the world, and you are still sleeping. Wake up!" This is the message of Al Jazeera.

In aiming to "shake up" the region and help bring about such a cultural transformation, Al Jazeera aimed its efforts not only at ordinary people, but also at their leaders. During its early years, particularly before other competitors emerged, the network became famous for its lively political talk shows, which often gave viewers the chance to ask direct questions of government ministers and other powerful figures who had rarely, if ever, made themselves available to the public in this way. Marc Lynch, the author of an influential book on the emergence of an "Arab public sphere" beginning in the 1990s, notes that in the process, "what would in the past have been a private discussion among elites" took on a "highly public character" (2006, 139).

As governments in the region began to lose a bit of their control over the flow of information, many found themselves at odds with Al Jazeera. The list of Middle Eastern governments that have accused the network of bias, closed its offices, or tried to ban its coverage ranges from Iraq to Egypt to Israel. Given the network's popularity and influence among ordinary people throughout the region, however, most governments have also found it difficult to say "no" when given the opportunity to appear on its programs. More recently, a number of Al Jazeera journalists have been arrested for various lengths of time by the Egyptian authorities in the aftermath of the 2013 military coup in that country.

Al Jazeera has also succeeded in "shaking up" patterns of representation that stretch well beyond the Middle East. The channel came into the consciousness of many in the Global North through its decision to broadcast statements released by al-Qaeda leader Osama bin Laden. While such moves generated significant controversy, including occasional charges that it was providing ideological support to terrorist organizations, Al Jazeera defended its decisions on the grounds that it was simply providing coverage of newsworthy events and perspectives. Such an argument obviously grated on the sensibilities of viewers who had become accustomed to networks that had long provided disproportionate coverage of what leaders of powerful Global North nations were saying. The often tense relationship between Al Jazeera and its critics in the United States is also represented by two U.S. missile strikes on Al Jazeera offices in Afghanistan and Iraq in 2001 and 2003, respectively, with the second strike killing Tareq Ayyoub, one of the network's reporters.

Also important from a global studies perspective is the nature of Al Jazeera's news coverage. Many of the basic elements of Al Jazeera's reporting and broadcasting style follow standards and models established long ago in the wider news industry—which is hardly surprising, given that many of the network's early hires were journalists who had previously worked for the BBC and other major broadcasters. As a result, Al Jazeera's on-air programming features news headlines read by anchors and presenters sitting behind desks or standing in front of large monitors; studio shows featuring commentary, debate, and analysis; reporters covering major political events and institutions; live and investigative coverage of on-the-ground events; and so forth. Similarly, the basic design of its news websites echoes broader patterns within the industry by featuring video clips, headlines of "top stories" and "trending" topics, content organized by various geographic and thematic categories, and links to information about on-air and social media content.

Beyond these structural similarities, however, it is also clear that Al Jazeera "selectively articulates" the world in its own distinct way. Given the company's location, it is not surprising to find that its main Arabic-language and English-language websites both prominently feature a wide range of content from throughout the Middle East, Central and South Asia, and Africa. Its English broadcast schedule includes a variety of programs designed to feature Global South perspectives, including *South2North* (a global talk show hosted from South Africa), *Inside Syria* (focusing on the Syrian civil war that began in 2011), and *Empire* (its flagship discussion program, which often takes a critical look at the impact of Global North domination).

### The Stream

One of Al Jazeera's most popular and successful programs, *The Stream*, appeals to a young and global audience through a heavy use of social media to promote dialogue on current topics. It can be accessed online at http://stream.aljazeera.com/.

A comparison of the main websites of Al Jazeera America and CNN reveals that the former features fewer advertisements, a more consistent focus on what is often called serious or "hard" news (as opposed to stories about sports, entertainment, and the lives of celebrities), and a tendency to spotlight stories that are often underreported by mainstream U.S. news networks. In the months following the launch of Al Jazeera America, for example, its website devoted significant space to in-depth reporting about Native American issues, sexual assault on U.S. college campuses, and protests against hydraulic fracturing ("fracking"). Such coverage reveals a significant effort to shift the global "politics of representation," reversing the typical direction of representation: from the Global North trained on the Global South, to the Global South looking "northward."

## TeleSUR

TeleSUR (shorthand for La Nueva Televisora del Sur, or the New Television of the South), a Venezuela-based regional broadcast network founded in 2005, shows the influence of Al Jazeera's pioneering work, but it also has its own distinct mission grounded in the particular political-economic and cultural realities of twenty-first-century Latin America. Closely identified with the "Bolivarian Revolution" that transformed Venezuela into a socialist state under the leadership of the late Hugo Chavez beginning in the late 1990s, TeleSUR has sought to promote Latin American regional integration and a more independent form of cultural and political self-representation. Its slogan, "Nuestro Norte es el Sur" (Our North is the South), signals the network's desire to challenge prevailing hemispheric relations that have long placed the South (which it defines as "a geopolitical concept that promotes the people's struggle for peace, self-determination, respect for human rights and social justice") in a peripheral, subordinate relationship to the North in general, and the United States in particular.

While TeleSUR thus far has not had the same global impact or audience as Al Jazeera, both networks have benefited from rising revenues in the fossil fuel sector. TeleSUR's primary source of funding is the Venezuelan government's oil revenues, but it also receives significant support from several other Latin American states. Its board of directors includes prominent cultural figures from within and beyond the region, many of whom are prominent left-leaning critics of global capitalism and U.S. hegemony. Its broadcasts are available via satellite throughout Latin America and, increasingly, in other parts of the world. In addition to its standard Spanish-language content, it provides some video and other content in both English and Portuguese, with the latter aimed at audiences in Brazil and former Portuguese colonies in sub-Saharan Africa. The network's live programming also streams online for those who have Internet access.

TeleSUR content may be accessed online via the following websites:

http://www.telesurtv.net/ (main Spanish-language website)
http://www.telesurtv.net/el-canal/senal-en-vivo (live transmission in Spanish)
https://www.youtube.com/user/telesurtv (Spanish-language video)
https://www.youtube.com/user/telesurenglish (English-language video)

Analysis of TeleSUR is inevitably shaped by its close relationship to Chavez, whose role in recent Venezuelan and global political history—even following his death in 2013—has been characterized in terms of everything from dictatorship to authoritarian populism to revolutionary democracy. Most analysts agree, however, that the network's emergence and orientation must be placed in a wider context that reaches beyond Venezuela to include recent changes in the regional media environment, political and cultural challenges to longstanding patterns of geopolitical hierarchy, and regionally based responses to globalization.

Mass media scholars who focus on Latin America highlight the widespread privatization of the media in the region in recent decades, which is part of a broader wave of neoliberal restructuring that left the media largely in the hands of a small number of private conglomerates such as Televisa in Mexico and TV Globo in Brazil. As in the United States and elsewhere, this consolidation has led to a growing emphasis on celebrity and entertainment coverage—sometimes referred to by critics as "tabloidization" or "infotainment"—and has also made it difficult for other voices to break into the public conversation. With the rise of left-leaning governments in several countries, along with associated popular social move-ments, however, demand for more democratic control of media created a space for alterna-tives to the private media.

At the same time, many observers note that, given the history of repressive military dic-tatorships in the region, Latin Americans have strong historical reasons to be wary of state-controlled media. This presents a significant challenge for TeleSUR, given its close ties to the Venezuelan state. The Chavez government's 2006 decision not to renew the public broad-cast license of the private RCTV (Radio Caracas Televisión) fueled these concerns even as government supporters justified the move as part of building a communications infrastruc-ture to aid the larger project of resisting neoliberalism and promoting twenty-first-century socialism.

The political economy of the media sector has direct implications for the politics of rep-resentation and for TeleSUR's larger cultural mission, which is often overlooked amid the polemical debate regarding Chavez and the Bolivarian Revolution. Sally Burch notes that for decades most television programming in Latin America came from outside the region and that most Latin Americans got their news from CNN's Spanish-language service or other Global North outlets. She quotes Aram Aharonian, an Uruguayan journalist who served as the network's first general director, and who emphasizes the importance of creating spaces where Latin Americans can bypass external representations and learn about one another more directly: "From the North they see us in black and white—mostly in black; we only appear in the news when a calamity occurs—and in reality, we are a continent in Technicolor" (quoted in Burch 2007, 228). In this sense one can view TeleSUR as seeking to create a new kind of public sphere in Latin America, much as Al Jazeera has tried to do in the Middle East.

Moving to the global level, many analysts emphasize the network's mission of providing a critical and distinctly Latin American response to the dominant forces driving what Philip McMichael (2012) calls the "globalization project." The Mexican scholar Armando Carbal-lal Cano, for example, notes that "the globalizing ideology and its simplistic metaphors, apologetic and uncritical, are transmitted in the field of global communication" (2009, 131; translation by author) and characterizes TeleSUR as promoting "an editorial line critical of the globalizing process, neoliberalism, the role of the United States in the region and in favor of [regional] integration" (134; translation by author).

In this sense, TeleSUR can be viewed as operating within two overlapping traditions that are influential both within and beyond Latin America. The first is the broad tradition of anticolonialism that extends back for centuries, including the Latin American independence movements of the early nineteenth century and the subsequent wave of global decoloniza-tion in the mid-to-late twentieth century. This tradition includes not only strong elements of nationalism and national self-determination, but also elements of transnational solidarity among people seeking to free themselves from colonial domination. The second, more spe-cific tradition is the history of critiques of the global communications system going back to the NWICO debate. Much like the global activists connected with the World Social Forum, many of TeleSUR's supporters see the democratization of communication as a central ele-ment in the fight for global justice.

Like Al Jazeera, TeleSUR structures its news gathering and reporting operations according to well-established television journalism formats and conventions, from its staff of presenters and correspondents to its use of scrolling headlines across the bottom of the screen. Its flag-ship programs such as *Edición Central, Conexión Global,* and *Dossier* address national, regional, and global events with a mix of news coverage, analysis, and debate. Other programs address the economy, regional issues, cultural themes, sports, science and technology, and environmental news. In keeping with the growing popularity of user-generated content, the network also features video from ordinary citizens on *Soy Reportero* (http://www.telesurtv. net/seccion/imreporter/index.html).

TeleSUR's particular mode of "selective articulation" is visible in at least three ways. First, the network can be quite open in its promotion of the policies and values associated with the Bolivarian Revolution and its leaders and allies. This tendency was visible during the 2006 national elections, when coverage was generally favorable toward Chavez and critical toward opposition figures, who were viewed by the regime as preparing a campaign to undermine democracy in the country. The same tendency emerged, albeit in a more conflicted way, in TeleSUR's coverage of the Arab Spring protests beginning in late 2010. As Massimo Di Ricco (2012) notes, the coverage was initially very sympathetic to the grassroots protesters in Tunisia and Egypt, but later became much more sympathetic to the Arab regimes in response to the multilateral intervention in Libya, an intervention heavily criticized as imperialist by the Chavez government. More generally, the selection of news items on the network's website reveals a preference for stories that highlight positive aspects of governments (e.g., Cuba or Bolivia) and grassroots movements that are more sympathetic to the revolution, whereas governments (in neighboring Colombia, for instance) and opposition movements reflecting the interests of upper-class populations are treated more critically.

For some analysts, such as the former BBC editor James Painter (2008), this alignment with the Venezuelan state, its national goals, and its geopolitical stance signals a lack of "editorial independence" (57) and a tendency to provide news coverage that is "agenda-driven" (71) rather than "objective." Others point out that the very concept of "objectivity" emerged out of the professionalization of journalists in the Global North, many of whom work for private media outlets that tend to privilege establishment voices. As Burch asks, "[H]as similar criticism [of a lack of independence from state power and dominant ideological frameworks] not been leveled at times at the BBC or CNN?" (2007, 231).

Second, in keeping with its focus on regional integration and self-representation, TeleSUR clearly looks at the world from a Latin American perspective that seeks to spotlight the experiences of ordinary people throughout the region and to connect those experiences with global processes. One example is *Entre Fronteras*, a program addressing themes of global migration. An edition of the program in early 2014 began with a series of brief items such as a news report on migrant workers facing discrimination in Europe, the opening of an office in Guatemala designed to assist workers planning to migrate north, and an update on policy debates and grassroots action related to immigration policy in the United States. These were followed by a more detailed exploration of how internal migration in Peru, particularly involving socially disadvantaged indigenous and Afro-Peruvian people, has led to a public discourse of multiculturalism that may obscure longstanding patterns of racism. While the program's focus is on one of the key themes of globalization (human migration), its particular orientation toward this theme, consistent with the populist leanings of the Bolivarian Revolution, is to prioritize the experiences of marginalized populations.

Finally, TeleSUR also echoes Al Jazeera America in offering critical coverage of stories that often go underreported in the traditionally dominant global media outlets, especially private media that typically concentrate their attention on immediate events and the actions and words of political and other elites, rather than on longer-term structural processes. Just as Al Jazeera America provided extensive coverage of Native American issues, for example, TeleSUR regularly covers the actions of indigenous social movements. Its English and Spanish video sites contain dozens of reports spotlighting topics such as indigenous activists fighting against major construction projects (e.g., in Brazil or Mexico) and the struggles of indigenous communities facing poverty and structural violence (e.g., in Paraguay or Guatemala). TeleSUR has also devoted significant attention to news from Haiti. While much of this coverage is designed to present Venezuela and its allies in a positive light by highlighting the assistance they are providing to Haiti, it does represent a more sustained level of journalistic engagement with the country than that provided by global private media, which tend to ignore Haiti except when there is a major disaster, such as the 2010 earthquake.

External responses to the emergence of TeleSUR mirror some of the responses to Al Jazeera. Some Latin American governments, perhaps pressured by private telecommunications conglomerates based in their countries, have sought to limit TeleSUR's access to their cable television markets. Others have objected to specific elements of the network's content, as in 2007, when officials in Colombia accused a TeleSUR correspondent of being sympathetic to the FARC rebel group in that country. Politicians in the United States, offended by Chavez's critiques of the country, and of the Bush administration in particular, have accused the network of being a propaganda vehicle for Chavez and his successor, Nicolás Maduro, and even of promoting terrorism. Many of these responses reflect dissatisfaction at the political level with the emergence of a strong, socialist state in Venezuela. As Nikolas Kozloff (2011) notes, however, U.S. officials have also expressed concern about the cultural impact of TeleSUR: according to U.S. diplomatic cables released by WikiLeaks, officials at the U.S. embassy in Caracas worried in 2005 that a successful experiment in locally controlled news media might lead to "endogenous (non-US) cultural development."

## References and Further Research

Anderson, Benedict. 2006. *Imagined Communities: Reflections on the Origin and Spread of Nationalism*. Rev. ed. New York: Verso.

Arnett, Peter. 1998. "State of the American Newspaper: Goodbye, World." *American Journalism Review*, November. http://ajrarchive.org/Article.asp?id=3288.

Burch, Sally. 2007. "Telesur and the New Agenda for Latin American Integration." *Global Media and Communication* 3, no. 2: 227–232.

Carballal Cano, Armando. 2009. "TeleSUR: Construyendo una televisión para la integración latinoamericana." *Estudios Latinoamericanos, nueva época* 24. http://www.revistas.unam.mx/index.php/rel/article/view/20253.

Di Ricco, Massimo. 2012. "The Arab Spring Is a Latin American Winter: TeleSUR's 'Ideological Approach' and the Breakaway from the *Al-Jazeera* Network." *Global Media Journal* (German Edition) 2, no. 1 (Spring/Summer). http://www.globalmediajournal.de/2012/05/07/the-arab-spring-is-a-latin-american-winter-telesurs-%E2%80%9Cideological-approach%E2%80%9D-and-the-breakaway-from-the-al-jazeera-network/.

El-Nawawy, Mohammed, and Adel Iskander. 2002. *Al-Jazeera: How the Free Arab News Network Scooped the World and Changed the Middle East*. Cambridge, MA: Westview.

Enda, Jodi. 2010–2011. "Retreating from the World." *American Journalism Review*, December/January. http://ajrarchive.org/article.asp?id=4985.

Fenton, Natalie, ed. 2010. *New Media, Old News: Journalism and Democracy in the Digital Age*. Los Angeles: SAGE.

Grossberg, Lawrence, Ellen Wartella, and D. Charles Whitney. 1998. *MediaMaking: Mass Media in a Popular Culture*. Thousand Oaks, CA: SAGE.

Habermas, Jürgen. 1989. *The Structural Transformation of the Public Sphere: An Inquiry Into a Category of Bourgeois Society*. Cambridge, MA: MIT Press.

Hackett, Robert A., and Yuezhi Zhao, eds. 2005. *Democratizing Global Media: One World, Many Struggles*. Lanham, MD: Rowman & Littlefield.

Hall, Stuart, Chas Critcher, Tony Jefferson, John Clarke, and Brian Roberts. 1978. *Policing the Crisis: Mugging, the State, and Law and Order*. New York: Holmes & Meier.

Herman, Edward, and Noam Chomsky. 1988. *Manufacturing Consent: The Political Economy of the Mass Media*. New York: Pantheon.

Herman, Edward S., and Robert W. McChesney. 1997. *The Global Media: The New Missionaries of Global Capitalism*. London and Washington, DC: Cassell.

Hudson Mohawk Independent Media Center, prod. 2003. *Independent Media in a Time of War*. Featuring Amy Goodman. DVD. Northampton, MA: Media Education Foundation.

Jansen, Sue Curry. 2002. *Critical Communication Theory: Power, Media, Gender, and Technology*. Lanham, MD: Rowman & Littlefield.

Kozloff, Nikolas. 2011. "Beware of 'Al-Chavezeera'." *Al Jazeera*, October 4. http://www.aljazeera.com/indepth/opinion/2011/10/2011101131015237289.html.

Lynch, Marc. 2006. *Voices of the New Arab Public: Iraq, Al-Jazeera, and Middle East Politics Today*. New York: Columbia University Press.

McLuhan, Marshall. 1964. *Understanding Media: The Extensions of Man*. New York: McGraw Hill.

McMichael, Philip. 2012. *Development and Social Change: A Global Perspective*. 5th ed. Los Angeles: SAGE.

Painter, James. 2008. *Counter-Hegemonic News: A Case Study of Al-Jazeera English and Telesur*. Oxford: Reuters Institute for the Study of Journalism.

Said, Edward. 1997. *Covering Islam: How the Media and the Experts Determine How We See the Rest of the World*. Rev. ed. New York: Vintage.

Schiller, Herbert I. 1989. *Culture, Inc.: The Corporate Takeover of Public Expression*. New York: Oxford University Press.

Stephanson, Hilde C. 2012. "Media Activism in the World Social Forum." *openDemocracy*, October 3. http://www.opendemocracy.net/hilde-c-stephansen/media-activism-in-world-social-forum.

van Ginneken, Jaap. 1998. *Understanding Global News: A Critical Introduction*. London and Thousand Oaks, CA: SAGE.

Waldman, Steven, and The Working Group on Information Needs of Communities. 2011. *Information Needs of Communities: The Changing Media Landscape in a Broadband Age*. Washington, DC: Federal Communications Commission. http://www.fcc.gov/info-needs-communities.

Williams, Raymond. 1973. "Base and Superstructure in Marxist Cultural Theory." *New Left Review* I/82, November-December. http://newleftreview.org/I/82/raymond-williams-base-and-superstructure-in-marxist-cultural-theory.

# 6

# Indigenous Peoples and Intellectual Property Rights

> We address and offer thanks to the earth where human beings dwell, to the streams, the pools, and the lakes, the corn and fruits, the medicines and trees, to the forests for their usefulness, and to the animals that are food and give their pelts for clothing, to the great winds, and the lesser ones, to the thunder; to the Sun, the mighty warrior, to the moon; to the messengers of the Creator who reveal his wishes and to the Creator who dwells in the heavens above who gives all things useful to humans, and who is the source and the ruler of health and life.
>
> Taiaiake Alfred, *Peace, Power, Righteousness: An Indigenous Manifesto*

There is a paradox in speaking of "global indigenous peoples," in that the term "global" signifies transnational flows, whereas "indigenous" signifies an attachment to a particular place. Nonetheless, in the age of globalization, relatively small groups of indigenous peoples, otherwise marginalized from the global political economy, and also marginalized within the state where they live, have found global alliances to be useful in strengthening their struggles for recognition and for human rights. This case study examines how indigeneity is defined today, as well as some of the particular challenges facing indigenous peoples in maintaining and reclaiming their cultural practices in the face of intellectual property regimes. Intellectual property rights are designed to protect the rights of those who discover or create new knowledge. When scientists or corporations "discover" the healing properties of plants that indigenous peoples have been using for centuries, suddenly those plants belong to corporations and the indigenous people have no more right to them than anyone else. The first part of the chapter will examine North American examples of the problems inherent in defining indigenous identities, and the discussion will then turn to Latin America for examples of clashes between indigenous lifeways and corporate capitalism.

## Background

The state boundaries of the contemporary world have little to do with the cultural groupings of people who have in many cases been in place for thousands of years. Most national boundaries were drawn by colonial powers, such as France and Great Britain in Africa, dividing some groups and throwing others together. In the wake of the decolonization movements of the mid-twentieth century, as well as the redrawing of boundaries during and after various wars, many of the newly independent states have engaged in nation-building projects, seeking to create a common national identity where none existed before. That is particularly true in sub-Saharan Africa. In other areas, states have broken down into smaller ethno-nations as in the former Yugoslavia. In the Americas, most states achieved independence from their colonizers by the end of the nineteenth century, but the new states retained elite settler classes descended from the colonizers and kept indigenous populations impoverished and marginalized.

Since the 1980s there have been a number of groups and working papers concerned with indigenous peoples' rights within the UN, the most important of which were the 1982 Martinez Cobo Report, the 1993 Draft Declaration on the Rights of Indigenous Peoples, and establishment in 2000 of the Permanent Forum on Indigenous Peoples.

---

**Major Steps in Global Recognition of Indigenous Peoples**

International Labour Organization conventions in response to forced labor:

1957: Convention 107 (The Indigenous and Tribal Populations Convention)
1989: Convention 169 (The Indigenous and Tribal Peoples Convention)

UN Processes:

1947: Establishment of Sub-Commission on Prevention of Discrimination and
    Protection of Minorities
1982: Working Group on Indigenous Populations report by Martinez Cobo
1983: First inclusion of indigenous peoples in working groups
1993: Draft Declaration on the Rights of Indigenous Peoples
1993: International Year of the World's Indigenous Peoples
1995–2004: International Decade of the World's Indigenous Peoples
2000: UN Permanent Forum on Indigenous Issues (UNPFII) established
2005–2014: Second International Decade of the World's Indigenous Peoples
2007: Declaration on the Rights of Indigenous Peoples adopted by UN General Assembly
2007: Expert Mechanism on the Rights of Indigenous Peoples established

---

The Working Group on Indigenous Populations was first formed in 1982. At that time, Jose R. Martinez Cobo, the Special Rapporteur of the Sub-Commission on Prevention of Discrimination and Protection of Minorities for the UN, proposed a definition of indigenous peoples that has been important in discussions of indigeneity ever since. In Cobo's definition, one that this case study draws on heavily, the idea of historical continuity—of a group of people extending back prior to colonial settlement—is critical, as is the right to self-definition by the indigenous peoples themselves.

---

**Cobo's Concept of Indigenous Peoples**

The following is Jose R. Martinez Cobo's working definition of indigenous peoples:

> Indigenous communities, peoples and nations are those which, having a historical continuity with pre-invasion and pre-colonial societies that developed on their territories, consider themselves distinct from other sectors of the societies now prevailing on those territories, or parts of them. They form at present non-dominant sectors of society and are determined to preserve, develop and transmit to future generations their ancestral territories, and their ethnic identity, as the basis of their continued existence as peoples, in accordance with their own cultural patterns, social institutions and legal system.

This historical continuity may consist of the continuation, for an extended period reaching into the present of one or more of the following factors:

a) Occupation of ancestral lands, or at least of part of them;
b) Common ancestry with the original occupants of these lands;
c) Culture in general, or in specific manifestations (such as religion, living under a tribal system, membership of an indigenous community, dress, means of livelihood, lifestyle, etc.);
d) Language (whether used as the only language, as mother-tongue, as the habitual means of communication at home or in the family, or as the main, preferred, habitual, general, or normal language);
e) Residence on certain parts of the country, or in certain regions of the world;
f) Other relevant factors.

On an individual basis, an indigenous person is one who belongs to these indigenous populations through self-identification as indigenous (group consciousness) and is recognized and accepted by these populations as one of its members (acceptance by the group).

This preserves for these communities the sovereign right and power to decide who belongs to them, without external interference.

—from *The Concept of Indigenous Peoples*, background paper prepared by the Secretariat of the UN Permanent Forum on Indigenous Issues, PFII/2004/WS.1/3.

## Identifying Who Is Indigenous

Despite these efforts to establish working definitions, it is not always obvious which peoples and cultures are "indigenous." For example, virtually all of Africa was colonized, but only certain ethnic groups have identified themselves as indigenous in the sense defined by the United Nations. Mostly, they are hunter-gatherers and nomadic peoples who wish to stay on their lands and continue at least some aspects of their traditional way of life. As Cobo noted, indigeneity is largely a matter of self-definition, based on a long historical memory; identification with a specific place; and a desire to preserve key elements of ways of life, place-related knowledge, language, and identity. Cobo emphasized that indigenous peoples see themselves as distinct from other populations now living within the state in which they are located. Examples include various Native American groups; Canadian First Peoples; Central American *indios*; South American native peoples; South Asian and Southeast Asian "hill tribes;" the Maori of New Zealand; the many Aboriginal peoples of Australia, the Polynesians, and many more.

According to the United Nations 2009 report *State of the World's Indigenous Peoples* (Kipuri), approximately 370 million people who identify as indigenous are spread across about ninety countries today. Of the approximately seven thousand indigenous languages existing today, four thousand are spoken by small groups of indigenous peoples, and are consequently threatened with extinction. For more information on the world's indigenous peoples, including access to the report (under "Library and Documents"), see the website of the United Nations Permanent Forum on Indigenous Issues (http://undesadspd.org/IndigenousPeoples.aspx).

These ideas may sound simple, but they are exceedingly complex in practice. To illustrate the complexities caused by past colonization, the redrawing of boundaries, and evolving state policies, the situations of some Native American indigenous peoples are instructive. In the United States, for example, determining what native groups should be called or how to divide native peoples into separate groups is a process that has been obfuscated by official federal policy over hundreds of years. Once the United States achieved independence from Great Britain, the federal government went through many attempts to assimilate the surviving native people and to take their land. In the 1830s the Indian Removal Act confiscated all the native-held land in the Southeast and drove the native people in that region west of the Mississippi. The Cherokees went to the Supreme Court in a case against the state of Georgia and won, but to no avail. The Indian General Allotment Act of 1887 (or Dawes Act, administered by the Dawes Commission) took the tribal lands of the "Five Civilized Tribes," whose members had adopted Western-style clothing and manners. The idea was to give them private, individual allotments of land and thereby break down native practices of collective land use and territorial sovereignty. In this process, official tribal roles were created for each of these five tribes, authoritatively determining their membership from then on. However, in the 1930s, as part of the New Deal, John Collier, the commissioner of the Bureau of Indian Affairs, reversed the carving up of native lands and instead supported the sovereignty of tribal lands and native religious practices.

Some of the issues involved in defining membership in Native American tribes today illustrate the challenges of establishing indigenous peoples' identities after so many years of colonial destruction. To some degree, the ways colonial governments imposed definitions onto indigenous peoples has shaped their own self-definitions. For example, the Mohawk, or Kanien'kehá:ka, people, part of the Iroquois or Haudenosaunee Confederation, once occupied much of eastern New York State. As a result of supporting the British during the American Revolution and the French during the War of 1812, the Kanien'kehá:ka people ended up in smaller groupings along the U.S.-Canadian border in Ontario and outside Montreal in Quebec. The largest group lives straddling the border in and around the St. Lawrence River. With a population of twelve thousand, the Akwesasne/St. Regis community has to deal with two national governments, two Canadian provinces, and New York State. Further complexity over tribal governance is caused by the existence of both a traditional council of chiefs and separate (and often opposed) Canadian and U.S. tribal governments, elected according to the "democratic" guidelines of the national states. In the case of the Akwesasne, the traditional council of chiefs is appointed by the mothers of the "tribe," which is a matriarchal society. The chiefs are male, but they are subject to the approval of the mothers, who can remove them. This is but one example of the effects of colonial divide-and-conquer policies. Nonetheless, the strong will of the people to maintain their culture and identity has triumphed.

---

**Terminology**

The language used to describe groups of indigenous people carries negative connotations dating from first contact and colonization. Europeans often viewed non-Europeans as "primitive savages," but they sometimes romanticized them as "noble savages," who were not corrupted by "civilization." The colonized people were usually referred to in English as the "natives," and the word "tribe" was used to label specific cultures or ethnic groups.

Today, the word "native" has no inherently negative meaning; it simply means born in a particular place. However, if a Western person were to use the term "native" to refer to an African or Asian person today, it would likely be offensive, because it carries the suggestion of inferiority rooted in colonial history.

The word "tribe" has similar problems. In fact, in today's fashion and interior decorating magazines, you will see the word "tribal" used generically to refer to any markedly ethnic design, beading, or fabric from the Global South. The word has stuck in reference to African ethnic groups, Native American groups, and Asian indigenous groups. Like the word "native," it had no inherently negative meaning when it was first applied to the ethnic groups the Europeans came into contact with during the period from sixteenth to the nineteenth centuries. Deriving from the Latin word for "three," it was used as a label for any social grouping. However it acquired a connotation of otherness, inferiority, or proximity to nature through its use on colonized subjects, and that connotation has carried over into the present.

Today, the term "ethnic group" should be used in an African context. In Canada the indigenous people are "First Nations" and in Australia, native groups are referred to as "Aboriginal" people, though there are many different cultural groups among them. In the United States and India, the word "tribe" still has official usage, but it is preferable to say "people" or "ethnic group," or simply to use the proper name of the group. In discussing Native American groups later, the word "tribe" will be used in the context of official distinctions based on federal tribal enrollment and tribal recognition.

Prior to European colonization, different Native American cultures had different ways of determining membership in their nation. Some were much more open to intermarriage and the adoption of outsiders than others. However, starting soon after the first American colonies were established and up through the first half of the twentieth century, both states and the federal government have imposed their own ways of identifying who is an "Indian" and who belongs to specific tribes. These governmental methods were based on "blood quantum," the percentage of tribal ancestry an individual can prove. This method was originally used to discriminate against native people. In some cases, a person who had 1/32 native blood was defined as a person of color or an Indian in order to draw a line between privileged white people and people of color. Especially in the South, states often recognized people only as white or black/colored up until the Civil Rights Act of 1964. However, in the 1960s and 1970s, in the wake of the civil rights movement and the American Indian Movement (AIM), it became more fashionable to have native ancestry, and more people claimed it. Some people sought to claim tribal membership in order to profit from things like mineral rights or casino profits. Since 1960 the U.S. Census allows every individual to determine his or her own ethnic identity, and Native American population numbers have been increasing since that time. However, an individual's choice to identify as Native American does not equal tribal membership. Tribes now control who is recognized as a member, but in many cases that recognition is dependent on U.S. government tribal enrollments that took place up through the 1950s.

Most Native American tribes require from one-sixteenth to one-half "blood quantum" for membership in the group to be sanctioned. One of the problems with blood quantum as a method for determining tribal membership is that it depends on the enrollment of an ancestor on the government registers at some time in the first half of the twentieth century. Thus, some tribes are beginning to reject the blood quantum method, which was imposed originally by the federal government. In 2013, for instance, the White Earth Band of Ojibwe tribal members—living in the upper Midwest of the United

States—approved a new constitution that eliminates their 25 percent blood quantum requirement for membership in favor of criteria more loosely based on family lineage. Another group in Canada, the Kahnawake Mohawks outside Montreal, established a 50 percent blood quantum requirement in 1981, which was initially defined by the Canadian government. Because only members of the tribe could live on their land, people who were less than 50 percent Mohawk had to leave the territory where they and their families had been living and working. In 2003, this led to a more culturally defined approach, one based on both lineage and residency as well as commitment to the language and culture of the Kanien'kehá:ka. It is this cultural commitment to maintaining a particular way of life in a specific place that is definitive of indigenous status around the world today.

---

For information on meetings and documents pertaining to indigenous peoples, see the following:

Declaration on the Rights of Indigenous Peoples (http://www.un.org/esa/socdev/unpfii/documents/DRIPS_en.pdf)

*Operational Policy on Indigenous Peoples and Strategy for Indigenous Development*, Inter-American Development Bank (http://idbdocs.iadb.org/wsdocs/getdocument.aspx?docnum=1442299)

*State of the World's Indigenous Peoples*, UN Permanent Forum on Indigenous Issues (http://www.un.org/esa/socdev/unpfii/documents/SOWIP/en/SOWIP_web.pdf)

*Study of the Problem of Discrimination Against Indigenous Populations*, UN Doc. E/CN.4/Sub.2/1986/7 and Add. 1–4, by José Martínez Cobo (http://www.un.org/esa/socdev/unpfii/documents/MCS_xvii_en.pdf)

UN Permanent Forum on Indigenous Issues (https://www.un.org/development/desa/indigenouspeoples/unpfii-sessions-2.html)

---

## Indigenous Knowledge and Intellectual Property Rights

The world's indigenous groups face other challenges beyond establishing recognition for their peoples' cultures and international status. These include extreme poverty, threats to health, cultural assimilation, deprivation of their traditional lands, and commodification of their cultures. For this case study, the focus is on the theft of traditional knowledge, especially in Latin America. Because, by definition, indigenous peoples have lived for centuries in relation to specific ecosystems, they often have sustainable webs of relationships with the climate, flora, and fauna of those systems. Many know how to survive in challenging conditions, how to heal or prevent illness with plants, how to plant crops in specific combinations and at precise times, and so forth. Much of this knowledge is now labeled "traditional knowledge," passed down from generation to generation through oral means and collectively owned by the community or under the domain of particular occupations within the community. This knowledge, and in many cases the lifeways, of indigenous groups can be valuable in preserving both cultural and biological diversity in a world threatened by climate change and the cultural homogenization wrought by consumer capitalism.

**The United Nations on Protecting Traditional Knowledge**

Article 31 of the Declaration of the Rights of Indigenous Peoples and Traditional Knowledge, adopted by the UN General Assembly in 2008, states the following:

1.  Indigenous peoples have the right to maintain, control, protect and develop their cultural heritage, traditional knowledge and traditional cultural expressions, as well as the manifestations of their sciences, technologies and cultures, including human and genetic resources, seeds, medicines, knowledge of the properties of fauna and flora, oral traditions, literatures, designs, sports and traditional games and visual and performing arts. They also have the right to maintain, control, protect and develop their intellectual property over such cultural heritage, traditional knowledge, and traditional cultural expressions.
2.  In conjunction with indigenous peoples, States shall take effective measures to recognize and protect the exercise of these rights. (http://www.un.org/esa/socdev/unpfii/documents/DRIPS_en.pdf)

Protecting this traditional knowledge is critical for the survival of indigenous groups; however, the major mechanism for protecting knowledge, ideas, and inventions is intellectual property law. And, in an ironically cruel twist, the increasing global recognition of the value and validity of indigenous knowledge has in fact had a negative impact on indigenous communities. Indigenous communities have been the site of clashes between collective ownership based on traditional and Western (now global) legal definitions of property, patents, and copyrights.

Intellectual property laws are based on ideas about private ownership and individual originality, enshrined in Western values and legal instruments, and they are an important element of neoliberal globalization as enshrined in the World Trade Organization (WTO) and World Intellectual Property Organization (WIPO). From a Western perspective, intellectual property rights are a way to protect one's ideas and inventions from piracy or copying by others. This ideology of property rights is rooted in Western societies' intellectual history: it was enshrined by John Locke in his 1689 *Second Treatise of Government*, a rationale for the English Glorious Revolution of 1688–1689 and for the American Declaration of Independence. One of Locke's central premises is that private property is created when an individual mixes his or her labor with the raw materials of nature. Thus, a lump of clay becomes private property when a potter makes it into a bowl. *Intellectual* property focuses on inventions and innovations, as opposed to objects. To obtain a patent on an "invention," it must be original, arising from the work of specific individuals, and it must have commercial potential. Once an individual or group takes out a patent on an invention, they own it exclusively for a certain amount of time, the *term of patent*.

For more information on intellectual property rights, consult the *WIPO Intellectual Property Handbook* (http://www.wipo.int/about-ip/en/iprm/). For details on the controversy between patent protection for drug companies and the HIV/AIDS crisis in Africa, see the WIPO report *Patent Protection and Access to HIV/AIDS Pharmaceuticals in Sub-Saharan Africa* (http://www.wipo.int/export/sites/www/about-ip/en/studies/pdf/iipi_hiv.pdf).

Many claim that the term of ownership is critical to innovation and invention in the United States. In this way of thinking, owners of patents—of intellectual property, that is—hope to obtain the maximum period of control in order to earn revenues to pay for the cost of developing the invention and bringing it to market. Patent terms in the United States were seventeen years until 1995 when the United States signed onto the Agreement on Trade Related Aspects of Intellectual Property Rights (TRIPS), which lengthened the term to twenty years. However, companies that own patents often work creatively to extend a patent further. For instance, a drug company might simply change the delivery system of a drug in order to take out a new patent when the old one is running out.

## Intellectual Property Rights or Biopiracy?

The case of indigenous knowledge is quite different from the patent issues that are part of global agreements to protect intellectual property. Whereas intellectual property claims reside in new products originated at a specific time by a particular entity, the knowledge of an indigenous community is passed down over long periods of time through oral tradition, and its origin might be attributed to a god or mythic figure. The knowledge, practice, or plant belongs to the group and is meant to be possessed by them forever. To Western eyes, this means the knowledge is "in the public domain" and can be taken by anyone. This ideology goes back to the ideas of John Locke, summarized earlier. In the West, private property is fundamental to the organization of society. As capitalism and the Industrial Revolution developed through the eighteenth and nineteenth centuries, more and more land in Britain went from being public grazing land to private property through acts, or laws, of enclosure. Intellectual property law is the latest version of those acts of enclosure. Copyrights, patents, and trademarks delineate what is privately owned from that which is in the "public domain." Most of what is in the public domain is old and has passed its term of patent or copyright. For example an old version of a Shakespeare play might be out of copyright and thus in the public domain, meaning it can be photocopied and used without restrictions. However, a number of scholars have created new editions of Shakespeare's plays, with new introductions and footnotes, and perhaps some changes to punctuation and wording. These versions are then under copyright.

Some elements of nature remain in the public domain. These are the "global commons," parts of the Earth not under any jurisdiction, including the oceans beyond national borders, space, and part of the Earth's polar regions (some would include cyberspace as well). Arguably, the natural settings within which indigenous peoples live, such as the Amazon rainforest, should be considered part of the global commons, but they are not. Therefore, a pharmaceutical company can take an Amazonian plant traditionally used by local people for healing and adapt it to pill form, obtain a patent, and own it exclusively for twenty years.

Insightful discussion of intellectual property issues relating to indigenous peoples can be found in the issue paper *Indigenous/Traditional Knowledge and Intellectual Property Law* (http://web.law.duke.edu/cspd/itkpaper#ackn), prepared by Jane Anderson for Duke University's Center for the Study of the Public Domain. It can also be downloaded as a PDF (http://web.law.duke.edu/cspd/pdf/ip_indigenous-traditionalknowledge.pdf).

As indigenous knowledge has become more widely respected over recent decades, transnational corporations have not only appropriated this knowledge for their own profits, but in many cases, once the traditional knowledge becomes patented, the people to whom it belonged no longer have free access to it. This is particularly true of knowledge about the uses of plants, whether for agriculture or for healing. The International Union for the Protection of New Varieties of Plants (UPOV), established in 1961, specifically states as a goal the rewarding of innovation in plant varieties with intellectual property rights for twenty to twenty-five years. The plant varieties have to be "new" in the sense that they have not previously been commercialized or sold. This means that a company can appropriate any plant in use by an indigenous community, claim ownership of it, and have exclusive rights to market it and profit by it for up to twenty-five years. Once this happens, the indigenous community has no right to use the plant any more without paying the new owner.

The term that has been coined for this privatization and commodification of indigenous knowledge and practices is "biopiracy." The Indian ecofeminist and activist Dr. Vendana Shiva has been at the forefront of struggles to preserve biodiverse seeds as collective traditional knowledge in the face of corporate patenting of seeds. Navdanya, meaning "nine seeds," is an organization she started across India to protect the rights of local farmers to use the seeds that have been developed and saved over many generations as best adapted to local conditions. Navdanya has set up 111 seed banks across India. Along with less well-known corporations, Monsanto has patented many of the seeds in use by Indian farmers, and it insists that the farmers pay Monsanto to use them. Monsanto has also flooded the market with genetically modified seeds that can blow from one field to another, so that when the farmers harvest seeds to use in next year's crop they are likely to be harvesting the GMO (genetically modified organism) versions owned by Monsanto. Since the Monsanto Corporation began marketing genetically engineered cotton and soybeans, it has investigated 475 farmers suspected of saving seed from the patented plants. Some of the farmers who were found to have violated patents have had to pay Monsanto tens of thousands of dollars each. This led to a rash of suicides, because such high prices are simply out of the reach of these small farmers.

These activists dressed up like eggplants for a protest outside Bangalore in January 2011 as India's environment minister traveled the country for hearings concerning the GMO version of the vegetable produced by Monsanto/Mayhco. Eggplants are an important food crop in India.

*Source:* Wikimedia Commons. https://commons.wikimedia.org/wiki/File:BT_Brinjal_Protest_Bangalore_India_TV_Interview.jpg

See the Navdanya website (http://www.navdanya.org/campaigns/biopiracy) for information on biopiracy and the network's challenges to corporate patents on traditional seeds essential to Indian agriculture.

See the website of the Seed Freedom network (http://seedfreedom.info) for more information on activism against corporate biopiracy.

Anup Shah's article "Food Patents—Stealing Indigenous Knowledge?" also covers these issues, and is available on the Global Issues website (http://www.globalissues.org/article/191/food-patents-stealing-indigenous-knowledge).

For information on Latin American resistance to Monsanto, the world's largest seed company, see the following links:

"Latin America Strikes Back Against Imperialist Monsanto, Monsanto," *Natural News* (http://www.naturalnews.com/045001_latin_america_monsanto_gmos.html)

Occupy Monsanto (http://occupy-monsanto.com/tag/south-america/)

"Women Take a Stand Against Monsanto Across Latin America," Association for Women's Rights in Development (http://www.awid.org/news-and-analysis/women-take-stand-against-monsanto-across-latin-america)

A national protest against Monsanto's patenting of GMO seeds in Chile on August 1, 2013. Protesters carry signs saying, "Monsanto sows death."

*Source:* Mapuexpress Informativo Mapuche/Wikimedia Commons. https://commons.wikimedia.org/wiki/File:March_Against_Monsanto_Chile.jpg

## A Focus on Latin America

In Central America, Monsanto's role in the genetic modification of corn carries huge symbolic value. Corn is the main staple of many Central American diets and has a sacred meaning to many peoples. The earliest civilization in Central America, the Olmec culture (1200–400 BCE), honored a god associated with maize (corn), and a staple of their diet was cornmeal ground with ashes, lime, or seashells (tortillas are made of a similar mix). The *Popol Vuh*, an indigenous Mexican creation narrative, presents humans and corn as inextricably mixed. Similarly, Native American peoples have stories of the Corn Mother, from whom corn first sprouted for the benefit of the people. Monsanto is now genetically modifying the seeds of the corn cultivated as far back as cultural memory can go in this region. These GMO seeds are shifting agriculture everywhere they exist, from biologically diverse varieties of crops to monocrops—single crops grown for export or single plant varieties grown widely in a region. Aside from the intrinsic value of biodiversity to future life on the planet, monocrops are highly vulnerable to new forms of disease or blight, opening the possibility that an entire region's agricultural production could be wiped out by a particular disease or insect.

The genetic mutations in many of Monsanto's seeds are designed to make them immune to the herbicidal effects of Roundup, another product produced by Monsanto. In this innovation, Roundup can be applied indiscriminately to a field and will kill everything growing there except the GMO seeds. A 2014 report by Bloomberg Business states that Monsanto's earnings have risen greatly because of increased Roundup sales. Without the genetically modified seeds, farmers would have options in how they deal with weeds, but they are virtually forced to use the GMO seeds, and then forced to use Roundup. According to Bloomberg, Monsanto's goal is to increase future profits by increasing sales of GMO seeds to Latin America.

For Monsanto's view of its own corporate activities, see its website for information on its Seedbed of the Future project (http://www.monsanto.com/improvingagriculture/pages/seed-bed-of-the-future-in-latin-america.aspx; http://www.monsantofund.org/programs/south-america/).

The article "Monsanto Profit Tops Estimates on Soybeans and Roundup," by Jack Kaskey, is available on the Bloomberg Business website (http://www.bloomberg.com/news/2014-01-08/monsanto-profit-tops-estimates-as-latin-america-soybeans-gain.html).

The Bloomberg article also says that South American farmers are planting more soybeans than corn because profits are higher with soybeans, yet corn is needed to feed huge populations within Latin America. This benefits U.S. corn farmers, who have too much corn and would like to export it under beneficial terms created by NAFTA (the North American Free Trade Agreement). Thus, Mexico's imports of U.S. corn doubled from 2012 to 2013. Nonetheless, Mexico has fifty-nine strains of indigenous corn.

The Latin American countries that consume corn as a staple of their diets are the ones whose cultures have the strongest indigenous base, as well as large indigenous populations. For example, Mexico is the second-largest consumer of U.S. corn, and it has the second-largest indigenous population in Latin America, after Peru. Its indigenous population, descended largely from the Mayans, speaks fifty-six languages and makes up around 13 percent of the overall population. Whereas the majority population in Mexico speaks Spanish and follows the Roman Catholic religion, indigenous peoples retain their lifestyle and language, and in many cases have been deprived of their land and autonomy.

**Indigenous Resistance to Neoliberal Policies: Chiapas, Mexico**

Recognizing early the kind of impact globalization would have on their indigenous lifeways, one indigenous group in Chiapas, Mexico, brought itself to the attention of the world when it rebelled in 1994 against the NAFTA, an agreement between Canada, the United States, and Mexico to reduce trade barriers and promote transnational flows of production and consumption. The Zapatista National Liberation Army (Ejército Zapatista de Liberación Nacional, or ELZN) initially used armed insurrection to fight against the Mexican government, but they quickly abandoned that approach for the use of global public relations, first through journalism and then through new media, including cell phones and the Internet, to win global support for their claims to profit from resources extracted from their region and for autonomy from governmental control.

The Zapatistas' ideology synthesizes traditional Mayan beliefs with leftist politics and assertions of women's rights. They have also expressed solidarity with other indigenous peoples of the Americas through the Intercontinental Indigenous Encounter at the end of 2007. Their successful use of new media to make known their oppression and their goals to the world is an instance of the local-global dynamics in indigenous struggles today. Their struggle was a model for the power of new media and global alliances in the struggles of indigenous peoples globally.

## Bioprospecting for Pharmaceuticals

Along with the patenting of essential agricultural plants, plants with healing properties are a key area of conflict between indigenous peoples and intellectual property law, especially in Latin America. "Bioprospecting" is the term coined to describe the quests by pharmaceutical companies and scientists for potentially marketable healing plants. Approximately 130 prescription drugs, 25 percent of all prescription drugs bought in the West, are derived from plants, according to some reports (see, for example, Veeresham 2012), and the vast majority were originally used by traditional healers. Three decades ago these drugs sold for about $43 billion ("Medicinal Treasures"). About two-thirds of all the plant species in the world are concentrated in tropical forests, which cover only 6 percent of the Earth's surface and are home to about fifty million indigenous people. Almost half of these tropical rainforests are in South America. Brazil is thought to have the richest plant diversity in the world (about 22 percent), with about fifty-five thousand plant species.

These statistics demonstrate why South America faces enormous challenges from biopiracy. As of 2000, about seven thousand patents had been acquired globally through biopiracy, or the illegitimate ownership of traditional knowledge. Two examples that have received a lot of attention from critics are the neem tree in India, used as an antiseptic and now as a pesticide, and the ayahuasca plant of the Amazon basin. Ayahuasca (*Banisteriopsis caapi* vine) is a plant indigenous to the Peruvian Amazon basin and viewed as sacred by a large number of indigenous groups, who use it in sacred ceremonies and for healing. In order to produce the hallucinogenic medicine used by shamans, the ayahuasca plant is combined with another plant and brewed as a tea. The tea is known as ayahuasca in the Quechua language, but by other names in other indigenous languages. When taken, it produces visions that are used for psychological healing and transformation. Archeological finds suggest that it has been used in the Amazonian region since at least 500 BCE.

The ayahuasca plant is known as a teacher or doctor of the shamans, or *vegetalistas*, who use it. In the Amazonian cultures that use ayahuasca, all plants are regarded as having spirits. According to the Peruvian anthropologist Luis Eduardo Luna, the cosmology of the *vegetalistas* is composed of two worlds, one on earth and one in water. Many legends concern the abduction of humans by creatures of the water. Certain visionary rituals involving plants might allow shamans to enter the world of the water. Strict diets and sexual abstinence are required before initiation into the teaching of the plants. The spirits of the plants teach melodies that the shamans use in their practice.

A number of Westerners, both spiritual seekers and botanists, "discovered" the visionary healing powers of ayahuasca. One of the substances produced by the tea is dimethyltriptamine (DMT), a Schedule I controlled substance under U.S. law (meaning the U.S. Drug Enforcement Agency considers it to have the highest potential for abuse or dependency). The reason why ayahuasca has to be combined with another plant in the tea is to allow the DMT to bypass enzymes in the digestive system that break it down and render it ineffective. The indigenous people who use it figured out this chemistry thousands of years ago. Until recently, it was illegal to use ayahuasca in the United States, even though it is a traditional part of some religious practices in U.S. churches formed by Amazonian people. In 2006 the Supreme Court ruled in favor of these churches under the Religious Freedom Restoration Act of 1993. The Court recognized the valid traditional use of the drug by a particular church. Some psychotherapists, trained in its use in Peru, were conducting ayahuasca sessions in which they guided the subjects' visions for healing purposes.

An American director of the International Plant Medicine Corporation, Loren Miller, took out a patent on ayahuasca in 1986 that was successfully challenged in 1999 by the Center for International Environmental Law (CIEL) along with the Coordinating Body of Indigenous Organizations of the Amazon Basin (COICA) and the Coalition for Amazonian Peoples and Their Environment (Amazon Coalition). COICA objected to the patent because it purported to appropriate for a U.S. citizen a plant that is sacred to many indigenous peoples of the Amazon, used by them in religious and healing ceremonies. The patent office allowed the patent to continue until 2003 when it expired, and it cannot be renewed. This was a huge triumph for indigenous knowledge over the intellectual property regime. In 2008 ayahuasca was declared part of the cultural patrimony of Peru, further protecting it from the incursions of those wishing to privatize and profit from its use.

However, ayahuasca has been commodified through what might be called "spiritual tourism" as Westerners travel to Iquitos, Peru, to participate in the experience. Ayahuasca is an extremely powerful drug, a purgative that causes vomiting and diarrhea. Its visions produce what many describe as an experience of death and rebirth. It traditionally would be taken after careful strict preparations and under strict spiritual guidance, but with a boom in interest, ayahuasca lodges have sprung up for tourists that are not always run by creditable shamans.

For information on the chemical and ethnobotanical properties of ayahuasca, see the Choque Chinchay Spirit Quest website (http://biopark.org/peru/ayahuasca.html).

Information on the Center for International Environmental Law's patent case on ayahuasca can be found on the center's website (http://www.ciel.org/project-update/protecting-traditional-knowledge-ayahuasca/).

On ayahuasca tourism, see "The Dark Side of Ayahuasca," by Kelly Hearn, published in *Men's Journal* (http://www.mensjournal.com/magazine/the-dark-side-of-ayahuasca-20130215); or "Magnificent Visions," by Ted Mann, in *Vanity Fair* (http://www.vanityfair.com/culture/features/2011/12/amazon-201112).

On the use of ayahuasca within the United States, see Bob Morris's article "Ayahuasca: A Strong Cup of Tea," published in the *New York Times* (http://www.nytimes.com/2014/06/15/fashion/ayahuasca-a-strong-cup-of-tea.html?_r=0).

---

**Drugs Derived or Taken from Native Latin American Animals and Plants**

- A small frog from the rainforests of Ecuador yields a toxin, epibatidine, which is a pain killer two hundred times more potent than morphine.
- The antimalarial drug quinine is made by boiling the bark of cinchona trees (Peru).
- Tubocurarine, made from the South American vine *Chondodendron tomentosum*, is widely used as a muscle relaxant during surgery.
- An Argentine soil microorganism has already been turned into an approved drug, Synercid, that fights antibiotic-resistant bacteria.
- Of the three thousand plants identified by the National Cancer Institute as having anticancer properties, 70 percent live only in the tropics.
- More than 260 South American plants appear to have potential fertility control applications.

*Source:* Quezada 2007, 14.

---

The case of ayahuasca has raised numerous issues relating to indigenous knowledge and how it has become caught up in transnational flows of information and people. Its patenting in the United States is an example of biopiracy, and the ban on its use, even for sacred purposes, by the U.S. Drug Enforcement Agency (DEA) demonstrates a transnational clash of cultures. To some degree these challenges to its place within Amazonian spiritual practices have been resolved through the expiration of the patent, the Supreme Court case allowing specific worshippers to use it, and its recognition as Peruvian cultural patrimony. Nonetheless, the commodification that accompanies global capitalism still exerts its pressure. The increasing publicity about tourists heading to ayahuasca lodges in Iquitos, Peru, suggests that its status as cultural patrimony does not protect against all forms of exploitation for profit. It remains to be seen whether the plant teacher will maintain its embeddedness within shamanistic regimes in its indigenous location, or whether the lure of commodification for tourists will have a destructive impact.

\* \* \*

To return to the paradox with which this case study began—namely, the tension between the "global" and the "indigenous"—the fact is that indigenous peoples have no choice but to use global mechanisms to protect their very local interests. At the same time, many global agreements support neoliberal premises about individualism and private property that threaten indigenous peoples and their traditional knowledge and practices, especially when these are tied to a specific place and ecosystem.

The cases discussed here involve a number of conflicting international agreements, including the 1993 Convention on Biological Diversity (CBD) and the Agreement on Trade-Related Aspects of Intellectual Property Rights (the "TRIPs agreement"), which supports private rights to intellectual property. The Convention on Biological Diversity was written under the auspices of the UN and was opened for signature at the United Nations Conference on Environment and Development (the 1992 Rio "Earth Summit"). The convention recognizes the links between biological and cultural diversity and the need to support their interconnections. The countries that are party to the convention are supposed to respect and preserve traditional knowledge, but they are not required by international law to do so.

Further, indigenous peoples are mostly marginalized minorities who either choose to remain outside the mainstream institutions or are excluded from them. There is no guarantee that the state will protect their interests against the forces of capitalism and privatization. Even within South American nations, scientists seek to block Northern scientists or corporations from patenting plants in Brazil or Peru because they themselves want control over their nation's potential products under the same intellectual property regimes used by North American and European companies.

Yet despite the huge forces of corporate capitalism, there have been political successes for indigenous peoples and their ecosystems. One of the most important occurred in Brazil, where Bioamazônia, the Brazilian Association for the Sustainable Use of the Biodiversity of Amazonia, was set up in 1999 to manage the biodiversity of the Amazon region and empowered to make business deals regarding the flora and fauna of this incredibly rich environment. In 2000 Bioamazônia sold exclusive rights to the Amazon region to Novartis Pharma AG, a Swiss pharmaceutical company. According to the agreement, Novartis is allowed to take ten thousand samples from the region's forest and exercise sole rights over any commercial products derived from them, for a paltry total of $4 million and 1 percent of the profits resulting the sale of these products. After huge protests, however, the agreement was dissolved by Brazil's government, which has put in place a commission to control bioprospecting (Quezada 2007, 39). It is hoped that more nations will move to protect their biodiversity, water, and land, which have been the sources and repositories of cultural memory and identity for many indigenous peoples.

## References and Further Research

African Commission on Human and Peoples' Rights (ACHPR). 2005. *Report of the African Commission's Working Group of Experts on Indigenous Populations/Communities*. Banjul, the Gambia: African Commission on Human and Peoples' Rights/Copenhagen: International Work Group for Indigenous Affairs. http://www.iwgia.org/iwgia_files_publications_files/African_Commission_book.pdf.

Alfred, Taiaiake. 1999. *Peace, Power, Righteousness: An Indigenous Manifesto*. Don Mills, ON: Oxford University Press.

Dodson, Michael. 2007. *Report on Indigenous Traditional Knowledge*. Presented at the Sixth Session of the UNPFII. UN Doc. E/C.19/2007/10. New York: United Nations Permanent Forum on Indigenous Issues (UNPFII). http://www.un.org/esa/socdev/unpfii/documents/6_session_dodson.pdf.

Kipuri, Naomi. 2009. "Culture." In *The State of the World's Indigenous Peoples*, 52–79. New York: UN Department of Economic and Social Affairs, Secretariat of the Permanent Forum on Indigenous Issues. http://www.un.org/esa/socdev/unpfii/documents/SOWIP/en/SOWIP_web.pdf.

Laird, Sarah A., ed. 2002. *Biodiversity and Traditional Knowledge: Equitable Partnerships in Practice*. London: Earthscan.

Luna, Luis Eduardo. "Towards an Exploration of the Mind of a Conquered Continent: Sacred Plants and Amerindian Epistemology." http://www.grahamhancock.com/forum/LunaLE2.php.

———. *Vegetalismo: Shamanism among the Mestizo Population of the Peruvian Amazon*. 1986. Stockholm, Sweden: Almqvist & Wiksell International.

"Medicinal Treasures of the Rainforest." *Adventure Life*. http://www.adventure-life.com/articles/rainforest-medicine-78.

Mgbeoji, Ikechi. 2006. *Global Biopiracy: Patents, Plants, and Indigenous Knowledge*. Ithaca, NY: Cornell University Press.

Oguamanam, Chidi. 2006. *International Law and Indigenous Knowledge: Intellectual Property, Plant Biodiversity, and Traditional Medicine*. Toronto: University of Toronto Press.

Quezada, Fernando. 2007. *Status and Potential of Commercial Bioprospecting Activities in Latin America and the Caribbean*. Santiago, Chile: Sustainable Development and Human Settlements Division, UN CEPAL. http://www.eclac.cl/publicaciones/xml/5/29455/LCL2742-P.pdf.

Rainforest Foundation UK. http://www.rainforestfoundationuk.org.

Shiva, Vendana. 1997. *Biopiracy: The Plunder of Nature and Knowledge*. Boston: South End Press.

———. 2001. *Protect or Plunder? Understanding Intellectual Property Rights*. London: Zed.

Tourism Concern. 2002. "Why Tourism Concern is Cautious about the International Year of Ecotourism." *Press Release*. January 25. http://www.travelmole.com/news_feature.php?news_id= 70460&c=setreg&region=4.

*Traditional Knowledge Bulletin*. http://tkbulletin.wordpress.com.

Veeresham, Ciddi. 2012. "Natural Products Derived from Plants as a Source of Drugs." *Journal of Advanced Pharmaceutical Technology and Research* 3, no. 4: 200–201. http://www.ncbi.nlm.nih.gov/ pmc/articles/PMC3560124/.

# 7

# NGOs, Humanitarianism, and the Cultural Construction of Global Hierarchy

An increasingly visible part of contemporary popular culture is the phenomenon of celebrities from the Global North using their fame to draw attention to social problems in the Global South, particularly sub-Saharan Africa. Megastars such as Madonna and Angelina Jolie, for example, have adopted children from Africa and Southeast Asia and become the public face of the increasingly popular process of transnational adoption. Big-name celebrities have lent their star power to campaigns organized by major humanitarian organizations such as UNICEF (for which the actress Audrey Hepburn served as Goodwill Ambassador), Oxfam (which has worked with numerous "celebrity ambassadors," including the British actress Helen Mirren and U.S. football star Larry Fitzgerald), and the Christian Children's Fund (which created a famous campaign of late-night, "adopt-a-child" ads featuring the actress Sally Struthers). Other Global North celebrities have played a more direct role in helping to organize their own humanitarian campaigns, such as when the singer Bob Geldof spearheaded the famous 1985 Live Aid concert to support famine relief for Ethiopia. More recently, one of the most famous and decorated journalists in the world, Nicholas Kristof of the *New York Times*, joined his wife, Sheryl WuDunn, to lead the Half the Sky Movement. The *Half the Sky* documentary film features a series of prominent actresses, including Meg Ryan and Eva Mendes, as they travel around the world with Kristof and WuDunn in an effort to promote women's empowerment.

All of these activities have generated public criticism of one form or another, often from those who argue that celebrity "do-gooders" are acting primarily out of a desire to promote themselves. Charitable organizations, however, may view the use of celebrity spokespersons as one among several strategies designed to break through the apathy and cynicism that often characterize public responses to their appeals in an era of what some have called "post-humanitarianism." As the public becomes more media savvy and media saturated, those engaged in humanitarian action find themselves needing to become more aware of what scholars such as Irene Bruna Seu describe as the "politics of pity," the complex and changing relations of power between distant sufferers and potential donors. There is also significant evidence that Global North audiences are becoming ever more removed from the realities of distant suffering, even though technologies increase the efficiency with which they can learn of and respond to such suffering.

In addition to examining the impact of media and technology, using a global studies framework to examine humanitarianism and post-humanitarianism, which this case study does, requires addressing other levels of analysis connected with the ongoing legacy of colonialism and its impact on the global politics of representation. Humanitarian nongovernmental organizations (NGOs) that seek to remedy human suffering in the

Global South rely on financial support from ordinary people and must use a variety of techniques to appeal to the consciences of potential donors. In doing so, they inevitably find themselves appealing to attitudes, emotions, and identities that bear the traces of longstanding, unequal North–South relations. Exploring these processes reveals both the changing nature of global cultural flows and the stubborn staying power of racialized constructions of "white superiority" and "brown neediness" that are grounded in colonial histories.

Questions raised by such an approach include: Where do humanitarian NGOs fit into larger structures of power in the era of globalization? What are the factors that shape the changing meanings of charity and humanitarianism, and how does the circulation of humanitarian images shape social identities? Is humanitarianism becoming more narcissistic in the age of social media? How can we understand the contemporary nature of humanitarianism given its often close relationship with political and military intervention, when outside forces frequently deliver aid as part of military operations? How does the expanding role of humanitarian NGOs contribute to the cultural construction of racial, gender, national, and other forms of global hierarchy? Finally, is it possible to imagine organized forms of transnational "helping" that would challenge such hierarchies rather than reinforcing them?

## NGOs: A Brief History

As the era of state-centered development gave way to the Washington Consensus era of neoliberal globalization, which focuses on individual freedoms and free trade and advocates the reduction of state-funded social services, NGOs have come to play an increasingly central role. In their influential 2000 book *Empire*, Michael Hardt and Antonio Negri describe an NGO as "any organization that purports to represent the People and operate in its interest, separate from (and often against) the structures of the state." Yet they also acknowledge that any attempt to "characterize the functioning of this fast and heterogeneous set of organizations under one single definition" would be ultimately "futile" (310). Indeed, if there is one thing that scholars writing about NGOs agree on, it is the impossibility of arriving at a universal definition. Nonetheless, there is a broad consensus that such organizations are a key part of what is often called *civil society*, the sector through which citizens engage in public affairs outside of the formal workings of government. NGOs, therefore, exist to provide alternatives to both government programs and the strictly for-profit private sector (even as their work often leads them to cooperate with both).

While some of the oldest NGOs date back to the abolitionist movements of the nineteenth century, and a number of major NGOs—such as the International Woman Suffrage Alliance (later renamed the International Alliance of Women) and Save the Children—were created in the early part of the twentieth century, the exponential growth in the number and reach of NGOs did not begin until after World War II. The increase in the number, diversity, and global reach of NGOs in recent decades is quite remarkable. By some estimates, there are now millions of NGOs in the world addressing issues such as poverty, health, education, community development, human rights, environmental sustainability, women's rights, antiracism, and sexual freedom. They range from small, locally based initiatives such as southern Kenya's Maji Moto (http://majimoto.org/), to national NGOs such as India's Navdanya (http://www.navdanya.org/), to transnational NGOs such as Accion International that function as umbrella organizations employing people in all corners of the world.

**Major Humanitarian NGOs**

These are some of the largest and most longstanding international humanitarian NGOs:

Accion International (http://www.accion.org)
CARE (http://www.care-international.org)
Catholic Relief Services (http://www.crs.org)
Heifer International (http://www.heifer.org)
Médecins Sans Frontières (http://www.msf.org)
Oxfam (http://www.oxfam.org)
Save the Children (www.savethechildren.org)
World Vision (http://www.worldvision.org)

Given the role that Christianity played in the long process of European colonization in terms of ideological justification, missionary activity, and forced conversion, it is not surprising that many NGOs are animated by various forms of religious commitment. Catholic Relief Services (founded in 1943), for example, uses a social justice orientation in its work of providing humanitarian assistance in poor communities throughout the world. There are many similar organizations operating on the progressive end of the Protestant theological

This image shows an Oxfam shop in Headingley, Leeds, West Yorkshire (UK) in late 2014. There are currently more than seven hundred Oxfam shops in the UK alone, and approximately twelve hundred worldwide.

*Source:* Michael Taylor/Wikimedia Commons. https://commons.wikimedia.org/wiki/File:Another_Oxfam_shop,_Otley_Road,_Headingley,_Leeds_(30th_December_2014).jpg

spectrum. Most mainline Protestant denominations, such as Methodism and Presbyterianism, support a variety of charity and solidarity-based work—sometimes in continuation of longstanding missionary activities, and sometimes in ways that are almost indistinguishable from the work of secular NGOs. Also on the Protestant side are more evangelical NGOs, ranging from those that openly seek to convert non-Christians and push socially conservative causes to those that place a greater emphasis on inclusiveness and social responsibility.

Whether religious or secular, NGOs are now so ubiquitous and so thoroughly woven into the fabric of social life that it is impossible to imagine any society functioning effectively without them. The need for their work derives largely from the impact of global neoliberal restructuring and privatization, which have resulted in what Philip McMichael (2012, 287) calls a "hollowing out of social democracy" as governments have gradually withdrawn from their previous role as providers of many social services. Thus, the daily work of many NGOs involves basic social tasks such as distributing food, providing primary health care and education, and building infrastructure for local communities. Much of this work is also inseparable from the disruptions created by certain elements of the state that have not been "hollowed out," such as social control, incarceration, war, and military intervention. While longstanding humanitarian actors such as the Red Cross and the United Nations have been active in conflict zones for decades, the relationship between state violence and NGO work has become even more tightly woven in recent years.

Hand in hand with this development, the world has seen a gradual professionalization of NGO work, with many NGOs now resembling governments and corporations in the complexity of their organizational plans, missions, and financial structures. For this reason, many grassroots activists have begun to question the role of what INCITE! Women of Color Against Violence (a North American radical feminist coalition) calls the "non-profit industrial complex" and its tendency to serve its own interests as much as the interests of ordinary people.

Most recently, the rise of social media as a communication and organizing tool has dramatically altered the work of many NGOs, the public face of humanitarian work, and the process of soliciting public support for this work. A number of high-profile cases involving human rights violations in sub-Saharan Africa reveal the rapidly shifting and often controversial relationships among NGOs, social media, "viral" marketing strategies, and techniques of individual and organizational branding. Discussed in more detail later, these cases include the Kony 2012 campaign (an offshoot of the earlier *Invisible Children* documentary), the Save Darfur movement, and the #BringBackOurGirls campaign launched in 2014 in response to the kidnapping of Nigerian schoolgirls by the Boko Haram rebel group.

## The Cultural Analysis of Global North Humanitarianism

*Humanitarianism* is a powerful philosophical and ideological concept. It is constructed through discourses that shape social identities and ideas about how different social groups relate to one another. Analysis of how humanitarianism manifests itself in global culture, therefore, must be attentive both to what "discourse" is and to what it does. More specifically, it is important to examine the complex relationship between humanitarianism and social hierarchies. On the one hand, humanitarianism assistance is one way of making the existence of such hierarchies visible, since it is the hierarchies that often create the need for assistance. On the other hand, the very act of humanitarian assistance can also be seen as reproducing those very hierarchies. As scholars such as Bruce Lincoln remind us, discourse analysis is especially suited to understanding such dynamics because of the fundamental role of discourse in the construction of all societies. In this case, a look at the history of colonization and its long-term reach into the eras of development and globalization can help us see how current global hierarchies, both within and across specific societies, are socially constructed through discourse.

## Discourse 101

*Discourse* is one of the most complex and debated terms in social and cultural theory. One useful definition holds that discourse refers to "ways of systematically organizing human experience of the social world in language and thereby constituting modes of knowledge" (Edgar and Sedgwick 1999, 117). Discourse has at least five basic, overlapping characteristics:

1.  Discourse is social. It is produced by human beings, is subject to social change, and plays a key role in the social construction of meaning and of society itself.
2.  Discourse is productive. It shapes our identities, defines the limits of acceptable speech and activity, and influences everything we do. What this tells us is that we are never entirely in control of discourse; it also controls us.
3.  Discourse is cumulative. It gathers "weight" over time as it continues to circulate socially; each time a discourse is invoked, it is reinforced and made to seem more "natural." This process of reinforcement is also limiting: because of the weight of a discourse, we can't just say anything; in order to be understood and be taken seriously, we must follow the conventions of the discourse.
4.  Discourse, however, is still contestable. While discourses gather "weight" over time, they can never fully close off other possibilities. This tells us that any discourse, no matter how seemingly powerful, is always open to struggle and change; indeed, it is one of the most important arenas through which people struggle over most fundamental social issues.
5.  Discourse is ideological. It is connected with the relationship between meaning and power. Through the use of discourse, particular groups seek (consciously or unconsciously) to give meaning to reality in a way that reflects their interests and experiences.

While European colonial projects were typically animated by the drive for capital accumulation, territorial acquisition, and resource extraction, they always had a significant cultural component that set in motion a complex process of transnational identity formation. This process, in turn, played a central role in the discursive construction of the modern concept of race and of various forms of racism that are built on hierarchical distinctions between "Self" and "Other." Perhaps the most famous example is the idea of "the white man's burden," first articulated in Rudyard Kipling's 1899 poem "The White Man's Burden," written in response to the American colonization of the Philippines. In calling on the United States to follow in Europe's footsteps, the first stanza of the poem encapsulates some of the cultural attitudes used to justify colonial expansion:

> Take up the White Man's burden—
> Send forth the best ye breed–
> Go bind your sons to exile
> To serve your captives' need;
> To wait in heavy harness,
> On fluttered folk and wild–
> Your new-caught, sullen peoples,
> Half devil and half child.

The poem is often cited as an example of the "civilizing mission" (*la mission civilisatrice* in French), an ideological concept that positioned colonized peoples as "half devil and half child," and therefore in need of some combination of Western guidance and discipline on the road to becoming "civilized."

There is a rich field of interdisciplinary scholarship exploring the emergence, operation, and social effects of colonial discourse. This literature provides a conceptual toolbox for

This 1899 ad for Pears' Soap draws on Kipling's poem "The White Man's Burden" (published a year earlier) and features images linking Western commerce, warfare, and missionary activity with notions of white supremacy. In the center is Admiral George Dewey, who led U.S. forces in the 1898 Battle of Manila Bay, a key battle in the Spanish-American war that launched U.S. colonial rule in the Philippines.

*Source:* Wikimedia Commons. https://commons.wikimedia.org/wiki/File:1890sc_Pears_Soap_Ad.jpg

understanding how colonialism was motivated, shaped, and justified by these kinds of cultural constructions and how they lent discursive support to unequal power relations associated with domination, slavery, charity, and religious conversion. David Spurr, for example, provides a useful list of twelve "rhetorical modes" that crop up regularly in examples of colonial discourse, both fictional and nonfictional. These include modes that exoticize colonized people, look down upon them from on high, equate them with nature, see them as objects of charity or conversion, or debase them through discourses of "savagery" and "darkness."

Other scholars, such as postcolonial theorist Gayatri Chakravorty Spivak, call attention to how colonial powers used dominant Western constructions of gender to justify their privileged position in cultural terms. In her famous essay "Can the Subaltern Speak?," Spivak discusses how British colonial authorities in India outlawed the practice of *sati* (in which some Indian widows burned themselves to death on their husbands' funeral pyres), taking what was actually a very rare phenomenon and presenting it as if it were typical of India in general. She notes that the British decision to oppose the practice in the name of defending Indian women can be interpreted as a case of "white men saving brown women from brown men," thereby reinforcing a set of racial, gender, and national hierarchies. In addition to identifying what was self-serving about the colonizer's attempt to "save" Indian women, Spivak argues provocatively that even when scholars seek to reconstruct the voices of the widows through colonial documents, they are ironically perpetuating the logic of a violent colonial system (see the discussion of subaltern studies in Chapter 3).

What emerges from these critiques of colonial discourse is a strong sense of how colonialism put in place a whole series of linguistic, cognitive, cultural, and psychological mechanisms that governed how colonizers and colonized were socially constructed, both in and of themselves and in terms of their relationship to one another. While colonial discourse was never free of internal contradictions, it tended to construct the colonized as relatively passive, childlike, and "backward" when compared with the active, mature, and "advanced" colonizers. Such discourses are fundamentally Eurocentric: they place European experiences, ideas, and desires at the center of their explanations of the world and assume a position of superiority in relation to non-European people. In their landmark 1994 book *Unthinking Eurocentrism*, Ella Shohat and Robert Stam argue that while Eurocentrism "first emerged as a discursive rationale for colonialism" during the long period of European expansion and conquest, it also "permeates and structures *contemporary* practices and representations even after the formal end of colonialism" (2, original emphasis). Eurocentrism, they argue, "'normalizes' the hierarchical power relations generated by colonialism and imperialism," making these relations seem "natural" rather than socially constructed.

As the era of formal colonial rule gradually came to an end after World War II, the discourse of the "civilizing mission" was replaced by the discourse of "development." While the latter discourse was less explicitly cultural and more focused on socioeconomic transformation, it nonetheless drew on a whole series of inherited categories and assumptions about "the West" and "the rest." The newly independent nations of the Global South, according to development discourse, were "underdeveloped" and thus "behind" or "below" the more established nations of the Global North. Whether viewed temporally as a set of historical stages or spatially as a ladder to be climbed, the idea of development reinforced existing geopolitical hierarchies. Southern nations were positioned as recipients of transnational assistance, while Northern nations were positioned as generous benefactors through their domination of the Bretton Woods institutions, such as the World Bank, which helped to implement the neoliberal Washington Consensus. When these relationships left many in the South mired in cycles of indebtedness, critical analysts such as Samir Amin and Andre Gunder Frank began using the concept of "dependency" to describe the perpetuation of these hierarchical relationships. For its part, the dominant discourse of development was also articulated, at least partly, in cultural terms. Rather than blaming poverty in the South on the ongoing influence of colonialism and colonial relations, the discourse located the problem in a kind of cultural deficit: only by overcoming "tradition" and embracing "modernity" could they hope to join the "developed world."

While the discourse of development remains influential in the twenty-first century, it has also given way somewhat to the discourse of North-South humanitarianism. As with the transition from the colonial era to the development era, the transition to the globalization era and its discourse of humanitarianism reveals the continuing power of old hierarchical patterns. People in the Global South remain constructed primarily as passive victims in need of outside assistance from the North. Whereas the development discourse defined the problem in terms of "underdevelopment," however, the discourse of humanitarianism locates the problem in terms of local corruption, anti-Western governments and movements, and a lack of individual "opportunity" to participate freely in the global market. The complexity of this discourse helps explain the flexibility of humanitarianism itself: it can mean anything from using military force to distribute food as part of the "global war on terrorism" to using microfinance to empower rural women.

The sociologist Keith Tester (2010, vii) argues that while humanitarianism can be defined generically in terms of "a moral sensibility demanding action on the part of the safe and secure towards the suffering and endangered," in practice the term carries with it a set of geopolitical and cultural coordinates: "Humanitarianism is about how the West understands and acts out of a sense of moral responsibility toward the impoverished parts of the world and their threatened inhabitants." This acknowledgment of what Tester calls the "vestiges of a distinctly imperial mindset" raises the question of who gets to define "impoverished parts of the world" and how the focus on suffering in faraway places might deflect attention away from structural inequality at home. He uses the example of Bob Geldof and the Live Aid project to illustrate how much of the dominant notion of what he calls "common-sense humanitarianism" is built upon a series of myths and stereotypes about the place that Western discourses have constructed as "Africa." Noting the central role of the media in shaping popular attitudes about the world, he ultimately provides a more critical definition:

> What is common-sense humanitarianism? It is the humanitarianism of media audiences who rely on unquestioned myths to make sense of the suffering of others. Common-sense humanitarianism is the naturalized cultural creation through which we make sense of the news from out of "Africa."
>
> (34)

Humanitarianism, as Tester points out, is not about removing once and for all the conditions that leave some people threatened or in poverty; it is about making an effort to "do something" by helping those in immediate need. For most people, engaging in humanitarian action means contributing to the efforts of existing, organized actors that have some specialized knowledge or access: states, corporations, and especially major Global North NGOs. Yet, as Hardt and Negri (2000, 37) note, the often tight relationship between humanitarian action and interventionist states raises a number of troubling questions. Is humanitarian action really a form of "moral intervention" that "often serves as the first act that prepares the stage for military intervention"? Do geopolitical actors who engage in military intervention treat NGOs as a way to outsource the work of cleaning up the mess after the fighting is over? And are such connections visible to ordinary citizens who see and respond to charity appeals asking for help for people in need on the other side of the world?

## Charity Appeals

During the 1960s and 1970s, a fairly standard pattern was established in terms of how mass public appeals from humanitarian organizations were constructed, and this pattern continues to influence appeals today. Many present fairly generic portrayals that confirm existing stereotypes about endemic suffering in the Global South. Seeking to play on feelings of sympathy, pity, and guilt, such appeals typically begin by presenting eye-opening statistics (for example, a 1990 Save the Children ad asked, "Did you know in many countries 2 out of 5 little ones never even make it to their fifth birthday?") or poignant and visually arresting images of suffering, such as a helpless mother holding a starving child, a refugee desperate to return home, or a family needing shelter after a natural disaster. Having gotten the viewer's attention, the appeals then move to identify a specific way in which the viewer can "do something" about the problem: by making a donation to the organization to support its work. The aforementioned Save the Children ad featured the actress Phylicia Rashad, famous for her role on *The Cosby Show*, appealing to viewers to help provide immunizations, clean water, and other necessities to children in poor countries.

The videos of charitable appeals referenced in this section can be viewed online at the following links:

- The 1990 Save the Children ad with Phylicia Rashad can be found at https://www.youtube.com/watch?v=BddddBZhYBU.
- The 2007 Christian Children's Fund ad is at https://www.youtube.com/watch?v=AHffiDYUMy0.
- The 2008 Oxfam "Be Humankind" video is at https://www.youtube.com/watch?v=eQK6ODxDfDY.
- The 2010 Heifer International video on women in India is at https://www.youtube.com/watch?v=674Xv9Gmicg.

Other appeals try to move beyond generic portrayals to provide something more personalized by spotlighting the needs of a single named person who serves as a stand-in for a larger category of people in need. Those responding to such an appeal can then feel like they are helping that specific individual (or someone similar), rather than simply sending money to an organization. For example, an ad from Christian Children's Fund begins with a close-up of a young girl named Michelle, who spends her days picking up trash in an unnamed country in the Global South. The narrator offers viewers the chance to sponsor "a child like Michelle" for "just 80 cents a day," promising that CCF will send the sponsor detailed biographical information about the child. While aiming to humanize the recipients of humanitarian aid in a certain way, such appeals may go further in the other direction by reinforcing stereotypes and many of the same hierarchical patterns of representation, focusing mostly on white donors thinking altruistically about mostly brown and black victims.

The long tradition of "adopt-a-child" ads in the Global North is a reminder of how humanitarian appeals are often built on a combination of cultural, gender, and age hierarchies. As the psychologist Erica Burman (1994, 2) argues, the child in such appeals "functions as the quintessential recipient of aid," combining innocence and neediness. These representations, however, can never be separated from their geopolitical context. The children, in this line of thinking, are being used not only as symbols of poverty, but also as symbols of entire societies that are constructed in development discourse as childlike and unable to stand on their own without Northern assistance. In this sense, when the sympathetic viewer is asked to "adopt" a child, this "adoption" mirrors not only the actions of celebrities such as Madonna and Angelina Jolie, but also the self-representations of "developed countries" that claim to act, as Burman asserts, "in loco parentis" (3) within an unequal international system.

Over time, such campaigns also become vulnerable to the critique that they result in a particular kind of "compassion fatigue" as the public becomes desensitized after viewing so many images of faraway suffering. Susan Moeller extended this critique to the media in general in a 1998 book, arguing that compassion fatigue contributes to superficial news coverage of complex global problems. Similarly, many aid organizations have come under scrutiny for devoting a large percentage of funds to operating costs, or for being content to provide "handouts" rather than support for sustainable changes on the ground. These critiques have led some organizations to craft ads that go beyond appeals to compassion and portrayals of passive victims. Seeking to inspire donations from people who are interested in making a more tangible, long-term difference in the lives of people in the Global South, this new type of ad presents the recipients of aid as active agents working to improve their lives with assistance from external donors. A 2010 video produced by Heifer International, for instance, spotlights the organization's role in helping poor women in Rajasthan, India, as they seek to empower themselves and one another.

Most recently, as Lilie Chouliaraki demonstrates in her book *The Ironic Spectator* (2013), humanitarian organizations have begun to respond to an increasingly narcissistic culture of social media by crafting appeals that play on the desire of individual donors to feel good about themselves. Many of these ads use postmodern composition styles such as animation and rapid jump cuts, creating videos that are designed to provide the viewer a brief sense of aesthetic pleasure rather than the sense of guilt or discomfort that may have come from earlier ads presenting the reality of Global South suffering more directly. As an example, Chouliaraki discusses Oxfam's "Be Humankind" series, in which animated figures confront a Hollywood-style "monster of injustice" in their town square, spontaneously choosing to join others in taking heroic action against the "monster" (68–69). These ads present humanitarianism as desirable because of the emotional reward one can derive from making a temporary "lifestyle choice." Such a shift toward a "self-oriented morality" fits smoothly within a neoliberal model of competitive individualism.

Along with such a shift, Chouliaraki argues, comes the risk that people in the West/Global North will lose any meaningful sense of

> the world beyond the West as a really existing, albeit different, world, which confronts us with the uncomfortable but vital questions of power, otherness and justice and, in so doing, keeps the possibility of social change in the global divisions of our world alive.
>
> (4)

This conclusion is supported by Irene Seu's (2010) research on audience responses to Amnesty International appeals. Using the tools of discourse analysis, Seu demonstrates how audiences increasingly respond to such appeals by engaging in complex forms of denial masquerading as critical analysis of the appeals themselves. Such responses include critiquing the "emotional manipulation" used in the appeals, questioning whether the appeals are fully truthful, and speculating about whether donated funds will make any difference at all. By positioning themselves as skeptical and media-savvy consumers, and even as victims of dishonest NGOs, audiences are able to avoid dealing directly with the reality of human suffering that lies behind the appeals. The result, she argues, is a "deafening" silence with respect to the recognition of "distant suffering," a lack of "altruistic emotional responses such as empathy, compassion and pity" (454) and, ultimately, a greater likelihood of inaction.

## The Half the Sky Movement

Nicholas Kristof and Sheryl WuDunn's Half the Sky project exemplifies some of the tensions that characterize the world of humanitarianism as it continues to change along with the broader culture. The project includes a best-selling 2009 book of the same name, a documentary film launched in the United States in 2012 on PBS, games for Facebook and mobile phone users, and a website spotlighting individuals and organizations featured in the film along with ways for people to get involved. Numerous prominent female artists have lent their support by donating songs, participating in the film, and speaking publicly about issues affecting girls and women worldwide.

Drawing on the work of Nobel Prize–winning economist Amartya Sen, Kristof and WuDunn (2009) seek to call attention to structures of gender discrimination that have resulted in millions of "missing women" around the world. The project's core message is that helping women and girls in the Global South to thrive should be a central commitment of Global North humanitarian activists and that the empowerment of women and girls is the key to addressing broader issues of development, poverty alleviation, and human rights. In articulating this message, the authors draw on preexisting representations of victimization while also seeking to emphasize the more positive theme of empowerment: "Women aren't the problem but the solution. The plight of girls is no more a tragedy than an opportunity" (xviii). Consequently, the project's basic approach is to expose the reader/viewer to some of the most troubling realities of female suffering while also spotlighting the efforts of women and girls to better their circumstances through local forms of activism and entrepreneurship. Half the Sky, they emphasize, invites people to "join an incipient movement to emancipate women and fight global poverty by unlocking women's power as economic catalysts."

Kristof and WuDunn are clearly aware of the long history of Western domination, as well as some of the problems associated with conventional forms of humanitarianism. Given the project's focus and its North-to-South angle of vision, however, it is not surprising that it reinforces many of the discourses and hierarchies discussed earlier. Like many humanitarian appeals, for example, the *Half the Sky* book begins with the story of a single representative individual, in this case a Cambodian girl who was forced into the sex trade after relocating to Thailand in search of income for her family. In the absence of the kind of close-up visual representation typically found in charitable appeals, the authors provide a physical description:

> Srey Rath is a self-confident Cambodian teenager whose black hair tumbles over a round, light brown face . . . Rath is short and small-boned, pretty, vibrant, and bubbly, a wisp of a girl whose negligible stature contrasts with an outsized and outgoing personality.

(xi)

Through this description, Rath is presented as something more than a stereotypically passive victim, yet she is also racialized in a way that establishes her "otherness" in relation to a predominately white audience. The authors return to Rath's story later in the introduction, showing how she has been able to transform her life.

Other elements of the book's approach reveal the authors' assumptions about their audience and its cultural and geopolitical orientations. The portrayal of girls and women who are disadvantaged, yet strong and active, appeals to Global North readers who are tired of only hearing "bad news," but who also are trained to expect it. The emphasis on "solutions such as girls' education and microfinance, which are working right now" is attractive to those who have been enculturated to expect immediate results. The project's geographic focus is squarely on the Global South. The three core issues spotlighted in the book ("sex trafficking and forced prostitution; gender-based violence, including honor killings and mass rape; and maternal mortality" [xxi]) reinforce this orientation, with the examples of honor killings and mass rape effectively ruling out the possibility of making a connection with gender-based violence in the North, such as the high rates of sexual violence. Northern women are present in the book primarily in their role as creators and supporters of organizations, such as Girls Learn International, that seek to address problems elsewhere.

The authors' implicit justification for limiting their "worldwide" discussion of gender-based injustices to the Global South lies in the idea of development. They make an explicit link with the development discourse that has been adopted by policy elites throughout the world, noting that women are central to the "development strategies" of many poor countries. In arguing that helping women can be a more effective way of promoting development, they refer to scholars such as Sen and Paul Farmer, investment firms such as Goldman Sachs, multilateral institutions such as the World Bank, major NGOs such as CARE, and major philanthropic foundations such as the NoVo Foundation. It is worth noting that the language of "opportunity" and economic empowerment invoked regularly in the book sits well with those who are comfortable seeing the Global South as a set of "emerging markets" for outside investment.

The Half the Sky project has sparked fierce criticism from scholars and activists who argue that the project is really about reinforcing a particular idea of white, Western moral authority and superiority. Many critics point to Kristof's particular reporting style, which often places him at the center of the story as a kind of "celebrity journalist" seeking to "save" women in a way that recalls Spivak's criticism of British colonialism in India. In a 2012 blog post for *Racialicious*, for example, Santayani DasGupta notes that despite the film's sympathetic presentation of many female activists in the Global South, it relies heavily on the use of what Kristof calls "bridge characters," the famous actresses with whom Western viewers are assumed to identify as they struggle to relate to the far-away people and issues in the film. The resulting binary distinction between "their women" and "our women," DasGupta suggests, has the unfortunate effect of undermining "global sisterhood" and hiding the reality of gender oppression "at home." Germaine Greer, a prominent Australian feminist, echoes this concern in a review of the *Half the Sky* book, pointing out that the authors missed an opportunity to use examples of sexual violence and other forms of gender injustice drawn from the United States and elsewhere in the Global North.

DasGupta also argues persuasively that some of the reporting strategies used in the project would be considered exploitative and even offensive if used in a Western context. "For example," she asks, "would Kristof, a middle-aged male reporter, so blithely ask a 14-year-old U.S. rape survivor to describe her experiences in front of cameras, her family, and other onlookers? Would he sit smilingly in a European woman's house asking her to describe the state of her genitals to him?" By calling attention to such taken-for-granted patterns of cultural representation, DasGupta points the reader toward broader questions about how humanitarianism shapes the cultural construction of identity.

The Half the Sky Movement has a significant online presence. See the following links for more information and perspectives:

- The official website for the project is at http://www.halftheskymovement.org/.
- The trailer for the film, along with footage and interviews, is available from PBS at http://www.pbs.org/independentlens/half-the-sky/video/.
- The Facebook page for Half the Sky Movement: The Game is at https://www.facebook.com/HalftheGame.
- Santayani DasGupta's *Racialicious* blog post can be found at http://www.conspireforchange.org/?p=964.
- Germaine Greer's review of the *Half the Sky* book is available on the website of the *Guardian* (http://www.theguardian.com/lifeandstyle/2010/jul/31/half-the-sky-germaine-greer).

## Viral Humanitarianism

The rise of social media in recent years has brought new opportunities for people to participate in the work of transnational humanitarianism by sharing informational videos and articles; making charitable donations directly from their mobile phones during major crises, such as the 2004 Asian tsunami; and devising their own "viral" social media campaigns. The ability of such campaigns to promote rapid public awareness of urgent global issues has led to a significant celebration of social media's humanitarian potential. At the same time, many have observed that such highly mediated forms of action constitute a kind of "slacktivism" that minimizes the need to understand the context surrounding political issues and become personally invested in the search for solutions. Other critics argue that while well intentioned, many forms of "viral humanitarianism" can also serve to reinforce discourses of cultural superiority and lend support to Western military intervention.

Three of the most prominent early twenty-first-century examples of technology-mediated humanitarian activism demonstrate the complexity of the factors shaping these dynamics: the Save Darfur movement, the Kony 2012 controversy, and the 2014 #BringBackOurGirls campaign. While each case is quite distinct, the fact that all of them concern humanitarian action focused on sub-Saharan Africa reveals the staying power of discourses and hierarchical relations grounded in the colonial era. At the same time, all three can be distinguished from earlier cases such as Live Aid in two important ways: the prominent role of social media and the overriding influence of geopolitical factors associated with the post-2001 "global war on terrorism" (GWOT), in which Africa is constructed as playing an increasingly prominent role.

Beginning in 2004, the Save Darfur Coalition played a key role in promoting public awareness of atrocities taking place in Darfur, a region located in Western Sudan, in connection with violent conflict between local rebel groups and the Sudanese government. Of particular concern were the killings reportedly carried out against civilians in Darfur by militias known as the Janjaweed. While estimates on the number of people killed and displaced during the war were (and are) difficult to confirm, Save Darfur and many others argued that what was taking place in Darfur constituted an ongoing genocide. Celebrities such as the actor George Clooney lent their faces and voices to the movement, which drew much of its strength from idealistic young people who organized campaigns in their high schools and universities.

Many public appeals at the time played on people's memories of the international community's relatively slow and ineffective response to the 1994 Rwandan genocide. This discursive connection promoted a highly simplified view of both the Rwanda and Sudan cases, relying on stereotypical constructions regarding African "tribalism" and binary constructions of "good" and "evil" characters. In the Darfur case, these constructions were overlaid with post-9/11 narratives that emphasized the Arab and Islamic components of the Sudanese government and the Janjaweed. In retrospect, it is clear that such narratives, while highly seductive for Western audiences, downplayed the role of other local factors, such as land and water disputes, as well as the less visible impact of climate change and transnational resource extraction on the conflict.

Several years later came what is arguably the most controversial example of "viral humanitarianism" to date. Jason Russell, cofounder of the anti–human trafficking group Invisible Children, released the documentary film *Kony 2012*, accompanied by an intensive social media campaign using the #Kony2012 hashtag, all designed to spotlight human rights violations, including the use of child soldiers by Joseph Kony and his Lord's Resistance Army (LRA) fighting in northern Uganda. As many analysts have noted, Kony made the perfect early-twenty-first-century villain for audiences raised on the specter of global insecurity and the promise of instant fame through social entrepreneurship and heroic cosmopolitan activism. The Ethiopian-American novelist Dinaw Mengestu, the prominent Ugandan scholar Mahmood Mamdani, and other critics took Russell to task for drastically oversimplifying a complex situation, manipulating the naïveté and narcissism of Western audiences, and brushing aside the sustained efforts of regional actors to address the political problems in Uganda and surrounding countries. Others, such as the Swedish anthropologist Sverker Finnström, noted how easily the public's fear and outrage concerning Kony could be manipulated into support for the growing level of overt and covert Western military intervention in postcolonial East Africa as part of the GWOT.

The cultural and geopolitical structures associated with the GWOT also played a key role in the public's response to the 2014 kidnapping of more than two hundred Nigerian schoolgirls by the Islamist rebel group Boko Haram. The kidnappers played on Western fears of Islamic terrorism by releasing videos that were menacing, often exaggeratedly so, suggesting an effort to copy or even exceed the impact of previous videos issued by other insurgent groups. On the other hand, the resulting social media campaign differed significantly from the Kony 2012 campaign in that the origins of the #BringBackOurGirls hashtag were located in Nigeria, not in Europe or the United States. As a result, the campaign was focused more fully on the victims themselves, rather than on celebrities and movement leaders in the North. Public outrage about the kidnappings was widespread and deeply felt, particularly in many communities in the African diaspora. At the same time, despite these understandable reactions, the #BringBackOurGirls campaign dovetailed significantly with the thematic focus of the Half the Sky project, contributing to a broader narrative of a presumed gender-progressive North helping girls and women in a presumed gender-regressive South.

Despite their differences, these three cases of viral humanitarianism can be viewed as symbolizing and contributing to global hierarchies in a number of ways. First, by promoting activism through social media, they reinforced the relative privilege of those whose engagement with social and political issues is shaped (and limited) by their extensive use of new technologies and their immersion in virtual culture. Whether viewed as "slacktivism" or simply as naïve idealism, critics argue, such engagement often ends up encouraging particularly shallow and simplistic forms of understanding that further obscure global power relations, rather than forcing audiences to confront them critically. Second, to varying degrees, the three cases cultivate Chouliaraki's position of the "ironic spectator" while combining this position with long-established forms of racial hierarchy. Taken to their logical conclusion, these patterns are connected with an emerging cultural phenomenon bitterly satirized by *The Onion*, *Reductress*, and others: the phenomenon of young white women posing with black African children, then posting their photos on Facebook or Instagram as symbols of personal transformation and philanthropy.

Third, by emphasizing poignant stories and charismatic personalities, viral humanitarianism can be seen as promoting the emergence of what the Nigerian-American writer Teju Cole labels the "white savior industrial complex." Writing in immediate response to the Kony 2012 phenomenon, Cole issued a controversial series of seven Tweets that pointed out the organic relationship between Western violence and self-congratulatory Western humanitarianism. In Cole's view, this humanitarianism is simultaneously naïve ("The world is nothing but a problem to be solved by enthusiasm"), dangerous ("The white savior supports brutal policies in the morning, founds charities in the afternoon, and receives awards in the evening"), and hypocritical ("Feverish worry over that awful African warlord. But close to 1.5 million Iraqis died from an American war of choice. Worry about that.") Here Cole connects directly with Hardt and Negri's discussion of the organic relationship between NGOs and Global North militarism.

> For critical responses to the campaigns of viral humanitarianism discussed in this section, see the following links:
>
> Teju Cole's Tweets on the "white savior industrial complex" can be found at http://www.theatlantic.com/international/archive/2012/03/the-white-savior-industrial-complex/254843/.
>
> Mahmood Mamdani's article "Joseph Kony and the Lord's Resistance Army" is available at http://www.aljazeera.com/indepth/opinion/2012/03/20123138139642455.html.
>
> Dinaw Mengestu's article on *Kony 2012* is at http://www.warscapes.com/reportage/not-click-away-joseph-kony-real-world.
>
> Satires on the phenomenon of young white women posing for photos with African children can be found on the websites of *The Onion* (http://www.theonion.com/article/6-day-visit-to-rural-african-village-completely-ch-35083) and *Reductress* (http://reductress.com/cutest-ways-photograph-hugging-third-world-children/).

## Alternatives to North-South Humanitarianism

As critiques of traditional humanitarian appeals become more common, and as more people begin to take on the role of "ironic spectator," it is tempting to agree with those who argue the world has entered a "post-humanitarian" age. At the same time, it is clear that the long-established patterns of representation associated with humanitarianism have shown a strong ability to reinvent themselves in response to changing geopolitical conditions. Equally important, the kinds of chronic social injustices that spark feelings of basic human solidarity show no signs of abating. So what does the future hold? Are there viable alternatives to the hierarchies that have long animated the social relations of North-South humanitarianism?

As noted earlier, humanitarian NGOs have already begun to respond to existing critiques by creating appeals that represent people in the Global South as actively involved in working to better their own lives. This shift itself may be viewed as an attempt to create alternatives to the most hierarchical forms of humanitarianism. Taking this approach a step further, some would point to the emergence of "voluntourism" (the practice of doing a small amount of charitable work as part of a tourist experience) as a welcome shift toward a more equal relationship between individuals and communities from different parts of the world. Others argue that voluntourism remains overly focused on the emotional needs of the Global North tourists and that, in practice, it has resulted in the creation of new forms of exploitation. Even at the most progressive end of the spectrum, when voluntourism morphs into politically motivated solidarity activism, there are concerns about whether such work might still end up reinforcing patterns of inequality and a neocolonial politics of representation.

The growing importance of major humanitarian organizations based in the South constitutes another emerging alternative. While some of these rely to some extent on financial support from the North, they are less likely to operate on the basis of cultural assumptions about Euro-American superiority and less likely to prioritize the emotional needs of Northern donors. One example is the Green Belt Movement, a Kenya-based NGO founded by Nobel Peace Prize winner Wangari Maathai and focused on the interconnected work of community development, environmental sustainability, and women's empowerment. In addition to the work they do within their own local communities, Southern NGOs may be seen as part of the broader process of what is often called "South-South cooperation." The technologies associated with globalization have increased the possibilities for people and nations in the Global South to deepen the exchange of knowledge and resources, including humanitarian assistance, in ways that sometimes bypass Global North organizations and governments altogether.

Much less common, at least to date, is the phenomenon of humanitarian assistance flowing from the South to the North. In principle, there is no reason why donors in the South could not become benefactors of projects addressing major social problems such as poverty and gender injustice in the North. When the Gulf Coast of the United States was hit by Hurricane Katrina in 2005, for example, dozens of countries from all parts of the world offered to send assistance. Perhaps most provocative was the Cuban government's offer of more than a thousand doctors and tons of medical supplies, an offer that was refused by the U.S. government despite pleas from many local and regional elected officials. This example suggests that a significant reversal in the patterns of global humanitarianism would require a loosening of the political and cultural structures that have shaped colonial, postcolonial, and neocolonial identities for centuries.

## References and Further Research

Burman, Erica. 1994. "Poor Children: Charity Appeals and Ideologies of Childhood." *Changes: An International Journal of Psychology and Psychotherapy* 12, no. 1: 29–36.

Chouliaraki, Lilie. 2013. *The Ironic Spectator: Solidarity in the Age of Post-Humanitarianism*. Cambridge: Polity Press.

DasGupta, Santayani. 2012. "Your Women Are Oppressed, but Ours Are Awesome: How Nicholas Kristof and *Half The Sky* Use Women Against Each Other." *Racialicious*, October 8. http://www.racialicious.com/2012/10/08/your-women-are-oppressed-but-ours-are-awesome-how-nicholas-kristof-and-half-the-sky-use-women-against-each-other/.

Edgar, Andrew, and Peter Sedgwick, eds. 1999. *Key Concepts in Cultural Theory*. London: Routledge.

Finnström, Sverker. 2012. "KONY 2012, Military Humanitarianism, and the Magic of Occult Economies." *Africa Spectrum* 47, no. 2–3: 127–135. http://journals.sub.uni-hamburg.de/giga/afsp/article/view/554.

Hardt, Michael, and Antonio Negri. 2000. *Empire*. Cambridge, MA: Harvard University Press.

Höijer, Brigitta. 2004. "The Discourse of Global Compassion: The Audience and Media Reporting of Human Suffering." *Media, Culture & Society* 26, no. 4: 513–531.

INCITE! Women of Color Against Violence. 2009. *The Revolution Will Not be Funded: Beyond the Non-Profit Industrial Complex*. Cambridge, MA: South End Press.

Kristof, Nicholas, and Sheryl WuDunn. 2009. *Half the Sky: Turning Oppression Into Opportunity for Women Worldwide*. New York: Alfred A. Knopf.

Lincoln, Bruce. 1989. *Discourse and the Construction of Society: Comparative Studies of Myth, Ritual, and Classification*. New York: Oxford University Press.

McMichael, Philip. 2012. *Development and Social Change: A Global Perspective*. 5th ed. Los Angeles: SAGE.

Moeller, Susan. 1999. *Compassion Fatigue: How the Media Sell Disease, Famine, War and Death*. New York: Routledge.

Mpanya, Mutombo. 1995. "Stereotypes of Africa in U.S. Hunger Appeals." In *The Color of Hunger: Race and Hunger in National and International Perspective*, edited by David L. Shields, 25–33. Lanham, MD: Rowman & Littlefield.

O'Dell, Lindsay. 2008. "Representations of the 'Damaged' Child: 'Child Saving' in a British Children's Charity Ad Campaign." *Children & Society* 22, no. 5: 383–392.

Seu, Irene Bruna. 2010. "'Doing Denial': Audience Reaction to Human Rights Appeals." *Discourse and Society* 21, no. 4: 438–457.

Shohat, Ella, and Robert Stam. 1994. *Unthinking Eurocentrism: Multiculturalism and the Media*. London: Routledge.

Spivak, Gayatri Chakravorty. 1995. "Can the Subaltern Speak?" In *The Post-Colonial Studies Reader*, edited by Bill Ashcroft, Gareth Griffiths, and Helen Tiffin, 24–28. New York: Routledge.

Spurr, David. 1993. *The Rhetoric of Empire: Colonial Discourse in Journalism, Travel Writing, and Imperial Administration*. Durham, NC: Duke University Press.

Steensland, Brian, and Philip Goff, eds. 2014. *The New Evangelical Social Engagement*. New York: Oxford University Press.

Tester, Keith. 2010. *Humanitarianism and Modern Culture*. University Park: Pennsylvania State University Press.

# 8

## Climate Change and Changing Global Imaginaries

The human being is capable of everything. He is capable of the worst and capable of the best. The main thing is the context in which he was born, the culture surrounding him and the type of customs in which he is settled. And if there is a preoccupation to live in harmony with the nature in the system where he lives, then, he is capable to live in harmony with nature and to be most respectful to his environment . . . [I]f the system in which he lives is predatory, he is consequently going to develop a predatory tendency to overconsumption and a relation to his environment . . . [and] he will no longer be able to live in harmony with this world that surrounds him. The matter is not an issue of human nature, the issue is that of what type of human culture we are capable to instill in our children and even ourselves. What system generates this type of culture today and what kind of system generates the opposite?

—Sihem Bensedrine, Tunisian human rights activist, quoted at the 2006 Table of Free Voices

It has become almost a cliché to say that global climate change represents the defining challenge facing humanity in the twenty-first century. The consensus among climate scientists is that the challenge is existential: the effects of climate change, if not addressed proactively in the form of fundamental social and political changes, have the potential to bring human civilization to the brink of extinction. Activists, scientists, and policy makers who seek to promote such a proactive response, however, face a significant paradox that requires a special effort to help people make the connection between what they might be observing locally and what is happening at the planetary level. On the one hand, the sheer scale and dire nature of the problem mean that its importance should be obvious to everyone who learns about it, regardless of their social location. On the other hand, precisely because the problem is so all-encompassing, one can easily fail to "connect the dots" among various local manifestations. Similarly, because some changes occur very gradually over long periods of time, they may not be noticeable to those who are immersed in them.

What this paradox reveals is that climate change does more than pose a threat to social and ecological systems. It also poses a significant challenge to what cultural theorists call our existing "imaginaries"—the culturally conditioned ways in which we see the world. A complex, globalized world is a world of many such imaginaries that overlap in dynamic ways, regularly coming into contact, dialogue, and conflict with one another. These imaginaries are grounded in the operation of various cultures and subcultures associated with everything from particular ethnic, national, or religious groups to corporations, virtual communities, and social activists.

Examining debates over climate change—what it is, what it means, and what to do about it—is a good way to explore the changing politics of global imaginaries. What happens, for example, when different global imaginaries intersect in political debates or at major international climate change conferences? What happens when existing imaginaries are faced with radically new information? How is the awareness of climate change altering how we see ourselves and others, how we see our place within larger natural systems, and how we see the planet itself? How does this awareness interact with inherited structures of ethnocentrism and identity, cultural systems of meaning and value, and visions of the future? How are activists seeking to foster new imaginaries as part of their struggle to promote particular responses to climate change?

For basic information on the 15th Conference of the Parties to the UN Framework Convention on Climate Change (COP 15), held in Copenhagen as part of the 2009 United Nations Climate Change Conference, see the UNFCCC website (https://unfccc.int/meetings/copenhagen_dec_2009/meeting/6295.php).

For a variety of perspectives on the COP 15 from official government delegations, civil society representatives, and activists, see the following web pages:

- "Canada's National Statement at COP 15," Environment Canada (http://ec.gc.ca/default.asp?lang=En&n=976258C6-1&news=39E3CF9B-B654-401F-8EBD-6695E56327F1)
- "OPEC Statement to the United Nations Climate Change Conference (COP15)," Organization of the Petroleum Exporting Countries (http://www.opec.org/opec_web/en/press_room/378.htm)
- "A People's Declaration from Klimaforum09" (http://klimaforum.org/)
- "Statement of Climate Justice Now! On the COP 15," Climate Justice Now! (http://www.climate-justice-now.org/cjn-final-statement-in-copenhagen/)
- "Statement to COP15, UN Climate Conference Copenhagen," World Council of Churches (http://www.oikoumene.org/en/resources/documents/wcc-programmes/justice-diakonia-and-responsibility-for-creation/climate-change-water/statement-to-cop15-un-climate-conference-copenhagen)
- "Transcript of President Lula's Address in Copenhagen," Brazil's COP15 web page (http://www.cop15.gov.br/en-US/indexe17b.html?page=noticias/pres-lula-speech)
- "UN Climate Change Conference (COP15)," Conference European Commission (http://ec.europa.eu/clima/events/articles/0013_en.htm)
- United States Participation in COP 15," U.S. State Department (http://www.cop15.state.gov/)
- "Voices from Small Island States," *Democracy Now!* (http://www.democracynow.org/2009/12/17/voices_from_the_island_states_maldives)
- "Wen Jiabao speech to COP15 Copenhagen, December 18," Scribd (http://www.scribd.com/doc/24278538/Wen-Jiabao-speech-to-COP15-Copenhagen-December-18)

## Understanding Imaginaries

The "imaginary" is a theoretical concept with roots in psychoanalysis, critical Marxism, sociology, and cultural studies. Like all such concepts, its precise meaning is subject to constant debate and revision as scholars respond to one another's work and to the changing world around them. At its core, however, the imaginary concerns the question of how human perception of the world—whether the external world or one's inner world—is enabled, limited, and framed by social forces. Consequently, the idea bears a close relationship to other concepts, such as ideology, worldview, cosmology, identity, and discourse. In addition to exploring the imaginary as a singular, abstract concept, scholars have explored the operation of more specific, concrete imaginaries within particular social contexts ranging from Renaissance Europe to modern nation-states to today's transnational communities that are constituted through human migration and other elements of globalization.

In his 1984 book on theories of ideology, John B. Thompson discusses Greek-French philosopher Cornelius Castoriadis's pioneering work on the concept of the social imaginary. For Castoriadis, who was influenced by Jacques Lacan's work in psychoanalysis, the imaginary "creates for each historical period its singular way of living, seeing and making its own existence, its world and its relations to it" (quoted in Thompson 1984, 23). Thompson adds that the imaginary "accounts for the orientation of social institutions, for the constitution of motives and needs, for the existence of symbolism, tradition and myth" (23), in the process constituting "the laces which tie a society together and the forms which define what, for a given society, is 'real'" (24). In this sense, the imaginary has much in common with what Michel Foucault describes as "truth regimes": systems of power and knowledge that govern which kinds of statements will be accepted as "true" within a particular society.

Castoriadis's work, produced during the Cold War, posed a challenge to the taken-for-granted notion that Western capitalist democracy and Soviet-style communism represented radically different forms of social life. Rather than accept this notion, he insisted that both forms were products of the same basic imaginary: a modernist imaginary built upon industrialism, rationalism, a linear notion of history, and faith in science and technology as the engines of "progress." From this standpoint, capitalism and communism are simply two streams springing from a common source, a source that can be distinguished from a range of non-Western imaginaries animating many indigenous and so-called traditional societies.

Subsequent work by feminist theorists such as Donna Haraway has established that the dominant Western imaginary identified by Castoriadis is also masculinist and objectivist in its orientation: it privileges knowledge that is generated through a male gaze that seeks to "distance the knowing subject from everybody and everything in the interests of unfettered power" (Haraway 1988, 581). Haraway's framework reveals how different imaginaries produce their own "ways of seeing" (to use the title of a famous book by the British art critic John Berger), including ways of determining which vantage points will be privileged and which kinds of knowledge will be validated or delegitimized. In response to what she calls the "conquering gaze from nowhere" associated with the masculinist scientific establishment, she emphasizes the importance of "situated knowledge," or knowledge that is self-consciously grounded in a particular position and that would enable us to "become answerable for what we learn how to see" (583).

These observations have important implications for contemporary efforts to build a shared understanding of what is happening to global climate. It is impossible to think about climate change without thinking about the Earth itself and the nature of the ecological and social systems contained within it—issues on which different imaginaries can diverge in significant ways. As Thompson (1984, 18) notes, for example, the Western imaginary illuminated in Castoriadis's work contains within it a specific understanding of the relationship between humans and the natural world: "The whole idea of applying knowledge for technical development, of regarding nature as a domain to be exploited, requires a certain attitude which is by no means universal." While not "universal" in the sense of being shared by people of all cultures, this attitude has nonetheless become quite hegemonic within an unequal global system through the alliance between state policy, scientific knowledge, and the ideologies surrounding economic and social development.

What does the imaginary mean today, in an era of intense and uneven globalization? The anthropologist Arjun Appadurai (1996, 33) notes that the rapid circulation of people, capital, goods, images, and technologies has disrupted a world neatly divided into distinct imaginaries (if such a world ever existed). What we find instead are what he calls "imagined worlds," new and constantly shifting experiential worlds that are the product of people's transnational existence. "An important fact of the world we live in today," writes Appadurai, "is that many persons on the globe live in such imagined worlds . . . and thus are able to contest and sometimes even subvert the imagined worlds of the official mind." At the same time, the residual influence of older social imaginaries cannot be underestimated, as it is these that are inherited by today's global citizens and that continue to shape their lives in innumerable ways. The following section explores briefly the history of some of these imaginaries, particularly those that bear on contemporary debates surrounding the future of humanity and of the planet in the face of global climate change.

## Global Imaginaries: A Brief History

The recognition of anthropogenic (human-caused) global climate change represents one of the most important moments in the history of how humans have imagined the world. Some scientists have begun to use the term "Anthropocene" to designate a distinct geological era marked by the impact of human activity on the planet's various ecosystems. Whether understood to refer to the post–Industrial Revolution period or to a longer period reaching back to the initial development of agriculture, the idea of an Anthropocene represents a novel contribution to a long list of global imaginaries, ranging from ancient cosmologies to contemporary imaginaries grounded in film, warfare, and information technology.

The oldest group of global imaginaries, typically known as cosmologies, seeks to place the globe in relationship to the wider universe. These include cosmologies associated with major religious traditions such as Hinduism or Christianity, but also various forms of animism, pantheism, and neo-paganism. Some of these imaginaries locate the existence of the Earth and humanity in relation to concepts of linear or cyclical time, others emphasize origin stories that provide the foundation of wider social and cultural systems, and still others view the entire universe as timeless. On the scientific side, the development of global imaginaries has been marked by a number of revolutionary discoveries, often known as "paradigm shifts," in which new knowledge radically alters previously held theories and assumptions. The shift from the Ptolemaic system (which viewed the Earth as the center of the universe) to the Copernican system (with the Earth orbiting the Sun) is a classic example of such a paradigm shift in global scientific imaginaries. More recently, the so-called big bang theory revolutionized physical cosmology by arguing that the universe has been expanding since its origin billions of years ago. Particularly in the United States, conflicts among differing cosmologies tend to be concentrated in the debate between those who have accepted prevailing scientific theories and those who believe the universe was divinely created.

A second group of global imaginaries comprises the geopolitical and geocultural imaginaries through which humans understand the existing spatial distribution and organization of cultures and societies. Many ancient cultures, for example, believed in the idea of a flat Earth, while mapmakers in the early modern period often placed sacred cities such as Jerusalem at the center of their maps, with all other known or imagined territories and peoples surrounding them. Since that time, global maps have been shaped not only by improved knowledge of the planet's physical geography, but also by the construction of categories such as empires, nations, ecumenes, civilizations, and so forth. In their 1997 book critiquing the influence of what they call "metageography," Martin Lewis and Kären Wigen argue that even taken-for-granted geographical constructions such as the idea of distinct "continents" (Asia, Africa, Europe, etc.) or hemispheres (Eastern/Western, Northern/Southern) ultimately represent the products of imaginaries that are culturally constructed rather than natural.

The very concept of globalization has generated a new set of global imaginaries as humans have become increasingly aware of global interconnectedness and how it disrupts the centrality of older political and cultural categories (see Featherstone 2006). Recent decades have seen a similar shift in the construction of maps and other tools for visualizing the globe. The emergence of the so-called Gall-Peters projection map, for example, posed a direct challenge to the Mercator projection that had been the basis for many world maps since the sixteenth century. By publicizing what many believed to be a more accurate way of "projecting" a round, three-dimensional world onto a two-dimensional map, the geographer Arno Peters (who drew on the previous work of James Gall) was also able to show how the Mercator and other maps had systematically misrepresented the relative sizes of richer and poorer nations. Other alternatives to traditional, Eurocentric maps include "bottom-up" maps that place the Southern Hemisphere on the top half of the map.

More recently, a growing interest in globalization has enabled mapmakers to generate a wide range of creative, complex, and interactive maps that represent an infinite number of ways of seeing the world. Aided by new geospatial and information technologies, such maps include dynamic representations of historical processes as well as contemporary themes such as poverty, human migration, cultural identity, war and violence, ecological change, human rights, agriculture, consumer trends, and public health. While many of these more conceptual maps retain the nation-state as the basic unit of comparative analysis, others deliberately avoid highlighting national borders, hoping to call attention instead to processes that are inherently transnational. In one especially provocative contribution, Paul Amar proposes in his book *The Security Archipelago* (2013) the idea of a transnational territory made up of "a metaphorical island chain of what the global security industry calls 'hot spots.'"

Useful global maps are shown and discussed on the following websites and web pages:

"40 Maps That Explain the World," *Washington Post* (http://www.washingtonpost.com/blogs/worldviews/wp/2013/08/12/40-maps-that-explain-the-world/?lines)
The Upside Down Map Page (http://www.flourish.org/upsidedownmap/)
"World Maps," *The Guardian* (http://www.theguardian.com/global/gallery/2009/apr/17/world-maps-mercator-goode-robinson-peters-hammer)

The development of new technologies during the past century has enabled the creation of a third set of global imaginaries that enable people to "see" the world in new, often highly mediated ways. The invention of modern cinema, for example, has had a radical impact on human perception in general, and, as Shohat and Stam argue in *Unthinking Eurocentrism*

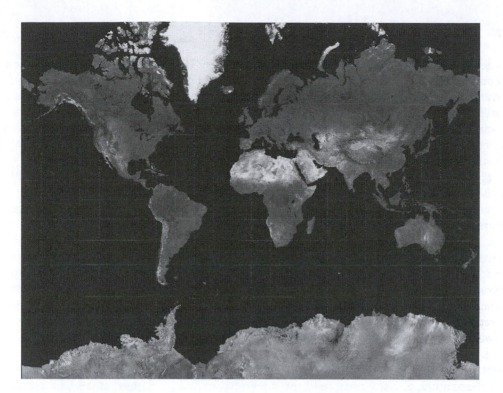

The Mercator Projection was originally created in 1569 by Flemish cartographer Gerardus Mercator. The source image for this version is from NASA's Earth Observatory "Blue Marble" series.

*Source:* Wikimedia Commons. https://commons.wikimedia.org/wiki/File:Mercator-projection.jpg

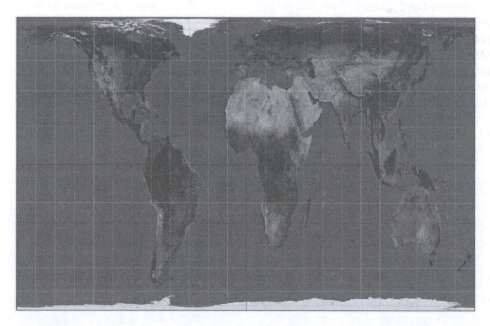

The Gall-Peters Projection offers a strikingly different vision of the world from the older Mercator projection, and the contrast between the two projections continues to provoke lively debate among cartographers. The source image for this version is a derivative of NASA's "Blue Marble" summer composite.

*Source:* Daniel R. Strebe/Wikimedia Commons. https://commons.wikimedia.org/wiki/File:Gall%E2%80%93Peters_projection_SW.jpg

(1994), on the construction of an "imperial imaginary" through which audiences came to "know" the world through the eyes of European colonizers. Another key moment was the invention of global satellite technologies that enabled powerful nations to develop their own capabilities of planetary observation and surveillance beginning in the late 1950s. The subsequent "space race" between the United States and the Soviet Union led to one of the iconic moments in the history of modern global imaginaries: the "Blue Marble" photograph of the Earth, taken by Apollo 17 astronauts in 1972.

The editors of a 2014 edition of the journal *Public Culture* note that while the "Blue Marble" image is often credited with sparking a new wave of global ecological awareness, its grounding in the highly militarized U.S. space program also demonstrates the close relationship between new visual technologies and the political structures associated with warfare and the drive for planetary control. Similarly, the French theorist Paul Virilio emphasizes that technologies of film and warfare represent "vision machines" that replace direct perception, thereby making it harder, not easier, for people to stay connected with reality. Most recently, the creation of the World Wide Web reveals once again the ongoing tension between the creation of new imaginaries for ordinary people and the creation of new tools of surveillance and control for political and economic elites.

Most obviously relevant to the issue of climate change are the imaginaries associated with ecological perspectives that seek to convince people of the need to see themselves as part of the biosphere rather than separate from it, to extend their ethical circle to include nonhuman life, and to understand the integrated nature of natural and social systems. The creation of the annual Earth Day celebration in 1970 represented one important moment in the emergence of a new ecological consciousness during the 1960s. Several years later, the scientists James Lovelock and Lynn Margulis developed the Gaia hypothesis, a controversial theory concerning the coevolution of living organisms and their surrounding environments. With its vision of the Earth as a self-regulating system, Gaia theory provided a compelling global imaginary for some in the scientific community, as well as for other ecologically minded people seeking alternatives to dominant religious and social systems. Some of the latter group included representatives of ecofeminism, although other feminists were strongly critical of some of the cultural assumptions embedded in the Gaia idea.

---

### Ecofeminism

Emerging in the 1970s and 1980s, ecofeminism represents a distinct global imaginary focused on what the philosopher Karen Warren (1996, x) calls "the nature of the connections between the domination of women (and other oppressed humans) and the domination of nature." The influential feminist author Carolyn Merchant identifies at least four basic types of ecofeminism: liberal, cultural, social, and socialist. A central debate among ecofeminists concerns whether the idea of a "natural" connection between women and nature should be used as a basis for political action, or whether such "biological reductionism and essentialism" (Sandilands 1999, 4) should be rejected on the grounds that it ultimately reinforces the binary divisions imposed by patriarchy itself. For ecofeminists who emphasize Earth-centered and goddess-centered spirituality, patriarchal forms of monotheism lie at the root of many contemporary problems, including gender oppression and ecological destruction. Other ecofeminists, particularly those based in the Global South, highlight how colonialism, capitalist expansion, and structures of gender inequality combine to make women more vulnerable to the impact of environmental degradation.

Ecofeminist perspectives continue to influence debates over how to mitigate the effects of global climate change, with feminist scholars and activists agreeing on several points, including (1) climate change hits already vulnerable populations the hardest, with women and girls falling disproportionately into this category; (2) policies on climate change are dominated by male decision makers; and (3) these policies too often ignore the specific needs of women and girls.

Debates among ecofeminists over possible solutions often mirror broader North-South debates at the government level. Many groups representing women in the Global South, such as Isis International (2014), reject "the re-emergence of views on a direct and simplistic connection between climate change and population growth"—a reference to arguments made by some environmental activists in the North. For Isis, the main cause behind climate change is "a refusal to limit production and consumption, particularly in the developed world," and the main challenge is how to make sure that women and girls are fully empowered and integrated into the process of creating sustainable solutions.

The invention of the Anthropocene concept coincided with the rise of significant human awareness of global climate change. As scientists have pooled their knowledge on the subject, major reports and international gatherings have provided opportunities to promote a new global imaginary in which the Earth's climate system is under dramatic threat. The first report of the Intergovernmental Panel on Climate Change (IPCC), released in 1990, was a watershed moment in this regard. Asserting directly that "emissions resulting from human activities . . . will enhance the greenhouse effect," the report brought to public consciousness the reality of increasing global mean temperatures ("global warming") and a consequent rise in sea levels. Subsequent IPCC reports, amplified by politicians and environmental activists across the world, have helped to cement the "paradigm shift" set in motion by awareness of global climate change. In addition to dire scenarios of widespread future conflict, environmental catastrophe, and even civilizational extinction, this awareness has prompted hopes of what Jeremy Rifkin (2009) calls an "Empathic Civilization" built on a new form of "biosphere consciousness."

## Perspectives From the Table of Free Voices

Despite all the talk of global imaginaries, and even of a singular "global consciousness" resulting from technological connectivity, people still live in local contexts and experience the impact of global climate change in ways that are often very local. The diversity of humanity itself, grounded in local specificity and producing a diversity of knowledge and perspectives, is arguably as important as biodiversity to the health of the planet.

One interesting attempt to think through the implications of these realities was the Table of Free Voices, a special event held in 2006 in Bebelplatz, a public square in Berlin. The sponsoring group, Dropping Knowledge, chose the square because of its historical significance in the struggle for free speech and thought: Bebelplatz was the site of one of the infamous book-burning ceremonies carried out by pro-Nazi groups in 1933. The 2006 event featured a large round table at which 112 prominent global activists, artists, and thinkers sat throughout the day and responded to a set of 100 "global questions," with each individual's response to each question captured on digital video. The final list of questions was selected from a much larger number that had been submitted by people throughout the world during the months leading up to the event. The questions were divided into eight categories:

- Reinventing Economics (example: "Are brands more powerful than governments?")
- Conscious Recognition (example: "Why do we consider some lives to be worth more than others?")
- Politics of Violence (example: "Who is profiting from terrorism?")
- Understanding Power (example: "What is the purpose of public international law if there are no effective enforcement mechanisms to apply it?")
- The Human Footprint (example: "How can everyone have sufficient clean water without conflict?")
- The New Global Frontier (example: "How do we determine 'truth' and 'fact' when we can manufacture either?")
- Innovation Acceleration (example: "Why does it seem that life gets more and more stressful with each thing we invent to save time?")
- A Perceiving Eye (example: "What does the future you want look like?")

The responses gathered then became the basis for a global dialogue platform on the Dropping Knowledge website. All of the materials from the project, including a variety of multimedia materials and transcripts of the responses, were made freely available to the public.

---

The Dropping Knowledge project has produced a wealth of materials related to the Table of Free Voices that are freely available online, including the following:

- An archive of all 11,200 video responses from the Table of Free Voices, sortable by question and by respondent, is available at http://www.droppingknowledge. org/bin/projects/archive.page.
- Profiles of the participants at the Table of Free Voices can be found at http:// www.droppingknowledge.org/bin/projects/participantList.page.
- A livestream of the original event can be downloaded from http://www.dropping knowledge.org/bin/projects/stream/quicktime.page.
- Question videos submitted from around the world as part of the project are available at http://www.droppingknowledge.org/bin/media/list/commercial.page.
- An introductory video, *This Is Dropping Knowledge*, is at http://www.dropping knowledge.org/bin/media/show/12284.page.
- *Problema*, a documentary film based on the Table of Free Voices, can be found at http://www.problema-thefilm.org.

---

One of the questions featured at the Table of Free Voices was, "Can a person be perceptive enough to see our planet in a way that tells them that they too are part of nature?" The question was submitted by the acclaimed Brazilian photojournalist Sebastiao Salgado, whose work has spotlighted themes of human migration, labor, environmental change, and indigeneity. Salgado's question, perhaps not surprisingly for a photographer, emphasized the issue of how people see the world and suggested that a change in perception might be necessary in order to maintain healthy ecosystems. A closer look at some of the responses to the question reveals how the interpretation of global climate change is shaped by the intersection of diverse imaginaries grounded in a range of traditions and experiences.

While Salgado's question did not explicitly invoke climate change, many of the respondents clearly had climate change in mind when they answered. Mae-Wan Ho, a biochemist from Hong Kong, insisted that the inability to perceive oneself as a part of nature is a modern problem and that those people who never fell into this trap in the first place would be the ones to "enable us to overcome the current crisis of climate change and energy depletion." Similarly, the Indian neuroscientist Mayank Mehta argued that people who are "living closer to nature" are in the best position to notice the immediate effects of global warming. Another panelist, the U.S. environmental activist Michael P. Totten, emphasized the importance of the voluminous information gathered and released by the IPCC and the Millennium Ecosystems Assessment. "The ability to be so protective about this planet on these issues," he noted, "is now accessible to anyone virtually on this planet that is in proximity to a computer and an Internet connection."

As some of these comments indicate, the theme of indigeneity played a key role in the responses, with numerous panelists (both indigenous and nonindigenous) making direct or indirect comparisons between indigenous imaginaries and those associated with highly industrialized, urbanized cultures. Thenmozhi Soundararajan, a filmmaker and community organizer from the Dalit community in India, emphasized the diversity of indigenous communities and indigenous knowledge systems around the world. "You have multiple world views, multiple ways people approach science," she observed, "and I think that's a very profound place to start to have this conversation." Among the indigenous people represented at the Table of Free Voices was Viviana Figueroa, a lawyer working to represent the Omaguaca-Kolla indigenous people in Argentina. Referring to the "particular vision" that indigenous people have in terms of "feeling as part of nature" and "caring for the land, caring for nature, just taking what is necessary," Figueroa drew a sharp contrast between this view and the view of cultures that emphasize private ownership of land. Two other indigenous activists, Donato Bayu Bay Bumacas from the Philippines and Oscar Olivera from Bolivia, emphasized the importance of community action in helping to change people's perceptions. For Olivera, the key lies in making sure that people truly "become part of communities . . . remembering the history of our ancestors."

Other respondents addressed Salgado's question by referring to themes of spirituality or by discussing how particular religious and cultural traditions have constructed the relationship between humans and nature. These perspectives effectively introduced other important global imaginaries into the conversation. Tu Weiming, a professor of Chinese history at Harvard University, invoked the "Confucian humanistic perspective" and its belief that "our defining characteristic of being human . . . is that intrinsically a person forms one body with heaven, earth and a myriad of things." The Algerian Islamic studies scholar Mohammed Arkoun and the Zimbabwean environmental activist Gladman Chibememe both noted that all major religious traditions insist on the connection of humanity with the natural world. For the Turkish-German scholar Sabiha El-Zayat-Erbakan, being part of "the Creation" and having a clear relationship with nature brings with it a concrete "responsibility" to act. She suggests that one way to spur the necessary action would be to try to "see nature and the environment as a juristic person with whom we have to negotiate a balance between a suitable exploitation and preservation."

The theme of global urbanization emerged repeatedly as panelists tried to explain how much of humanity has become distanced from its grounding in the natural world. In effect, they suggested, the growth of cities has helped produce a distinct kind of global imaginary. "I suppose it gets more difficult for young people growing up in urban environments on TV and game screens to see themselves as part of nature," said Elisabet Sahtouris, an evolution biologist and futurist from the United States. Yet even people in large cities can make connections with nature, she argued, by treating plants and animals as "intelligent beings" and trying to create a "communion" with them. Susan George, a prominent critic of neoliberal globalization, connected the growth of cities with the economic processes driving people away from the countryside, where this kind of "communion" is easier to maintain. "It is very hard to see yourself as a part of nature if you are living in a slum," observed George. "So, what's the answer to that? I think the answer is we have to green our cities."

Finally, many of the respondents at the Table of Free Voices grappled with the issue of perception itself, reflecting on which types of perception are most likely to generate a useful awareness of ecological interconnections. The French-American writer Raymond Federman recalled the wonder he felt when seeing the "Blue Marble" photograph. In the face of such an overwhelming image of the planet, he said, people "should feel that they are just a miniscule little thing living on this planet amongst such beautiful things as trees and grass and all and even the beautiful blue water that is so present in us." Rodrigo Baggio, a social entrepreneur from Brazil, lamented the tendency of many people in the modern world to "live their isolated lives, focused on their own personal questions." What is needed, he argued, is for people to develop a more "systemic view" that enables them to "act locally" in ways that are connected with larger global problems.

Interestingly, the issue of climate change denial or skepticism—the belief that climate change is either not occurring in an alarming way or not occurring as a result of human activity—was absent from the discussion. None of the panelists held such views themselves, and none made reference to them in their responses. In many cases, it is clear that such perspectives are the product of intense political lobbying (especially within the U.S. political system) by the fossil fuel industry. Yet climate change denial and skepticism appeal to those whose global imaginaries make them less likely to accept a consensus that is produced through scientific knowledge. Many Christian conservatives, for example, see the world through the lens of biblical creationism, and even for those who might recognize the existence of anthropogenic climate change, some might be inclined to see this is as hastening an apocalypse they view as inevitable or even desirable. The absence of such views at the Table of Free Voices speaks to the difficulty of finding dialogue among imaginaries that are radically opposed to one another.

## Visualizing Climate Change

Another panelist at the Table of Free Voices, the Danish artist and designer Kigge Hvid, insisted that the people who understand environmental problems best are those who are most directly affected by them, such as the people living near the Chernobyl nuclear accident, and that other people need to "see it for themselves" in order to be convinced. "This leaves a giant responsibility to those who either are experts or to those directly affected by it," Hvid argued, "to make sure that other people all over the world, who are necessary to change the global environmental situation, make sure that these people get these visual impressions, which ensure that one actually understands it." Hvid's call for efforts to help people "see for themselves" the impact of environmental problems such as climate change has been taken up in numerous ways by individuals and groups seeking to promote global imaginaries in which climate change plays a central role.

More information about the online materials discussed in this section may be found at the links listed here.

Artistic responses to climate change:

- Aksik—Stories about Adaptation and Subsistence: Native Voices from the Frontlines of Climate Change (http://aksik.org/)
- Cape Farewell: The Art (http://www.capefarewell.com/art.html)
- "Charismatic Megafauna: The Growing Power of Celebrities and Pop Culture in Climate Change Campaigns," by Max Boykoff, Mike Goodman, and Jo Littler (http://www.kcl.ac.uk/sspp/departments/geography/research/Research-Domains/Contested-Development/BoykoffetalWP28.pdf)
- Global Cool (http://www.globalcool.org/)
- Imagine 2020: Art and Climate Change (http://www.imagine2020.eu/)
- *An Inconvenient Truth*: The Official Website of the Award-Winning Film (http://www.takepart.com/an-inconvenient-truth/film)
- VII International Exhibition of Graphic Humor-Lima (http://www.irancartoon.com/vii-international-exhibition-of-graphic-humor-lima-2014-peru-1/)
- *Jadagen Warnkan Barnden: Changing Climate in Gija Country*, IDAIA (http://crossart.com.au/home/index.php/archive/197-jadagen-warnkan-barnden-changing-climate-in-gija-country)
- Kinnari Ecological Theatre Project (http://www.kinnarieco-theatre.org)
- 350.org (http://350.org/; for the press release on the planetary art show, go to http://art.350.org/press-room/nov20/)
- "Maldives Politicians Submerge," Reuters news report about underwater cabinet meeting in the Maldives (https://www.youtube.com/watch?v=odFmDiYWJ0M)
- Zero Carbon Africa (http://zerocarbonafrica.blogspot.com/2012_09_01_archive.html)

Citizen science links:

- "Citizen Scientists' Climate-Impact Survey Wraps Up," *Nature* (http://www.nature.com/news/citizen-scientists-climate-impact-survey-wraps-up-1.9697)
- eBird (http://ebird.org/)
- "The Rise of Citizen Science," Climate Council (http://www.climatecouncil.org.au/the-rise-of-citizen-science)
- "Weather@home," climateprediction.net (http://www.climateprediction.net/weatherathome/)

Climate change has proven to be a powerful inspiration for creative artists working in all artistic media across the world, often in dialogue with climate scientists. One exemplary 2013 exhibition from Australia, *Jadagen Warnkan Barnden: Changing Climate in Gija Country*, featured the work of a group of Aboriginal artists who collaborated with an environmental scientist and a local specialist in linguistics. The announcement of the exhibition highlights how an increase in extreme weather events, such as the major floods of 2011, has affected Aboriginal communities, how the adaptive nature of traditional knowledge systems has aided local people in "reading" these changes, and how the artists sought to visualize these dynamics in their work. An essential element of the work is the recognition that "climate change" is hardly a new concept for Aboriginal people in Australia:

> The renowned rock art paintings of the Kimberley document climate changes over thousands of years and are an important example of the use of art to conceptualize climate change. Today's Gija people live in a vastly different landscape to that of their ancestors. Even the invasion of the East Kimberley by Europeans as recently as 1884 made dramatic changes as cattle destroyed traditional water holes and springs. Yet, the traditional ecological knowledge depicted in rock art galleries has been passed down the generations through song, dance and story, remaining strong within contemporary Aboriginal life. Art encapsulates the multiple dimensions of socio-ecological relationships, allowing people to visualize concepts and think through issues on multiple levels of consciousness.
>
> (http://crossart.com.au/home/index.php/
> archive/197-jadagen-warnkan-barnden-changing-climate-in-gija-country)

Two UK-based projects, Cape Farewell and Imagine 2020, have made significant progress in supporting European artists who seek to respond to climate change in their work. Cape Farewell's basic mission is to "bring artists, scientists and communicators together to stimulate the production of art founded in scientific research" (http://www.cape farewell.com/art.html). The organization regularly leads expeditions to areas such as the Arctic and the Andes, with the goal of promoting climate-sensitive imaginaries that will stimulate new artistic work. Imagine 2020 seeks to "research new ways of producing and presenting exciting artworks with minimal environmental impact, and share its learning in order to get the European cultural sector as a whole to include climate change concerns in their everyday working practice" (http://www.imagine2020.eu/about-us/). Examples from outside Europe include the Kinnari Ecological Theater (Taiwan), which stages plays that highlight human–nature interconnectedness; the "ARTing Climate Change" event held in 2012 at the University of Lagos (Nigeria); and the VII International Exhibition of Graphic Humor, whose 2014 event in Lima, Peru, focused on climate change.

Using art to promote awareness of climate change is also a key strategy of organizations such as 350.org, which was created in 2008 by the environmental writer Bill McKibben and students at Middlebury College in Vermont, with the goal of promoting the need to reduce the amount of carbon dioxide in the atmosphere to 350 parts per million. Among its early actions was a 2010 "planetary art show" featuring large-scale art installations designed to be visible from space. 350.org also organized the 2009 International Day of Climate Action, which included more than five thousand actions in 181 countries, with the number "350" providing a common visual device for the demonstrations. In addition to helping people learn how to do their own organizing, the group devotes significant effort to projects with a strong visual component. These include a range of informational and mobilizational videos and an interactive map of local actions and activist groups around the world.

Many groups seeking to fight climate change, like conservation groups in general, have found that it is much easier to get the public's attention if they highlight what are often called "charismatic megafauna": large animals that trigger powerful emotional responses when humans perceive them to be under threat. A classic example is the World Wildlife Fund's decision to make the panda its organizational symbol, presumably on the assumption that people would be less likely to identify with a less "charismatic" endangered animal. In the case of climate change, the most "charismatic" animal to date has been the polar bear, which is threatened by glacier melting. YouTube, for example, features several thousand videos addressing climate change and polar bears.

In a working paper on the cultural politics of representing climate change, Max Boykoff, Goodman, and Littler (2010, 1) note that the image of "stranded polar bears" is among the first to come to mind when many people think of climate change. They also argue, however, that public discourse on climate change has become increasingly framed by the involvement of celebrities, who constitute "charismatic megafauna" in their own way because of their central role in today's entertainment and personality-heavy imaginaries. Examples include the award-winning documentary *An Inconvenient Truth*, dominated by the persona of former U.S. vice president Al Gore; the media coverage given to appearances at major climate change summits and demonstrations by public figures such as Archbishop Desmond Tutu, Arnold Schwarzenegger, and Bono; and the emergence of an NGO such as Global Cool, which the authors describe as using young celebrities to help promote "practical solutions for climate change mitigation for 'hipsters'" (7).

While climate change, by definition, affects all parts of the planet, some communities are seeing more drastic effects than others. Consequently, many activists are using the strategy of spotlighting the observations and experiences of people who are on the "front lines" of climate change in the Arctic or in low-lying areas at great risk from rising sea levels. One such effort, the Aksik project, uses citizen journalism and documentary filmmaking to focus attention on two native villages in Alaska (Savoonga and Shaktoolik) where people are struggling with the impact of chaotic weather patterns and sea-ice melt. Another example

The picture shows some of the efforts being done in Shaktoolik, Alaska, to protect a village of 250 people from increasingly dangerous storms that threaten to wipe it off the map. The village has stacked driftwood and placed derelict bulldozers strategically in order to defend a school and other critical infrastructure from the storm surge.

*Source:* Dr. Jon Rosales, St. Lawrence University.

is the well-publicized decision by the government of the Maldives, a low-lying island nation in the Indian Ocean, to hold the world's first underwater cabinet meeting in 2009. Submerged underwater in full scuba gear, the cabinet members signed an "SOS message" to be delivered to the subsequent COP 15 conference in Copenhagen.

For people in other locations that may be less drastically affected, "citizen science" initiatives have proven to be a useful way of documenting the realities of climate change. The basic idea behind citizen science is that ordinary citizens can use everyday local observation to help generate useful scientific data, which can then be aggregated using the tools of information technology. Cornell University's eBird project, for example, gathers information from birders throughout the world, producing aggregate data that is useful for conservation biologists, climate scientists, and educators. Another project, the Weather@home initiative, enables people to contribute data on local weather patterns to a global database that forms part of a major global climate modeling experiment. A third example is the five-year study carried out by the Earthwatch Institute in forests in Brazil, China, and India "in order to better understand the way that forests capture and release carbon, one of the least understood aspects of the global carbon cycle" (http://www.nature.com/news/citizen-scientists-climate-impact-survey-wraps-up-1.9697).

If social movements and citizen science initiatives represent strategies for shaping people's global imaginaries through active participation in work on climate change, big-budget feature films about climate apocalypse arguably represent the other, more passive end of the spectrum. The Hollywood film industry has a long history of using public fears about outsized global threats (from space aliens, communists, terrorists, birds, apes, etc.) into blockbuster movies. In many ways, the specter of climate change slides easily into this particular global imaginary, lending itself well to futuristic films that feature spectacular, visually appealing scenes of catastrophic fires and floods, along with heroic struggles for survival. Two famous examples from Hollywood are *Waterworld* (1995) and *The Day After Tomorrow* (2004), while films from other countries and genres include *The Colony* (a 2013 Canadian science fiction film), *Blood Glacier* (a 2013 Austrian horror film), and *Snowpiercer* (a 2013 South Korean action film).

## Climate Change and the Promise of Globalization

One of the core challenges of globalization is also one of its greatest promises: the possibility of developing a more detailed and empathetic understanding of what others are experiencing and of how others see the world. Because it represents a threat facing all of humanity (albeit in very uneven ways that often reflect longstanding global hierarchies), climate change can provide a concrete platform on which to foster such understanding, while also promoting new forms of cooperation across lines of cultural difference. The existence of diverse, sometimes clashing global imaginaries can be both a source of support for this work and a roadblock to it.

If "seeing is believing," as the old saying goes, then it is not a surprise that so many people have put so much effort into making the effects of climate change visible. Scientists, artists, activists, governments, and mapmakers have all played a role in producing powerful visual representations of climate change that both draw on and challenge particular global imaginaries. The cumulative impact of these efforts has been considerable, helping more and more people to "see" the influence of climate change when they experience local phenomena such as extreme weather patterns, a change in growing seasons, or rising sea levels. At the same time, because so much of the concern about climate change is connected with future prediction, there remains the challenge of reaching and shaping the imaginaries of people who may not perceive major changes in the present.

Moreover, as most activists know from experience, seeing and believing are no guarantee that people will engage in sustained and meaningful action. Here an analogy to the human rights field, where activists regularly struggle to promote a move from pity or shock into action, may be useful. In her powerful 2003 book *Regarding the Pain of Others*, Susan Sontag notes that even photographs documenting political atrocities "may give rise to opposing responses" ranging from calls for peace or revenge to "simply the bemused awareness . . . that terrible things happen" (13). The same is true of representations of climate change. A film such as *The Day After Tomorrow*, for example, might shock some viewers into action by helping them see what a future of catastrophic climate change might look like (at least through the eyes of a Hollywood filmmaker). Other viewers, however, might simply experience the film in the same way they experience any other blockbuster disaster movie, seeing it as just another collection of enjoyable visual stimuli. For still others, the film might serve as confirmation of the inevitability of global apocalypse and the futility of trying to prevent it.

The overlapping challenges of helping people see, believe, and act in relation to climate change reinforce the importance of understanding how global imaginaries work. These imaginaries are often viewed as being grounded in relatively separate social worlds, such as the worlds of scientific investigation, religious faith, economic activity, political activism, and moral/ethical philosophy. More specifically, the fundamental clash of imaginaries between Global North and Global South remains a central element of many discussions of climate change, whether at international policy gatherings or within environmental justice activism. Consequently, those seeking to promote awareness and collective mobilization in response to climate change need to engage with existing imaginaries on their own terms while also prioritizing key ethical points (such as notions of environmental stewardship or ideas about one's responsibility to future generations) in an effort to build common ground.

Even as climate scientists offer increasingly dire forecasts, it is clear that efforts to bring various global imaginaries together are slowly beginning to bear fruit. The current movement for climate justice, while marked by the ongoing political divisions and debates that animate any social movement, embodies some of the most optimistic possibilities of globalization and the search for global "unity in difference." Within the discourse of this movement, accessible forms of scientific data are often combined with provocative visual representations, inspiring calls to action, and firsthand stories from vulnerable local communities whose voices have typically been ignored. In this sense, the potential of climate change to disrupt or even destroy human civilization is matched by its potential to help humanity build new forms of understanding, solidarity, and collaboration.

## References and Further Research

Amar, Paul. 2013. *The Security Archipelago: Human-Security States, Sexuality Politics, and the End of Neoliberalism*. Durham, NC: Duke University Press.

Appadurai, Arjun. 1996. *Modernity at Large: Cultural Dimensions of Globalization*. Minneapolis: University of Minnesota Press.

Berger, John. 1972. *Ways of Seeing*. London: British Broadcasting Corporation; Penguin Books.

Boykoff, Max, Mike Goodman, and Jo Littler. 2010. "Charismatic Megafauna: The Growing Power of Celebrities and Pop Culture in Climate Change Campaigns." Environment, Politics and Development Working Paper 28. London: Department of Geography, King's College London. http://www.kcl.ac.uk/sspp/departments/geography/research/epd/BoykoffetalWP28.pdf.

Carruth, Allison, and Robert P. Marzec. 2014. "Environmental Visualization in the Anthropocene: Technologies, Aesthetics, Ethics." *Public Culture* 26, no. 2: 205–211. http://publicculture.org/articles/view/26/2/environmental-visualization-in-the-anthropocene-technologies-aesthetics-ethics.

Featherstone, Mike. 2006. "Genealogies of the Global." *Theory, Culture & Society* 23, no. 2–3: 387–392. http://www.sagepub.com/mcdonaldizationstudy5/articles/Globalization_Articles%20PDFs/Featherstone.pdf.

Haraway, Donna. 1988. "Situated Knowledges: The Science Question in Feminism and the Privilege of Partial Perspective." *Feminist Studies* 14, no. 3: 575–599.

Intergovernmental Panel on Climate Change. 1990. *IPCC First Assessment Report: Overview*. Geneva: IPCC. http://www.ipcc.ch/ipccreports/1992%20IPCC%20Supplement/IPCC_1990_and_1992_Assessments/English/ipcc_90_92_assessments_far_overview.pdf.

Isis International. 2014. "Forever Forward, Never Backward: Joint Statement of Women's Rights Civil Society Movements at the Asia-Pacific Civil Society Consultation for the 20-Year Review of the Implementation of the Beijing Platform for Action and for the 58th Session of the Commission on the Status of Women." Quezon City, Philippines: Isis International. http://www.isiswomen.org/index.php?option=com_content&view=article&id=1660:forever-forward-never-backward&catid=187:media-tools.

Lewis, Martin W., and Kären E. Wigen. 1997. *The Myth of Continents: A Critique of Metageography*. Berkeley: University of California Press.

Merchant, Carolyn. 1995. *Earthcare: Women and the Environment*. New York: Routledge.

Rifkin, Jeremy. 2009. *The Empathic Civilization: The Race to Global Consciousness in a World in Crisis*. New York: Tarcher/Penguin.

Sandilands, Catriona. 1999. *The Good-Natured Feminist: Ecofeminism and the Quest for Democracy*. Minneapolis: University of Minnesota Press.

Shohat, Ella, and Robert Stam. 1994. *Unthinking Eurocentrism: Multiculturalism and the Media*. London: Routledge.

Sontag, Susan. 2003. *Regarding the Pain of Others*. New York: Farrar, Straus and Giroux.

Thompson, John B. 1984. *Studies in the Theory of Ideology*. Berkeley: University of California Press.

Virilio, Paul. 1994. *The Vision Machine*. Translated by Julie Rose. Bloomington: Indiana University Press.

Warren, Karen J. 1996. *Ecological Feminist Philosophies*. Bloomington: Indiana University Press.

# 9

# Transnational LGBT Identities: Liberation or Westernization?[1]

In the United States, 2012 was a banner year for "gay rights," as gay marriage became legal in nine states. And by May 2014, gay marriage was legal in eighteen states plus the District of Columbia. Finally, on July 9, 2015, same-sex marriage became legal throughout the United States. As of 2015, twenty-one other countries have laws permitting same-sex marriage. However, as some nations promote recognition and equality for alternative forms of sexuality and gender, others enact harsh penalties for sexual practices outside what they perceive to be the norm. Thus, changes in national laws on gender and sexuality reflect bifurcated and increasingly polarized viewpoints across the world. The blog *Erasing 76 Crimes* reports on the seventy-six countries with laws against homosexual activities. A November 2011 United Nations Human Rights Council (UNHRC) report noted that five countries invoke the death penalty for same-sex relations: Iran, Mauritania, Saudi Arabia, Sudan, and Yemen. According to Human Rights Watch, in October 2014 the Singapore Supreme Court upheld its anti-homosexuality law. In 2013 Senegal's president Macky Sall proclaimed that homosexuality is incompatible with its national values (Refugee and Immigration Commission of Canada), and more recently, Sall and U.S. President Obama sparred over homosexual rights (Nossiter 2013). Also in 2013, thirty-four students were expelled from school in Ghana as suspected lesbians. And in May 2013 the UNHRC pressured Cameroon during the agency's periodic review to change its penal code, which gives jail sentences between six months and five years for same-sex intercourse. These are just a few examples of the kinds of gender and sexuality violence that prevail in much of the world today.

Globally, activism on behalf of alternative genders and sexualities ranges from preventing violence against nonheterosexual people to lobbying for marriage equality. About thirty countries have decriminalized homosexuality since the 1990s. In June 2011 the UNHRC passed Resolution 17/19 on "Human Rights, Sexual Orientation and Gender Identity," introduced by South Africa, the first nation to include gay rights in its constitution, calling for a global report on discrimination on the basis of sexual orientation and gender identity. The votes in the Human Rights Council were deeply divided, however, with twenty-three approving the resolution and nineteen opposing it. While the United States strongly supported the resolution, Russia and the Eastern European bloc insist that there is no basis in international law for nondiscrimination on the basis of gender identity or sexual orientation. Russia's bill to criminalize pro-gay propaganda caused much controversy in the lead-up to the 2014 Winter Olympics in Sochi.

A UN report followed in November 2011 focusing on violence against and criminalization of people worldwide on the basis of "sexual orientation or gender identity." Navi Pillay, the UN High Commissioner for Human Rights from 2008 to 2014, called on receiving countries to acknowledge sexual orientation or gender identity as a valid basis for granting asylum. Furthermore, and most controversially, she stated that in cases where there is a clash between freedom of religion or culture and basic human rights, human rights must prevail. A follow-up meeting was held in Oslo, Norway, in April 2013, cosponsored by South Africa and Norway. It was preceded by regional meetings in Brasilia, Kathmandu, and Paris, as well as nongovernmental meetings in several African locations.

---

The full text of the November 2011 UN Human Rights Council (UNHRC) report, *Discriminatory Laws and Practices and Acts of Violence Against Individuals Based on Their Sexual Orientation and Gender Identity*, can be found on the UNHRC website (http://www.ohchr.org/Documents/Issues/Discrimination/A.HRC.19.41_English.pdf).

The blog *Erasing 76 Crimes* (www.76crimes.com) provides extensive coverage on anti-homosexual activities in countries with anti-gay laws.

---

This case study about alternative conceptions of gender and sexuality across societies illustrates the ways that colonialism and globalization spread ideas and social movements across borders, but with unpredictable repercussions. Societies may embrace outside influences, or they may react harshly against them. Often, power relations among nations or cultures affect the ways that local people respond to transnational influences, and outside influences may bring greater freedom for citizens or they may bring stronger discrimination. In addition, marginalized groups within powerful nations may look to what they perceive as more traditional cultures to sanction their own practices. Thus practices involving "third genders" (neither male nor female) in non-Western societies have been taken as models by some transgender people in the West today. The entire concept of "traditional culture" is challenged by a deeper look at various societies' ways of practicing gender and sexuality. Ideas and values that seem to be traditional may have been introduced from outside the society centuries ago.

---

### Terminology in the United States

In the United States and other English-speaking countries, the letters "LGBT" stand for lesbian, gay, bisexual, and transgender. The four categories recognize various non-normative forms of gender and sexuality. More recently, "Q" has been added to the mix, for "queer," and subsequently, "I" was added, for "intersex." Queer is a more amorphous category than the others, a label that rejects neat categories of sex and gender, and to some degree of social conformity itself. "Queer" is a label that has been repurposed as a self-affirmation after having served as a derogatory label for homosexuality in the past. "Intersex" applies to people whose anatomy does not fit neatly into male or female categories. There are many other terms currently in use, such as "cisgender" for those who fit into the hegemonic binary norms, such as a person with a vagina identifying as feminine in gender. A further issue of language is what pronouns to use to refer to gender, particularly transgender, transitioning, or intersex people.

For more on these terms, see the 2013 *New York Times* article "Generation LGBTQIA" (http://www.nytimes.com/2013/01/10/fashion/generation-lgbtqia.html?_r=0), http://www.glaad.org/sites/default/files/allys-guide-to-terminology_1.pdf, and http://internationalspectrum.umich.edu/life/definitions.

For example, many countries' anti-homosexuality laws date from the colonial rule of Great Britain and other European powers. Barbados, for example, an otherwise quite progressive society, retains harsh anti-sodomy laws on its books, as do eleven other former British colonies in the Caribbean region. Thirty-eight African nations have laws against homosexuality, as do twelve in Asia and eleven in the Middle East. While many European nations now promote gender equality and gay rights, during the era of colonialism (sixteenth to mid-twentieth centuries) they were dominated by conservative Christian sexual morality, and they exported that morality to the countries they colonized. Part of the dynamic of colonialism is convincing the colonized that they are less civilized than the colonizers, thus encouraging the colonized people to "improve" themselves by adopting the values of the colonizers. In addition there are contemporary evangelical Christian missionary efforts emanating primarily from the United States and influencing countries like Uganda, as discussed later. Ironically while Western notions of identity and rights are the engine driving movements to repeal discriminatory laws and practices, in many cases Western colonizers and missionaries either instituted the laws or brought with them the idea that sodomy or "unnatural sexual practices" were to be equated with Satanism and sin.

In India, another former British colony, activists have been working for the repeal of Section 377 of the Indian Penal Code, drafted in 1860, by the British historian and politician Lord Macaulay, criminalizing what the code refers to as "unnatural offences":

> 377. Unnatural offences.—Whoever voluntarily has carnal intercourse against the order of nature with any man, woman or animal, shall be punished with imprisonment for life, or with imprisonment of either description for a term which may extend to ten years, and shall also be liable to fine.
>
> Explanation.—Penetration is sufficient to constitute the carnal intercourse necessary to the offence described in this section.

In fact, the Delhi High Court struck down the law as applied to consenting adults of the same gender having sex in private. It is notable that the law does not use the word "homosexual," and that it does not apply exclusively to male-on-male sex, though it has in the past been used to prosecute homosexual activity, and in particular the *hijra* (a caste of what we would call transgender people, males who live as females). In referring generally to "carnal intercourse against the order of nature" the law was interpreted to apply to bestiality and child molesting as well as to sex between two men or two women. However the Supreme Court of India subsequently upheld the criminalization of homosexuality. According to legal scholar R. S. Akila, "Gay rights activists' plea that Section 377 criminalises a group of people and deprives them of equal citizenship was also rejected by a Court that held on to a textual reading that the law only criminalises certain acts but not people or identity." The court's reasoning here illustrates the particularly modern, or postmodern, emphasis on sexual orientation as an identity rather than a form of activity or desire.

Nonetheless, laws don't tell the whole story. Some nations have harsh anti-homosexual laws but never apply them, and others, such as Iraq, don't have such laws but nevertheless suffer from rampant homophobia and do not punish attacks on homosexuals. The kinds of violence that take place outside the law are noted in the 2011 UN report. The UN also has a Special Rapporteur on Violence Against Women. In 2007 the Rapporteur noted that "lesbian women face an increased risk of becoming victims of violence, especially rape, because of widely held prejudices and myths," including, "for instance, that lesbian women would change their sexual orientation if they are raped by a man"

(UNHRC 2007). In the 2011 UNHRC report, the worldwide incidence of brutality against LGBT people is highlighted, and reports are noted of gang rapes, family violence, and murder experienced by lesbian, bisexual, and transgender women in El Salvador, Kyrgyzstan, and South Africa.

## Gender and Sexualities: Identities versus Practices

The socially and culturally determined categories of sex and gender, as well as the range of acceptable sexual practices, vary widely from society to society, past and present. Locally determined norms for gender and sexual behavior leave certain people and practices marginalized or subordinate. Western discourses of individual freedom and human rights are invoked by groups across the globe whose gender or sexual practices are stigmatized where they live. But social movements such as gay pride may carry with them entire cultural systems of thought and meaning. Specifically, along with the discourse of rights and nondiscrimination come Western ideas about gender and sexual identities. Key concepts in Western thought, especially since the time of the European Enlightenment (1660–1815), include individualism, identity, and formal constitutional rights based on individual freedom and equality. These are tightly linked with a number of historical developments, including the Protestant Reformation; the rise of modern science; and the increasing predominance of the middle class, capitalism, and industrialization, the last two of which were both sponsored and funded by the African slave trade and colonialism.

Within the industrialized middle classes of Europe and North America, specific gender roles evolved to suit modern ways of life. Men were aligned with the public sphere and women with the private, domestic sphere. In the West today, it is often assumed that women's maternal role is "natural," a product of a given biological role, and that heterosexual marriage is what both nature and the Judeo-Christian God ordained. However, these gender and sexual roles are historically and culturally specific constructs. The feminist philosopher Judith Butler (1990) sees gender as performative, a set of behaviors and practices that each of us learns and imitates. Precepts such as "boys don't cry" or "throwing like a girl" are parts of the scripts American society provides for the performance of gender.

In the West, personal and group identities are extremely important. Identities take a particular aspect of the self and make it a defining characteristic. Identity, or sameness, also implies its opposite, difference. If I identify as a woman or an American, that makes me different from nonwomen and non-Americans. The Enlightenment philosopher David Hume pointed out that personal identity is a necessary fiction imposed on a collection of memories and experiences to create a unified self. This applies to groups as well. In the United States recently, identity-based groups have become important political actors, using their "difference" and marginalized positions in society as the basis for seeking recognition and rights.

Some theorists argue that the process of social activism actually creates new identities. For example, the gay rights movement that began in 1969 with the Stonewall Riots was part of a series of identity-based liberation movements following from the civil rights movement of the 1950s and 1960s, in which African Americans sought to establish their equality under the law. On June 28, 1969, a group of gay patrons of the Stonewall Inn in Greenwich Village, New York City, gathered outside the bar to protest their mistreatment and harassment at the hands of the police; the confrontation with authorities sparked a riot that inflamed the passions of the gay community. Indeed, a year later, on June 28,

The image shows a participant in the 2011 Gay Pride celebration in Rio de Janeiro, Brazil. She wears a tie sporting the rainbow symbol of the LGBT movement.

*Source:* Eric Walter/Wikimedia Commons. https://commons.wikimedia.org/wiki/File:Cravat%C3% A9e.jpg

1970, the first gay pride parade took place. The LGBTQ movement has evolved a great deal since 1969, galvanized by the HIV/AIDS epidemic. Through the social movement for recognition and equality, the very identities signified by the word "gay" have become more complex as they have been debated and lived within the gay community. The LGBTQ label has evolved to represent differences within the non-normative community. As a result of transnational gay activism, gay pride parades are now celebrated in cities throughout the world. A gay pride calendar for 2013–2014 includes over two hundred events around the world. Certain tourist destinations market themselves as LGBTQ friendly—including Cape Town, South Africa, and Provincetown, Massachusetts—recognizing the economic benefits of doing so. However, full recognition and equality have yet to be achieved by any non-hegemonic group in the United States.

While sometimes individuals identify primarily with one aspect of identity, such as race or gender, the feminist concept of *intersectionality*, originated by Patricia Hill Collins, emphasizes that all individuals have multiple identities, some privileged by the dominant culture and some not. For example, a gay white male who comes from a wealthy family and works as a financial analyst on Wall Street is marginalized as a gay man, whereas a Latina lesbian struggling to support herself by working at McDonald's has multiple identities, including ethnicity, sexuality, and economic class, that are subordinated in U.S. society. Postmodern theorists, such as Judith Butler, who emphasizes the performative nature of gender identity, or Homi Bhabha, who emphasizes multiple or hybrid identities, sometimes also make room for the tactical use of *strategic essentialism*.

### Essentialism versus Social Construction

The terms *essentialism* and *social construction* are used to describe the opposing views that identities such as race or gender are based on biology, or some other universal and immutable principle, rather than taught or constructed by the society where one is raised.

The implication of social construction theories is that human behaviors are products of particular times and places and thus changeable. *Strategic essentialism*, on the other hand, a term coined by Gayatri Chakravorty Spivak, is a temporary use of an apparent essentialism for political purposes. Thus, while social construction argues that women may have any number of character traits and may or may not like children, a feminist political movement might choose to organize around the idea that women are often responsible for children in order to push for day care programs or paid maternity leave. They strategically draw on society's biases about female identity in order to achieve a specific political goal.

At first glance, the spread of gay pride and the recognition of LGBTQ identities sound unequivocally like something to celebrate. Persecution and violence are certainly not good anywhere. However, where new identities move in, old ways of conceiving of the world and alternative conceptions of selfhood and society may disappear; moreover, a reactionary backlash against Western influences may lead to harsh reprisals for newly constructed sexualities.

The dominant ideas and beliefs in a society, whether defined as hegemony or ideology, serving the interests of the ruling class and the state, make its cultural constructs appear to be natural or biological, not caused by sociohistorical forces. Thus, for many in the West, the idea of an individual identity defined by race or ethnicity or gender or sexuality seems "normal" and "natural." Specifically, as Lisa Downing writes, "commonplace wisdom says that sexuality belongs in the (often held to be unimpeachable) realms of the biological, the genetic, the psychological" (2008, 86). Yet all these identities are historical products of social construction. Specifically in the case of sexual and gender identities, the French philosopher and social theorist Michel Foucault (1926–1984) argued in his *History of Sexuality* that "the nineteenth century replaced the sin of sodomy with the 'personage' of the homosexual" (Downing 2008, 89). These ideas raise two issues. First, the Western concept of individual identity contrasts with alternative cultural understandings of personhood. A person might not have an individual identity, but rather a set of relationships to an extended family or to a series of age-defined roles that change from childhood to adolescence to young adulthood to elder status. For example, in a volume on cross-cultural conceptions of human rights, Kwasi Wiredu describes the Ghanaian "Akan conception of a person" (1996, 244). To the Akan, a "person" comprises an element from God, an element from the mother (lineage), and one from the father. Most importantly, the person comes into the world situated within "a network of kinship relations that generate a system of rights and obligations" (245). Akan people are expected to contribute to communal welfare and to make sure those in their network are provided for. In this kind of system, identity is mobile and relational, tied to age and position within the kinship network.

Second, the contemporary Western discourse of sexual identity implies that a particular category of sexual desire and behavior determines a person's identity. This contrasts with alternative, more fluid views which hold that sexuality is a matter of practices, not identities.

In classical Athens, older male mentors had sexual relations with the young men they mentored. The older men were usually married to women, and they took the active role in intercourse, penetrating the younger male with whom they had a relationship. The active or passive role was tied to the age and mentoring relationship of the males involved. Again, there was no question in that sexuality of a permanent, defining identity based on sexuality. Men went through a series of sexual roles. If they had what we might call an identity, it was probably that of Athenian citizen. These are relational ways of conceptualizing the person, and they allow for changing identities in different periods of life, or in different roles. Similarly, in the nineteenth and early twentieth centuries, upper-class British schoolboys might have sexual relationships with other boys at their boarding schools. However, they did not consider themselves to have a homosexual identity, and most would marry women and carry on heterosexual relations in their adult years. Sodomy, as male homosexual relations were labeled, was against the law.

Michel Foucault claimed that nineteenth-century European sexologists produced sexuality, constituting it as a discourse and a discipline. Foucault developed the idea of discourse as a web of truth claims through which power circulates. This power is both repressive and productive. Power and knowledge are productive of each other. Technologies of medicine and psychiatry divided normative sexuality from marginal or perverted sexualities. Foucault defined these discourses of sexual identities as particularly Western, based on a drive to identify "the underlying motivation for individual sexual behavior" and to "treat the sexually 'sick'" (Downing 2008, 91). The "pervert," in all his or her many guises, is a creation of the discourse of the normal. Thus the term *heteronormative* describes the belief that the right and natural way to be is heterosexual. Children are heavily socialized into the discourses of heteronormativity, leading many who feel no desire for the "opposite" sex to believe there is something wrong with them, even to the point of committing suicide.

John D'Emilio, a historian and professor of gender studies, argues that industrialization and mobile labor allowed for separating sexuality from procreation in the West, especially the United States:

> Thus capitalism has created conditions that allow some men and women to organize a personal life around their erotic/emotional attraction to their own sex . . . . Only when *individuals* began to make their living through wage labor, instead of as parts of an interdependent family unit, was it possible for homosexual desire to coalesce into a personal identity.
>
> (1993, 470)

D'Emilio argues that medicalization, the disciplinary knowledge of human health or sickness, followed in the early twentieth century, furthering the idea of homosexuality as an essential, defining aspect of a person's individuality. Today, ironically, a movement within the gay community aims to prove scientifically that homosexuality is a biological "essence," genetically caused. In large part this is a reaction to conservative, often Christian, efforts to retrain "effeminate" or gay boys and men into heterosexuality.

## LGBT Identities: Transnational Encounters

In "Sexual Identities: Western Imperialism?" (2006), Chilla Bulbeck states that "the notion of homosexual identity forged through shared lifestyles" is "almost exclusive to the West" (224), where "rigid bifurcation" characterizes gender and sexuality (230). She goes on to quote Eve Kosofsky Sedgewick: "It is in fact the gender of object choice which is defining of sexual identity in the West" (225). In other words, if a man chooses to have sex with a woman, he is heterosexual, whereas if he chooses sex with a man, he is homosexual. However, from the perspective of Bulbeck, Sedgewick, and others, sexual identity is more complex. Bulbeck notes Stephen Murray's cross-cultural analysis of different forms of male-on-male sex:

> Age-graded homosexuality is part of a rite of passage to manhood in which young boys graduate to male roles in the homosexual exchange. Profession-defined homosexuality occurs among performers and prostitutes who cross-dress or cross-gender as part of their occupations. Examples include shamans, dancing boys, transvestite singers and prostitutes, and the actors of the Noh and Kabuki theatres in Japan . . . . In the third form, the man who takes the 'passive' (insertee) role is defined as committing a homosexual act but not the man who takes the 'dominant' (inserter) role . . . . The fourth type is "purely to earn money."

(225)

Mark Padilla illustrates a similar variety of sexualities in his empirical studies of sex and tourism in the Dominican Republic. However, along with John D'Emilio, Padilla argues that urbanization and capitalism have created the dominant Western idea of homosexual identity: "Gay identity in the industrialized West has produced—through its consumption of 'foreign' bodies and identities—a market for particular performances of gender and sexuality" (2007, 245). Thus "an understanding of the contemporary meanings of Dominican homoeroticism requires an analysis of how local sexualities are being commodified by foreign gay tourists" (245). The two categories of men who have sex with men in the Dominican Republic are the *bugarrón,* "a man who engages in insertive anal sex with other men, often for money or other instrumental benefits, but who in other domains of life may not be noticeably different from 'normal' men," and the *sanky panky,* a type that emerged in the 1970s and 1980s in response to tourist demand (247). These are men with small dreadlocks who can be found on the beach near resorts. *Bugarrón* was a preexisting label in Dominican society. From 1999 through 2001, Padilla interviewed 199 male sex workers about their self-identification and found that 4 identified as "homosexual," 2 as "gay," 41 as "bisexual," 35 as "heterosexual," 72 as *bugarrón,* 33 as *sanky panky,* and 12 as other.

Whereas Padilla emphasizes the fluctuations and alternative constructs of male-on-male sexualities, Donald L. Donham celebrates the transmission of Western LGBTQ identities in Soweto, South Africa, as a side effect of the anti-apartheid movement, from 1960 to 1994. Donham uses the example of a male named Linda to illustrate the changes in gender and sexuality brought about through the globalized anti-apartheid movement. Before the movement, Linda, raised in a Zulu family, was born with a penis but exhibited feminine gender tendencies. S/he was raised within the family to wear women's clothes and perform women's work. S/he had sex with men, partly within a system that was a product of apartheid, whereby black men had to work far from their townships and therefore stayed in all-male hostels near their work. In those hostels many men developed sexual and social relations parallel to that of marriage, but they did not see themselves as "gay" or homosexual. As in many societies, the male taking the role of penetrator was considered to be in the masculine role and the one taking the receptive role was seen as feminine.

However, a major transformation occurred with the arrival in South Africa of European notions of homosexual identity through the anti-apartheid movement. Linda was anatomically a male but socially gendered a female, and in that sense socially heterosexual, despite having sex with other persons with penises. As she adopted Western constructs of sexuality and gender, however, she became a homosexual, a man having sex with other men. It was her gender—the idea of who she was—that changed, more than her sexual choices. In Zulu culture, there was a place for a person with a penis to play a feminine role, to dress as a female, to do the domestic labor of women. Western notions of a more rigid gender binary whereby biological attributes determine gender came along with the idea of gay identity. Gay liberation discourse encouraged the adoption of sexuality as an identity rather than a practice or activity. In South Africa that idea of sexual identity accompanied a liberal understanding of individually based rights, reflected in the new constitution.

In marked contrast to this case in South Africa, contemporary Uganda has received conflicting global attention for Draconian anti-homosexuality laws proposed by David Bahati, MP, in October 2009. Bahati is not a fringe member of Parliament, but rather part of the ruling party, and also chief of the Scout Board in Uganda. He did his undergraduate degree at Makerere University in Uganda, going on to earn an MBA from Cardiff University in Wales and then a certificate from the Wharton School at the University of Pennsylvania. Much controversy swirls around his involvement in the Fellowship (formerly The Family), "a conservative American religious and political organization" ("A Well-Locked Closet," 2010). The organization is reputed to be highly influential in the U.S. government, hosting the annual national Prayer Breakfast. According to *The Economist*, over half the anti-homosexual laws around the world are based on British anti-sodomy laws. Yet, ironically, in Uganda and other former African colonies, the West is seen as pro-gay and African societies as naturally opposed to homosexuality. Thus, in Uganda, even harsher laws and sentences are being proposed against what is seen as an un-African import from the West. The interconnectedness of old colonial laws and new attempts to demonize homosexuality as "Western" demonstrates the fundamentally transnational nature of this issue.

In what has been discussed so far, ideas about sexuality have flowed from Europe, and later the United States, to the Global South in at least three ways. First, they came from the legislation of colonizers who sought to "civilize" those they conquered as part of their rationale for occupation. Second, ideas of sexuality have flowed through Christian missionaries who have demonized same-sex relations from the nineteenth century on. While Foucault explicitly linked the rise of modern science with the decline of the importance of religion in the West, contemporary fundamentalisms among not just Christians, but Hindus and Muslims, have in fact demonstrated a powerful political presence today and have joined forces together, transnationally, to produce a homosexual "other." Third, ideas about sexuality have flowed to the Global South through the pro-gay social movements associated with liberation and equal rights. Gay pride parades, for example, now occur throughout the world, and the concept of LGBT identities has been exported with them.

## Gender as Identity

Judith Butler takes Foucault's work on sexuality and extends it to gender in her book *Gender Trouble* (1990). Using a deconstructive approach, she challenges the Western mapping of gender and sexuality onto a binary logic. In this sense, "binary oppositions" constrain thought between two and only two alternatives, such as male or female, white or black, mind or body. Butler critiques a commonly held feminist premise that there are two biological *sexes* (male versus female), whereas *gender* (masculine versus feminine) definitions are socially and culturally constructed. She argues that "gender must also designate the very apparatus of production whereby the sexes themselves are established" (7). In other words, the presumption of two genders, masculine and feminine, while now known to be historically and culturally variable, is projected backward onto bodies that are categorized into two and only two types by nature. Even in cases where anatomy does not clearly place the body into either male or female, the medical profession and families now often rush to shape the body through surgery into one clear sex. In Western cultures, one of the very first questions asked when a baby is born is whether it's a boy or a girl, though increasingly, the parents know that before the birth. Clothing and toys often are either pink or blue—girl's or boy's, respectively. In fact, however, human bodies display characteristics on an anatomical, chromosomal, and hormonal spectrum, established both in utero and afterward. Butler asks whether gender could be constructed differently.

Indeed, many people balk at the idea that humans cannot be reduced to two choices, male or female, penis or vagina. However, contemporary science is now recognizing that there is far more variability along a sex/gender continuum than formerly thought. Physical sex/gender possibilities include (1) multiple chromosomal patterns; (2) anatomical variations, including a spectrum of "female," "male," hermaphrodite, castration; (3) secondary sex characteristics on a spectrum from "male" to "female"; (4) transsexual surgeries; and (5) various levels of sex hormones in individuals. According to the authors of a World Health Organization (WHO) report, "Gender and Genetics," many possibilities for anatomy, hormonal influences, and gender construction and assignment exist:

> Developmental biology suggests that a strict belief in absolute sexual dimorphism is incorrect. Instead, Blackless et al. suggest two overlapping bell-shaped curves to conceptualize sexual variations across populations. Qualitative variation in chromosome complement [the allocation of X and Y chromosomes], genital morphology and hormonal activity falls under the area of overlap. Such an opinion challenges the need for medical intervention in cases of intersexuality.

> (WHO 2015, 2)

Gender then maps onto the body of the baby the socially and culturally defined behaviors, roles, dress, speech patterns, and other forms of meaning and practice. According to Butler, the emerging person learns to perform the appropriate gender through her or his behaviors and dress. Nonetheless different societies allow greater or lesser flexibility in gender roles. For instance, a person's official sex/gender in the United States is extremely important, and once it has been marked on a birth certificate it is hard to change. And in Western cultures, despite the fact of sex reassignment surgery, sex is conceptualized in fairly rigid binary oppositions. A man who undergoes surgery to become a woman is thought of not as a third gender but as a woman, now however, increasingly as a transwoman. Nonetheless, the idea of being transgender is slowly becoming more acceptable in the United States. Massachusetts now has a category on its Registry of Motor Vehicles site for changing one's gender on a driver's license.

> The entire text of the World Health Organization (WHO) article, "Gender and Genetics," is available on the Genomic Resource section of their website (http://www.who.int/genomics/gender/en/). Information on how to change one's gender on official documents is available from the National Center for Transgender Equality (http://transequality.org/Issues/federal_documents.html).

## Alternative Genders: Hybrid, Trans, or Third?

The story of "Linda" in Soweto illustrates alternative possibilities for gender and sexuality, as do what are sometimes called "third genders" in many societies. Linda grew up gendered as a girl although she had a penis. She practiced her sexuality with other penis-bearing humans, noting that the masculine-role-taking actors preferred to believe that the penises of those they had sex with were very small. Within a binary logic, Linda was performing the role of a female both in the family and sexually. Nonetheless, when she became exposed to Western-style homosexuality, she became a homosexual man. Today, homosexuality is considered a sexual identity or practice, but in Linda's case s/he became gay by affirming a masculine gender identity. S/he did not change his/her sexual objects (males). The aspect of gender as performative, which Butler discusses, is foregrounded in Linda's life as a girl or woman; however, his shift to masculine gender, based on having a penis, reflects a biological definition of gender. This shift from feminine to masculine gender came about through the influx of European ideas about gay rights that was part of the anti-apartheid movement in South Africa.

Many cultures have or have had gender roles that are loosely androgynous/hermaphroditic or transgender. In "Romancing the Transgender Native" (2002), Evan B. Towle and Lynn Marie Morgan critique the idea of using "cross-cultural examples to provide legitimacy to transgender movements in the United States" (469). However, the same can be said for the reverse process of using Western ideas of gay identity to bring emancipation to people cross-culturally. Nonetheless, Towle and Morgan catalogue many examples of gender variation from the anthropological literature, including "the *hijra* of India, the *berdache* of native North America, the *xanith* of the Arabian peninsula, the female husbands of western Africa" (469).

The term *third gender* was

> apparently introduced in 1975 by M. Kay Martin and Barbara Voorhies and began to be applied to behaviors that transcended or challenged dyadic male-female codes or norms. It was also applied to societies (most of them non-Western) that seemed to provide institutionalized "intermediate" gender concepts and practices.
>
> (Towle and Morgan 2002, 472)

Towle and Morgan demonstrate the difficulties for those of us raised with a binary perspective on gender to understand, let alone produce, alternative ways of thinking. They discuss the work of Marjorie Garber on cross-dressing, noting that "she rejects the idea that 'third' is principally a word, sex, or specific referent of any kind. It is, rather, 'a mode of articulation, a way of describing a space of possibility'" (475). This parallels the work of Homi Bhabha (1994) on hybrid racial, ethnic, and cultural identities and diasporic spaces as "third spaces" or "culture's in-between," where new or alternative ways of being are produced or invented. However, Garber's optimistic view of "thirds" as interrupting rigid binaries is criticized as being ahistorical. It is absolutely essential to place gender and sexual constructs within a specific historical and cultural context. Each cultural understanding of gender is distinct. The existence of a third gender, or a fourth or fifth, may or may not be more open and flexible than Western binaries. An example of the way that alternative constructions of gender may *not* be emancipatory, according to Anuja Agrawal, is that more categories of gender and sexuality may be more oppressive, rather than less, because "each may demand the conformity of the individual within increasingly narrower confines" (294). She argues, for example, that a "real" *hijra* is castrated and not a cross-dressing or feminine male (292–293).

On January 24, 2013, Al Jazeera carried a story titled "'Third Gender' Identity" (http://stream.aljazeera.com/story/201301240002-0022501), prompted by Nepal's decision to issue a citizenship certificate for sexual minorities, including a traditional third gender. The story reported that most of the individuals so labeled practiced male-on-male sex and are biological males who function as females in society. Traditionally, their genitals were cut off in a ritual and they played a spiritual role in society, including blessing weddings, similar to the *hijra* in India. Before this decision, LGBT and intersex (the contemporary term for people whose anatomy or physiology does not conform to the male–female dichotomy) people could not get documentation that would allow them to have official status in society, such as buying property, opening a bank account, and so forth.

Interestingly, the recognition of this non-Western gender category coincided with the first South Asian LGBT sports festival, held in Kathmandu in October 2012. The Blue Diamond Society of Nepal is an activist organization for LGBT rights. Their website shows pictures from their ninth and tenth gay parades, in 2010 and 2011, and a beauty contest, "Mr n Miss Third Gender 2010." They claim to have reached about 350,000 LGBT MSM (males having sex with males) in their work since 2001. The images portray a range of people dressed in saris and other forms of local traditional dress, as well as clothing from Africa and the West. They promote tourism for Nepal, as well as health care and leadership for "gender and sexual minorities."

One of the more well-known "third genders" today is that of the *kathoeys*, or "ladyboys," in Thailand. This performative identity cannot be equated with the "exotic" or "native" categories of gender and sexuality referred to by Towle and Morgan. Today's *kathoeys*, well-represented on the Internet, are a globalized or hybridized contemporary form of gender/sexuality. Insofar as they participate in Thailand's thriving sex tourism sector, they are partially a product of the Vietnam War's influence in creating a market for sex workers. According to Peter A. Jackson, an Australian who has written extensively on changes in Thai conceptualization of gender and sexuality from the nineteenth century to the present, the Thai concept of *phet* is a sexualized gender. Prior to the 1960s and the presence of U.S. soldiers involved in Vietnam, there were three main types of phet: *phu-chai* (normative masculine man who had sex with women), *phu-ying* (normative female who had sex with men), and *kathoey* (intermediate people who could be hermaphrodites or whose gender roles were not the same as their anatomies). The Thai word *kathoey* translates into English as "ladyboy," transgender, feminine male, or androgynous (Williams 2010, 505). Before Buddhism became the dominant religion in Thailand, *kathoeys* were considered to be twice as spiritual as other people, and were highly respected as a result. Thailand takes pride in never having been colonized, yet during the nineteenth century, King Rama V (1853–1910), crowned in 1868, navigated successfully between British and French imperialism, in part through acquiring Western knowledge and language and adopting Western dress. Westerners found the similarities in appearances between men and women in Siam to be very strange. Both had long hair, wore skirts, and wore little above the waist. Rama V had *kathoeys* dancing in his court. Rama VI, king from 1910 to 1925, is reputed to have had two male lovers. He brought a French lawyer, Rene Guyon, to his court to craft a modern legal code. Guyon had also written on sexual ethics, and the result was that Thailand has never criminalized any sexual activity.

According to Walter Williams, writing in the *Greenwood Encyclopedia*, Thai people do not make a rigid distinction between heterosexual and homosexual people, but rather view sexuality and gender on a continuum of behaviors and practices. Nonetheless, in contrast to contemporary Nepal, Thailand's passports will list only a person's birth sex, male or female. Some labels given to Thai gay men are clearly hybridized and transnational, based on English words but phonetic spellings. Examples are "gey king" as penetrator or "gey queen" as receiver, with "quing" referring to both. Other examples suggesting the influence of Anglophone constructs are female-to-male transgender "toms" versus femme "dees" (from "lady"). *Kathoeys* may practice sex in either the "active" or "passive" role. Thai women, *kathoeys*, and gay men often seek out wealthy foreign men as partners. Additionally, Bangkok is internationally known as a gay tourist destination, with a huge gay pride parade held annually, a Miss Annual Transgender Beauty Queen contest, and gay publications. Thailand has also become a global center for transsexual surgeries. However, according to Williams, increasing Western influence in the cities is also introducing homophobia that did not exist historically.

This picture shows a transwoman, known in Thailand as a "ladyboy" or *kathoey*, performing in a cabaret show in Pattaya, Thailand.

*Source:* Wikimedia Commons. https://commons.wikimedia.org/wiki/File:Pattaya_transwomen_2.jpg

More recently, in South Asia, Internet-initiated gay groups have emerged among higher socioeconomic groups of men, including Boys only Bangladesh, Gay Bangla, and Queer Bangla. An online Indian magazine called *Pink Pages* is oriented toward the rising professional classes. While showing a strong Western influence on how gay and lesbian identities are conceptualized, the contributors to the site also debate how to make these ways of life particularly Indian as well. One article concerns the beginnings of online social networking for gays in Bangladesh. The author, Udayan, writes about "The Boys of Bangladesh" based on an interview with thirty-year old Tanvir:

> It was Rengyu, a middle aged foreign educated guy from an indigenous tribe who came up with the first e-group for queer Bangladeshis called "GayBangladesh" in 1999. The group drew a good number of members (1000+) and was quite active online. But in 2004 Rengyu died in a road accident and the group's activities halted there. There was another active group before BoB by the name of Teen_Gay Bangladesh (TGB). In October 2002, the founder of BoB, Joy went to meet the moderators of this group (Prakash and Abrar) and first got the idea of helping the gay people from these two bright young boys. Since the name TGB exclusively was meant for teen gays, Joy decided to open BoB (Boys of Bangladesh) on 2nd November 2002.
>
> (http://pink-pages.co.in/features/neighbours/the-boy-of-bangladesh/)

Notably, Rengyu was "different" from mainstream Bangladeshi society in two ways: he was educated outside the country and presumably exposed to more open attitudes toward homosexuality, and he was not Bengali but from a minority indigenous group.

According to one writer on *Pink Pages*, it is often alleged that the Indian LGBT movement borrows too much from the movement in the West. In the West, for example, more left-wing or liberal political parties have been supportive of LGBTQ rights. Therefore most Indian LGBT people have assumed that center-right politics and politicians are essentially anti-gay. However, such an assumption may not be correct in the Indian context after all. The article "Is Right Right?" (http://pink-pages.co.in/features/politics-and-activism/is-right-right/) argues that the *Bharatiya Janata Party* (BJP), the conservative Hindu nationalist party, is more gay friendly in its efforts to distinguish itself from the Islamic state of Pakistan, and that the center-left Congress Party has more Christians and Muslims in it who are against homosexuality. Thus layers of Western influence are both oppressive and emancipatory, and local traditions of alternative sexualities and genders may be replaced by Western conceptions of LGBTQ identities and rights. Each local and national case has its own history of belief, law, and everyday practices. As noted at the beginning of this chapter, laws do not tell the whole story. No one has been prosecuted under Statute 377 in twenty years, and removing the discriminatory law would not guarantee that the public would or would not support alternative sexualities.

One writer, Valan, states in the *Pink Pages* that

> [t]he stark opposition to transexualism [sic] is of recent origin thereby easy to be wiped out. Extending from then until today is the practice of inviting transsexuals home to bless a new born infant or newly-wed couple. This practice originates from the epic Ramayana.

The *Pink Pages* article by Valan, titled "Transexualism: An Indian Perspective," tells the story from the Ramayana about the custom of transsexuals blessing newborn infants. It can be accessed on the *Pink Pages* website (http://pink-pages.co.in/the-gay-agenda/transexualism-an-indian-perspective/).

*Pink Pages* thus demonstrates an acute consciousness of the dynamics between traditional, local constructions of a "third" gender and contemporary globalized constructions of transsexuals. In one case, custom accords the *hijra* a specific place in society; in the other, rights are sought through the legal system. This takes place against a long history of occupation and colonization, as well as an independence movement that partitioned the Indian subcontinent eventually into three nations, two Muslim and one predominantly Hindu. Such are the complexities of social movements in today's world: there is no way to reduce the topic of gender and sexuality in South Asia to a set of binary oppositions between male and female, homosexual and heterosexual.

## Conclusion

This discussion of genders and sexualities illustrates the complexities of transnational movements from north and west to south and east. In this case, liberatory social movements along with consumer demands based on tourism have brought ideas of gay pride and LGBTQ lifestyles to many parts of the world. Yet earlier European colonization brought homophobia and statutes criminalizing "unnatural" sexual practices. Both waves of influence disrupted local understandings of gender and sexuality, for good or ill, and an anti-Western backlash threatens to aggravate homophobia. At the same time, Western transsexuals and intersex people appropriate anthropological accounts of "third gender" people in various other cultures to legitimize their own struggles.

Flows of ideas across national boundaries cannot be stopped. Neither can the efforts of people to better their status through appeals to cross-cultural role models, even where those are misunderstood. But it is critically important to try to understand, in all the historical and cultural specificities of each case, what is being changed or lost. In the West, the addition of "queer"—and to a much lesser extent, "intersex"—to the rainbow banner of LGBT suggests that efforts to open up a space for less binary identities is on the rise. Outside the West, Nepal's legal recognition of a nonbinary gender category indicates that liberation may also come through local or hybrid understandings.

## Note

1 D. Merika Wilson, a graduate of St. Lawrence University, inspired this case study with her 2011–2012 senior honors thesis in global studies. Merika's study-abroad experiences in both Thailand and Uganda led her to pursue the topic of homosexuality in Uganda, along with "third genders," or *kathoeys*, in Thailand.

## References and Further Research

Agrawal, Anuja. 1997. "Gendered Bodies: The Case of the 'Third Gender' in India." *Contributions to Indian Sociology* 31 (July): 273–297.

Akila, R. S. 2014. "Section 377: The Way Forward." *The Hindu*, March 1. http://www.thehindu.com/features/magazine/section-377-the-way-forward/article5740242.ece.

APA (American Psychological Association). *Answers to Your Questions about Transgender People, Gender Identity, and Gender Expression*. Washington, DC: APA. http://www.apa.org/topics/sexuality/transgender.aspx.

Beech, Hannah. 2008. "Where the 'Ladyboys' Are." *Time*, July 7. http://www.time.com/time/world/article/0,8599,1820633,00.html.

Bhabha, Homi. 1994. *The Location of Culture*. London: Routledge.

Blue Diamond Society of Nepal. http://www.bds.org.np/.

Bulbeck, Chilla. 2006. "Sexual Identities: Western Imperialism?" In *Beyond Borders: Thinking Critically about Global Issues*, edited by Paula S. Rothenburg, 224–244. New York: Worth. First published in *Re-Orienting Western Feminism: Women's Diversity in a Postcolonial World*, 129–166. Cambridge: Cambridge University Press, 1998.

Butler, Judith. 1990. *Gender Trouble: Feminism and the Subversion of Identity*. New York: Routledge.

Collins, Patricia Hill. 1998. "It's All in the Family: Intersections of Gender, Race, and Nation." *Hypatia* 13, no. 3 (Summer): 62–82.

Dellamora, Richard. 1990. *Masculine Desire: The Sexual Politics of Victorian Aestheticism*. Chapel Hill: University of North Carolina Press.

D'Emilio, John. 1993. "Capitalism and Gay Identity." In *The Lesbian and Gay Studies Reader*, edited by Henry Abelove, Michele Aina Barale, and David M. Halperin, 467–476. New York: Routledge.

Donham, Donald L. 2005. "Freeing South Africa: The 'Modernization' of Male-Male Sexuality in Soweto." In *Internationalizing Cultural Studies*, edited by Ackbar Abbas and John Nguyet Erni, 196–209. Malden, MA: Blackwell.

Downing, Lisa. 2008. *The Cambridge Introduction to Michel Foucault*. Cambridge: Cambridge University Press.

Duberman, Martin. 1993. *Stonewall*. New York: Plume.

*Erasing 76 Crimes*. http://76crimes.com/tag/adefho/. Freedom to Marry. http://www.freedomtomarry.org/states.

Foucault, Michel. 1984. *The Foucault Reader*. Edited by Paul Rabinow. New York: Pantheon.
———. 1990. *The History of Sexuality*. Vol. 1, *The Will to Knowledge*. Translated by Robert Hurley. Harmondsworth, UK: Penguin.
Gay, Peter. 1969. *The Enlightenment: An Interpretation*. Vol. 2, *The Science of Freedom*. New York: Norton.
Hossain, Adnan. 2010. "Bangladesh." In *Greenwood Encyclopedia of LGBT Issues Worldwide*. Vol. 1, edited by Chuck Stewart, 333–346. Santa Barbara, CA: Greenwood.
Human Rights Watch. "Lesbian, Gay, Bisexual, and Transgender Rights." http://www.hrw.org/topic/lgbt-rights.
———. 2014. "Singapore: Court Ruling a Major Setback for Gay Rights." October 29. http://www.hrw.org/news/2014/10/29/singapore-court-ruling-major-setback-gay-rights.
Hume, David. 1969. *The Essential David Hume*. Edited by Robert Paul Wolff. New York: New American Library. See pp. 129–139.
Immigration and Refugee Board of Canada. "Senegal: The Situation of Sexual Minorities in Senegal, Including Societal Attitudes and Whether There Is a Difference in the Treatment of Lesbians and Gay Men; State Protection (2010-April 2013)." http://www.refworld.org/docid/524bc6be4.html.
International Gay and Lesbian Human Rights Commission. http://www.iglhrc.org/.
Intersex Society of North America. "Does ISNA Think Children with Intersex Should Be Raised without a Gender, or in a Third Gender?" http://www.isna.org/faq/third-gender.
Jackson, Peter A. 1989. *Male Homosexuality in Thailand: An Interpretation of Contemporary Thai Sources*. Elmhurst, NY: Global Academic.
Jackson, Peter A., and Gerard Sullivan, eds. 1999. *Lady Boys, Tom Boys, and Rent Boys: Male and Female Homosexualities in Contemporary Thailand*. New York: Haworth.
The Leadership Conference. 2009. "Stonewall Riots: The Beginning of the LGBT Movement." http://www.civilrights.org/archives/2009/06/449-stonewall.html.
Locke, John. 1980. *Second Treatise of Government*. Edited by C. B. Macpherson. Indianapolis, IN: Hackett.
"Making Love a Crime: Criminalization of Same-Sex Conduct in Sub-Saharan Africa." Amnesty International, June 24, 2013. http://www.amnestyusa.org/research/reports/making-love-a-crime-criminalization-of-same-sex-conduct-in-sub-saharan-africa?page=show.
Mohanty, Chandra Talpady. 1988. "Under Western Eyes: Feminist Scholarship and Colonial Discourses." *Feminist Review* 30 (Autumn): 61–88.
Morris, Nigel. 2009. "Iraqi Leaders Attacked over Spate of Homophobic Murders." *The Independent*, April 13. http://www.independent.co.uk/news/world/middle-east/iraqi-leaders-attacked-over-spate-of-homophobic-murders-1668013.html.
National Public Radio. 2009. "The Secret Political Reach of 'the Family.'" *Fresh Air*, November 24. http://www.npr.org/templates/story/story.php?storyId=120746516.
Nossiter, Adam. 2013. "Senegal Cheers Its President for Standing up to Obama on Same-Sex Marriage." *New York Times*, June 28. http://www.nytimes.com/2013/06/29/world/africa/senegal-cheers-its-president-for-standing-up-to-obama-on-same-sex-marriage.html.
Padilla, Mark B. 2007. "'Western Union Daddies' and Their Quest for Authenticity: An Ethnographic Study of the Dominican Gay Sex Tourism Industry." *Journal of Homosexuality* 53, no. 1–2: 241–275.
Patterson, Orlando. 1991. *Freedom in the Making of Western Culture*. New York: Basic Books.
PBS (Public Broadcasting Service). "Background Readings: *Race: The Power of an Illusion*." http://www.pbs.org/race/000_About/002_04-background-02–05.htm.
———. "A Map of Gender-Diverse Cultures." http://www.pbs.org/independentlens/two-spirits/map.html.
PFLAG. http://community.pflag.org/Page.aspx?pid=194&srcid=-2. *Pink Pages: India's National Gay and Lesbian Magazine*. http://pink-pages.co.in.
Port Cities: Bristol. "Bristol and Transatlantic Slavery." http://discoveringbristol.org.uk/slavery/.
Racoma, Bernadine. 2013. "United Nations Human Rights Council to Discuss LGBT Issues in Geneva in June." *Day News*, May 6. http://www.daynews.com/world/society/2013/05/united-nations-human-rights-council-to-discuss-lgbt-issues-in-geneva-in-june-19998.
Solow, Barbara L. 1991. Introduction to *Slavery and the Rise of the Atlantic System*. Cambridge: Cambridge University Press.

Stewart, Chuck K., ed. 2010. *Greenwood Encyclopedia of LGBT Issues Worldwide*. Vol. 1. Santa Barbara, CA: Greenwood.

Tourism Authority of Thailand. http://www.tourismthailand.org/Thailand.

Towle, Evan B., and Lynn Marie Morgan. 2002. "Romancing the Transgender Native: Rethinking the Use of the 'Third Gender' Concept." *GLQ: A Journal of Lesbian and Gay Studies* 8, no. 4: 469–497.

UNESCO. "Slavery and Racism." http://www.unesco.org/bpi/eng/unescopress/2001/01–91e.shtml.

UNHRC (United Nations Human Rights Council). 2007. *Report of the Special Rapporteur on Violence against Women, Its Causes and Consequences: Addendum*. A/HRC/4/34/Add.1. New York: UNHRC, March 19. http://daccess-dds-ny.un.org/doc/UNDOC/GEN/G07/119/48/PDF/G0711948.pdf?OpenElement.

———. 2011. *Discriminatory Laws and Practices and Acts of Violence against Individuals Based on Their Sexual Orientation and Gender Identity: Report of the United Nations High Commissioner for Human Rights*. New York: UNHRC, November. A/HRC/19/41. http://www2.ohchr.org/english/bodies/hrcouncil/docs/19session/A.HRC.19.41_English.pdf.

Wahrman, Dror. 2006. *The Making of the Modern Self: Identity and Culture in Eighteenth- Century England*. New Haven, CT: Yale University Press.

"A Well-Locked Closet." 2010. *The Economist*, May 27, p. 335.

WHO (World Health Organization). 2015. "Gender and Genetics." http://www.who.int/genomics/gender/en.

Williams, Eric. 1966. *Capitalism and Slavery*. New York: Capricorn.

Williams, Walter L. 2010. "Thailand." In *Greenwood Encyclopedia of LGBT Issues Worldwide*, Vol. 1, edited by Chuck Stewart, 505–521. Santa Barbara, CA: Greenwood.

Wiredu, Kwasi. 1996. "An Akan Perspective on Human Rights." In *Cultural Universals and Particulars: An African Perspective*, 157–171. Bloomington: Indiana University Press.

World Outreach International. "Sex Tourism in Thailand." http://www.wouk.org/rahab_interna tional/pdf_files/Sex%20Tourism%20in%20Thailand.pdf.

# 10

# The Islamic Veil and the Global Politics of Gender

The various forms of veiling practiced by Muslim women have occupied a symbolic role in global encounters between Islam and the West, and they illustrate the ways that gendered "traditions" are subject to innovation and adaptation. The influences and counterinfluences of colonialism, globalization, migration, and information technologies can bring with them cultural hybridization, but they can also inspire a hardening of identities, an emphasis on difference and the purity of tradition. For example, in 1936 the first shah of Iran (Reza Khan Pahlavi) decreed that Iranian women should embrace modernization by throwing off the cloak known as a chador. In 1979, however, following the country's Islamic Revolution, the religious leader Ayatollah Khomeini decreed that they should put it back on. This one example (discussed more later) illustrates that societies do not progress along a linear continuum of social change, but rather shift and change according to both internal and external dynamics.

This case study will examine the veil in Islamic practice as a sliding signifier, a symbol whose meaning changes in different times and places—in this case, specifically in response to globalization. Using this concept, I will explore how the beliefs and practices surrounding veiling bring together gender, culture, and religion in different ways, depending on local conditions, exemplifying relations between the local and the global. After a brief account of various types of coverings for Muslim women and their relationship to the teachings of Islam, I will consider controversies surrounding the hijab (veil) in the predominantly Christian West, as well as in predominantly Muslim countries of the Middle East and Asia.

While many people perceive Islamic fundamentalism or Islamization in societies such as Iran, Afghanistan, and Egypt as a return to long-held beliefs and traditions, in actuality they are partially inventing conservative customs, formed as a political response against Westernization or globalization. Those Western influences may be cultural, as in images of women wearing bikinis or engaging in sexual behaviors outside of marriage. They also may be political, springing from a long history of Western intervention in Muslim spaces, whether by Britain and France under colonialism; by the United States and its allies during the Cold War; or by the United States today in its powerful support of Israel in its conflict with the Palestinians, or in its military intervention in the Middle East and South Asia in its "war on terror." Also considered will be the gendered nature of these reactions. For instance, women in these societies are typically placed in the role of bearers of tradition, while the men participate in modernity through economics and politics.

A major aspect of globalization, and another source of flow and flux in cultural meaning, is economic and political migration, or movements of people from one cultural space to another. Many people from Arab and Muslim countries have migrated to the metropolitan centers of their former colonial powers. Thus France is now home to populations of Algerian and Tunisian descent, while Britain is home to South Asians and Arabs from its former colonies. In these European nations, Muslim girls have encountered opposition to wearing the hijab in school. And, in an interesting twist, the political conflicts surrounding their wearing of the hijab have transformed its meaning for many of them. What had been for many a simple bow to tradition has become a signifier of their freedom to practice their religion within a multicultural state. In this way, the wearing of the hijab has thrown a spotlight on cultural globalization, particularly the challenges of multicultural citizenship.

### Historical Background on "Islam versus the West"

The relationship between Islam and the West, particularly the United States, is contentious for complex reasons. Some of them can be understood as a product of binary thinking, the knee-jerk assumption that there is inevitably a good guy and a bad guy, or "us versus them." But the antagonism between Islam and the West also has roots in historical events that have shaped the geopolitics of the post–World War II world.

In its fears of communism during the Cold War, the United States used its relationships with some Islamic countries to further its geopolitical goals. It supported military coups and oppressive governments, including a 1953 coup in Iran that gave power to the shah, coups in Tunisia and Algeria, the rule of Saddam Hussein in Iraq, and the royal family in Saudi Arabia—support that many across the world view negatively even today. Actions against—or in cooperation with—Islamic countries has also been motivated, since the Cold War, by the need for stability in oil supplies and prices. Although the United States produced more oil in 2013 than it imported (for the first time since 1995), protecting supplies of oil across the world has been a critical goal of its foreign policy. The United States will continue to be affected by the prices set by the Organization of Petroleum Exporting Countries, or OPEC, a cartel of countries, including many Islamic states, that sets production quotas and therefore contributes to the price of oil across the globe.

The United States has also engaged in direct military intervention in the Middle East. It waged a war against Saddam Hussein's Iraq in 1990–1991 to protect oil supplies when Hussein started to seize neighboring Kuwait's oil fields. Following this conflict, a U.S.-imposed embargo caused immense suffering of Iraqi civilians. And since the September 11, 2001, attacks in the United States, fighting more direct terrorist threats has been a high priority, used to justify two wars: against Iraq (again) and Afghanistan.

Additionally, and perhaps most importantly, U.S. foreign policy in the region has been dominated by supporting the State of Israel. Israel is unpopular with people from Islamic and Arab countries, among others, due to the fact that its creation in 1948 displaced millions of Palestinians living in the same territory, many of whom have been in refugee camps ever since. Also aggravating the situation is the fact that many people—from Islamic societies and Western countries alike—view Israel as intransigent in efforts to resolve the conflicts with its neighbors in the Middle East.

*unwilling or refusing to change one's views or to agree about something!*

### Key Concepts Critical to This Case Study

This case study is meant to illustrate several theoretical points and concepts related to cultural globalization:

1.  A signifier, such as the veil, gains its meaning only through context and in its differentiation from other signifiers.

2. The homogenizing, and to some degree Westernizing, tides of globalization pro-voke reactions in many locales that lead to a strengthening of identities as defined through difference.
3. These effects can be seen as both national in scale, as in some Middle Eastern and Arab countries, and as subcultural in scale, as in the responses of immigrant populations within France, Britain, and Canada.
4. The responses of Western democracies to Muslim practices have provoked crises in multicultural citizenship.
5. Within fundamentalist reactions against modernity, women are positioned as the primary bearers of alleged traditions.

## Dress as a Signifier of Identity and as an Instrument of Politics

The head covering or robes sometimes worn by Muslim women illustrate the many ways that human cultures can invest an arbitrary signifier with multiple, sometimes contradictory, meanings. This particular gendered symbol of cultural and religious belonging or identity can be interpreted differently by insiders and outsiders. And even to "insiders," it can have conflicted meanings.

The ambiguity of the veil or headscarf arises from the fact that it is merely a piece of cloth. Its meaning is dependent on context, and thus may differ between the wearer and the viewer, as well as among viewers. A square of silk worn as a head cover by a 1950s Hollywood star would be seen by outsiders very differently than a similar cloth worn as a hijab by a contemporary Muslim woman in New York. One might also compare the veil and robes worn by traditional Roman Catholic nuns or statues of the Virgin Mary to the hijab worn by many Muslim women. The idea that women should cover their heads can be found in all three of these contexts. For example, up until the early 1960s, Catholic girls and women had to cover their heads in church, while Orthodox Jewish women traditionally covered their hair or cut it off after marriage. In the New Testament of the Bible, in 1 Corinthians 11:5–6, Paul says, "every woman who prays or prophesies with her head uncovered dishonors her head." Roman Catholic nuns often shaved their heads and wore veils. In fact, there is some evidence of a revival of Catholic women covering their heads in church and for nuns to return to a habit with a veil. These practices all share an association between women's hair as sexually attractive to men and the idea that spiritual devotion by men precludes them being in the presence of sexually attractive women. However, what they mean to the practitioner, to the woman wearing the veil, can vary even within the same society. In one case a woman might be *compelled* by her family or religion to wear a head covering, and in another she might *choose* to do so in order to make a public statement of her identity or faith. Many Muslim women in the West feel that they are not only projecting their religious identity by wearing a scarf, but also that they do not want to be judged for their looks. Thus modest clothing is something that is enjoined by their faith, but it is also something that differentiates them from Western values surrounding sexuality and the objectification of women's bodies. It has also become simply a marker of Islamic identity for minority populations in the West.

## Religions of the Book: History, Beliefs, and Traditions

Judaism, Christianity, and Islam are known as the "religions of the Book," offshoots of the same roots in the Middle East. These religions based on sacred scripture also share, in various ways, distinctions between the commands or laws laid down in scripture, whether it be the Hebrew Bible, the Christian Bible (Old and New Testaments), or the Quran, on the one hand, and a body of theological and legal interpretations created by scholars, on the other. While the Quran is sacred revelation from Allah, the hadith are stories told by friends and witnesses of the Prophet Muhammad about his actions and sayings. These created models for the pious life of his followers. Judaism and Catholicism also have traditions of both scripture and law. While the sacred books do not change over time, the interpretations given to them and the social practices associated with these religions do evolve. All three reflect the patriarchal social system within which they developed, but different traditions within them have adapted, more or less, to contemporary social conditions and local social structures.

The religions of the Book have evolved into world religions, spreading through conquest and colonization in the cases of Christianity and Islam; through diasporas in the cases of all three; and through missionary activity, primarily in the case of Christianity. They have been syncretized, or transformed, to varying degrees as they have come into contact with the different cultures. For example, when Christianity came to Ireland in the fifth century CE, the Celtic goddess Brigid became the Catholic Saint Brigid. Sacred wells that were dedicated to Celtic spirits became incorporated into Christian religious practices. In Christianity, a schism between Orthodox and Roman Catholics occurred in 1054, and later the Protestant Reformation led to a vast number of new Christian sects, while Conservative and Reformed Judaism developed in the past two centuries as practitioners encountered environments outside their core communities of faith. Islam adapted as well to the various societies it spread to, such as India, Indonesia, and many areas of Africa.

Specific religious beliefs or practices are often attributed to sacred scriptures, even by believers, when in fact they are hybridizations between local traditions and globalizing theologies. In addition, many members of a culture or religion follow certain practices without really knowing why. Until the early 1960s, for example, Roman Catholics could not eat meat on Fridays, but they typically could not tell a non-Catholic the reason for their abstinence. The Second Vatican Council (1962–1965) removed the rule, but most Catholics would not be able to explain that either. However, when different cultures come into contact with each other, especially if one is dominant or viewed as dominant, the minority culture may suddenly cling to its traditional practices, which may then become important signifiers of collective belonging and identity. A devout Catholic, seeing vast cultural forces as a threat to her traditions, may choose to continue the practice of not eating meat on Friday. An Islamic woman, similarly seeing cultural forces pressing in around her, may also cling to wearing a veil. So, too, with devout Jews, or even those who are not so devout, who carry on their traditions, such as making a bar mitzvah, to claim their identities. With immigrants, this cultural dynamic is perhaps more urgent. Although some newcomers may choose to assimilate to the dominant culture, others may become more fervent in the beliefs and practices that differentiate them. In addition, one generation may assimilate, but their children may then develop a renewed interest in their traditions.

With more than 1.5 billion believers today, Islam originated in the early seventh century CE around the revelations of the Prophet Muhammad (570–632 CE), born in Mecca in what is now Saudi Arabia. The "five pillars of Islam," or obligations of believers, are generally shared throughout the otherwise varied populations of Muslims. They include the profession of the faith, the five daily prayers, fasting during Ramadan, giving alms to the poor, and making the *hajj*, or pilgrimage to Mecca. The shrine at Mecca is believed to sit on the site where the biblical Abraham went to sacrifice his son in response to a command by God—a narrative important in Islam, Christianity, and Judaism. However, while Jews and Christians believe this son was Isaac, Abraham's child by Sarah, Muslims believe it was Ishmael, his son by the slave woman Hagar. The shrine was near the trade routes connecting the Mediterranean with the Indian Ocean, thus facilitating the spread of the Prophet's teachings. Through the unifying influence of Islam, Muhammad launched a widespread Arab Empire that spread across the Middle East and the Mediterranean.

Jesus had been born six centuries earlier into a part of the far-flung Roman Empire. Earlier empires, including the Assyrian, Babylonian, and Persian, affected the history of the Jewish people. These political and cultural networks, along with the later Ottoman and Mughal Empires, helped spread what are now world religions from very local voices. The Arab Empire continued to expand through the ninth century, fusing its religion and culture with the cosmopolitan societies of Persia and Mediterranean Europe. Nonetheless, soon after Muhammad's death in the mid-seventh century, divisions occurred among his followers, most notably leading to the differences between Shiite and Sunni Muslims. Sunnis, the vast majority of Muslims, regard Shiites as "innovators," and even heretics, a division that has seeded many conflicts in the contemporary world. Sunnis regard Abu Bakr as the first caliph, and Ali, Muhammad's cousin and husband of his highly regarded daughter Fatima, as the fourth. Shiites consider Ali to be the appointed successor to the Prophet. Ali and his sons (Muhammad's grandsons), Hassan and Hussein, were martyred. Ali was assassinated, Hassan was poisoned by his wife in Medina, and Hussein was killed in a struggle over the inheritance of the caliphate at Karbala in Iraq. Shiite Muslims commemorate his martyrdom, believing, unlike Sunnis, that there should be an imam, or leader of Islam, who can trace his lineage to Muhammad. Today, Shiism is the state religion of Iran, with minority communities in Iraq and other Gulf states, as well as South Asia and the eastern Mediterranean. There are three major subsets holding significantly different beliefs within Shiism: Twelvers, Ismailis, and Zaidis.

> For a good explanation of the status of Sharia law in predominantly Muslim countries, see "Islam: Governing under Sharia," on the Council on Foreign Relations website (http://www.cfr.org/religion/islam-governing-under-sharia/p8034).

## Women in Sharia Law

In Islam there is no distinction between sacred and secular practices. Thus Sharia law, which is a body of rules based in Islam regulating Muslims' behavior, encompasses the family, economic practices, and politics, as well as religion and ethics. Sharia law developed in the centuries after Muhammad's death, often based on hadith, drawing inspiration from the Prophet's actions and teachings. However, Muhammad's ideas evolved over time, and eyewitness reports sometimes appear to conflict. Thus various schools of jurisprudence developed with different interpretations of particular hadith. Within Sunni Islam there are four widely accepted schools of jurisprudence, or legal reasoning, and a fifth that is not accepted by all. Different legal schools hold more or less strict views on family law and women's status. Certain Arab cultural practices that had no specific sanction in the Quran became accepted as part of Islamic teaching. Circumcision is an example of this.

Many argue that Muhammad sought to protect the status of women during his time by regulating for the equal support of multiple wives and for widows and divorced women. He also wrote many statements explicitly making men and women spiritual equals. In the Quran, however, women are sometimes given half the rights of men in inheritance and in legal testimony. For example a woman would inherit half what her brother would and two women's testimony before a judge would be required rather than just one. These restrictions on the status of women were echoed in many non-Muslim societies at the time of Muhammad and long after. For example, up until the twentieth century, in many parts of the world, including some U.S. states, women could not inherit property. Thus the issue for women in Islamic societies today is whether and how far interpretations of the Quran should change to adapt to today's world. The Quran itself cannot be altered, but examining the social context within which it was written can open up space for contemporary understandings. For example some Islamic feminists argue that the reason men inherited double what women did within the same family was that men were expected to provide for their wives—including multiple wives in the case of some followers of Islam—and thus needed more wealth. These feminists argue that the Prophet was not emphasizing gender inequality but rather a practical matter of providing for the family. Somewhat similar arguments, highlighting the societal "requirement" of men to support their women, as opposed to granting women's economic equality, were made to justify differences in men's and women's pay in the United States as late as the 1950s.

---

### Islam and Women's Dress Codes

Traditional coverings for Muslim women vary in different parts of the world. The most minimal is the *hijab*, or headscarf. The *abaya* is a cloak or long dark robe, with no face or head covering, worn by many Arab women. Variations on coverings include the following:

- The two-piece *al-amira* is a cap and scarf.
- The *shayla* is a long rectangular scarf.
- The *niqab* veils the face, leaving only the eyes visible; it is worn with a headscarf.
- The *burqa*, worn in parts of South Asia, especially Afghanistan, covers the entire body and face, with just a mesh screen through which the eyes can see.
- The *khimar* is a cape-like veil that covers the head and upper body.
- The *chador* is the Iranian cloak that covers the head and body, but is simply held closed by the wearer.

Drawings of these variations can be seen on the BBC News website (http://news.bbc.co.uk/2/shared/spl/hi/pop_ups/05/europe_muslim_veils/html/1.stm).

---

## Gender and Fundamentalism

Most predominantly Islamic countries have experienced a series of imperial rulers, resulting in competing cultural beliefs and values. Europeans in the nineteenth and early twentieth centuries brought with them Enlightenment rationality, individualism, languages, and educational and governmental structures. As the Europeans imposed their institutions, preexisting Islamic schools were left a much narrower sphere within which to operate. Thus they specialized in religious matters. Both under colonialism and under postcolonial authoritarian regimes, Friday prayers in the mosque became a space in which to articulate strong religious views that opposed the state. As anticolonial movements developed in the mid-twentieth century, nationalism was articulated in opposition to European culture, often as specifically Islamic. Nonetheless, postcolonial states that were predominantly Muslim emerged in a variety of forms of rule, from socialist to monarchist. More recently, a fundamentalist movement has grown within Islamic societies, mobilized to some degree in opposition to American military involvement in the Middle East and to globalized popular culture emanating largely from the United States. This "Islamism," or political Islam, should not be confused with Islam itself.

The Iranian Revolution of 1979 was a powerful indicator of anti-Western sentiment, as the Westernizing shah installed by the United States was overthrown in favor of a theocratic regime. The worldwide trends in Islamic countries show women returning to veiling where it had not been common practice. Islamist movements, like other religious fundamentalisms, claim to be returning to a pure-past tradition while actually being considerably modern—using modern forms of state power, participating in the global economy, using contemporary methods of communications technologies, and so forth.

Another case is the Muslim Brotherhood in Egypt, which has been in existence since the 1920s, but only gained political clout during the Arab Spring of 2011. The Brotherhood arose partly in opposition to British imperialism in the building of the Suez Canal. They also stood for opposition against Egypt's peace treaty with Israel and against the United States. In the elections held in 2012, the Brotherhood won the presidency by appearing to support democracy, but within a year it was overthrown and is currently out of favor in the country. One of the reasons given for the coup was the treatment of minorities and women under the Muslim Brotherhood's administration. In March 2013 the Egyptian government under the Brotherhood attacked a UN Convention against violence toward women, saying it would contravene Egypt's cultural specificity. Women had been highly active in the protests of the Arab Spring, and they continued their protests against the elected Islamist government.

The push toward Islamism can even be seen in Turkey, a secular state since 1924, with a population that is over 95 percent Muslim. Turkey had long banned the wearing of headscarves by women working in the public sector and attending universities. In recent decades, however, students have demanded the right to wear the veil, a movement associated with the rise of pro-Islamist politics in Turkey. The ban was strongly opposed by large numbers of people until a 2008 court decision lifted it.

The most extreme and clearly oppressive instance of Islamic fundamentalism up until 2014 was Taliban rule in Afghanistan during the 1990s. Women were deprived of all human rights and forced into extreme seclusion, not just by the burqa, but also by extensive restrictions on all their personal freedoms. While these deprivations were done in the name of Afghan "traditions" of purdah, or separation of the sexes, they illustrate, among other things, the destructive and reactionary response to imperial exploitation. Looking at the oppression of women from this perspective, while perhaps offering an incomplete narrative, is instructive. At a key point on the Silk Road, Afghanistan has been at the crossroads of numerous empires, and most recently was the subject of a tug of war between imperial Russia and British India in the nineteenth century, and between the United States and the Soviet Union during the Cold War. In 1979 more than a million Afghans died in a war between the rebel mujahideen, trained and armed by the United States, and the Afghan state, backed by the Soviet Union. The mujahideen morphed into the Taliban, which U.S. and international forces have been fighting since 2001. The extreme appropriation of Islam and so-called local tradition can be viewed as a reaction against the invasions and destruction caused by Western imperialisms. But it is women who have been forced to be the social and cultural pawns—the symbols of political Islam—in this reaction. Fortunately, the Taliban is an outlier within the Islamic world.

## Shifting the Meaning of Modest Dress in Islamic Countries

The Quran states that both women and men should dress modestly. An often-repeated hadith states that women should show only their faces and hands to those outside the family. The specific interpretation of these injunctions has evolved from cultural traditions in specific areas of the world where Islam has taken root. Islam originated in the Arabian Peninsula, and the long black robe, called the abaya, has spread outward from there along with the religion. The abaya is sometimes worn with a veil over the hair or a niqab over the head and face, especially in Saudi Arabia. The most conservative form of female Muslim attire, the burqa, is mentioned in Arabia prior to the advent of Islam as a covering both for animals and as a winter covering for women. In Indonesia, home to the largest population of Muslims in the world, many women wore no clothing above their waists prior to Islamicization. Today they usually wear the *kebaya* (a word derived from abaya), which is a particular style of jacket and dress, and a *kerudung*, a headscarf with a sewn-in visor. In South Asia, the *dupatta* is a long shawl-like piece of fabric that is worn over the head by both Hindu and Muslim women. In North Africa, women often wear brightly colored long robes such as kaftans.

While each region has its own history of clothing, and many have adapted their own forms of Muslim modesty for women, in recent decades the influence of Islamic fundamentalism has led to a trend of increasing conservatism, sometimes in reaction against the signifiers of the sexual revolution in the West, and sometimes as an expression of religious identity. On the east coast of Africa, for example, Swahili women have increasingly come to wear a black robe with a black hijab called *buibui*, a word probably also derived from abaya. However they also wear more traditional coverings—colorful rectangles of cloth printed with proverbs called *kangas*, which can be used to cover the head and body. Those women who cover themselves in the *buibuis* often wear fashionable Western-style dress underneath the black coverings, which are removed at home or in all-female social gatherings where the women dance and show off their finery. The increasing presence of the black *buibui* is at least in part

U.S. Secretary of State Hillary Clinton meeting with female Afghani politicians in 2011. All of the Afghan women are wearing hijabs, one of the most minimal versions of veiling worn by Muslim women.

*Source:* U.S. Embassy—Kabul, Afghanistan.

a result of funding and influence from Iran and Saudi Arabia—with their conservative forms of Islam—and the cultural insensitivity of European tourists who frequent the coastal beach resorts of Mombasa, Lamu, and Zanzibar in bikinis. The reaction against what is viewed as the immodesty of Western women has led to even small girls wearing *buibuis*, although that was not common practice in the recent past.

An additional complexity of the multidimensional meanings relating to women's dress in East Africa is class related: the shifting from the *kangas* to the black *buibuis* is a signifier of upward mobility. In fact, a number of writers on the practice of veiling note that, historically, veiling was a mark of elite status in many places. In Mesopotamia (now Iraq), servants and prostitutes were not allowed to wear veils. When the shah of Iran banned the veil in 1936, many women were horrified. After he left power in 1941, the enforcement of the law was relaxed and women could wear veils, but those who did were considered to be backwards or lacking in ambition. This changed in the 1979 Islamic Revolution, when his son, the second shah (Mohammad Reza Pahlavi), was overthrown and an Islamic republic was instituted, and the chador was required. Prior to the revolution, the chador was a light-colored garment, but now it is a black robe worn over other clothes. There is considerable variation in the strictness with which the hair is covered. The case of Iran illustrates how veiling and unveiling can shift their political meanings 180 degrees overnight. Many women who were opposed to the shah wore the veil as a revolutionary symbol of opposition, but a few years after the revolution, when they were forced to cover their heads by law, many saw the veil as a symbol of oppression.

## Failed Multiculturalism? Wearing the Hijab in France and Britain

Meanwhile, Muslim women in Europe have experienced a related yet different set of issues regarding how they dress in public. During the 1990s and early 2000s, a much-publicized controversy took place in France over the head coverings worn by Muslim girls. Similar conflicts have occurred in other liberal democracies such as Britain and Germany. "*L'affaire du foulard*," or "the scarf affair," brought together a number of complex cultural and political confrontations involving multiculturalism, the legacy of colonialism, cultural relativism, and the nature of identity and equality—specifically, both gender and religious identities and equalities. French national identity is a product of the European Enlightenment and the 1789 French Revolution, fought in the name of republican liberty, equality, and fraternity. During the revolution, France broke with the powerful Roman Catholic Church, but later reconnected with it. Thus the French have both an intellectual commitment to what they see as universal rational, secular values and a strong cultural tie to the Catholic religion. Because they view their national values as "universal," multiculturalism is a challenge. According to the 2013 Index Mundi, 83 to 88 percent of the population in France is Catholic, with only 2 percent Protestant and 1 percent Jewish, while 5 to 10 percent is Muslim, mostly from France's former African colonies of Algeria, Tunisia, and Senegal.

In 1989, three Muslim girls were expelled from their French schools for wearing headscarves, igniting a controversy that led to the expulsion of twenty-three Muslim girls from their schools in November 1996 and to the near unanimous passage of a law in 2004 against wearing or displaying religious symbols in state schools. This was followed in 2011 with a law banning the wearing of the burqa or niqab in French public spaces. The president at the time, Nicholas Sarkozy, stated that to wear a full veil (presumably covering the face as well as the hair) was a violation of the values of the republic. The law imposes a fine of 150 euros for covering one's face in any public space, including shops, movie theaters, and restaurants. Exceptions are made for fencing masks and masquerade masks, as well as welding masks, sunglasses, motorcycle helmets, and sunglasses. The law creates severe penalties for anyone forcing a woman to wear an Islamic veil—up to a 60,000-euro fine and two years in jail.

The controversy has shown no sign of abating. Attempts to enforce the law have resulted in riots in Paris suburbs and in Marseille, yet the vast majority of French people support it. In 2013 a French woman known as S. A. S. took this ban to the European Court of Human Rights; the court referred the case to its Grand Council, signaling the importance of the issue to the entire European Union. The woman explicitly stated that neither her husband nor any other family member has pressured her to wear the burqa. She chose to wear it in support of her faith and culture and to achieve inner peace.

In the case at the European Court of Human Rights, the French government argued that associations in public space are central to life in a democracy and that burqas and niqabs take away the dignity and identity of the wearer. These views clash with the view held by some, but not all, Muslim societies that women should not consort with nor reveal themselves to people who are not *mahram*, or family. Saudi Arabia is a prime example of a society ruled by this belief. Thus a Saudi woman visiting France would be placed in an impossible situation. As noted earlier, the Quran itself mandates only modesty, and the primary hadith on the subject is taken to say that women should reveal only their faces and hands. The niqab and burqa go beyond these standards in covering a woman's face. Nonetheless, many women are used to this degree of coverage and believe it is appropriate. Yet the French majority hold their beliefs just as strongly. This case shows the limitations of cultural relativism, and of tolerance for different cultural values, in resolving clashes between cultures. These two culture-based beliefs cannot co-exist side by side. Either the French must modify their beliefs about secularism, or Muslim women living in France must modify their dress code. Or some compromise must be achieved.

Initially, the conflict over veiling was represented in the international press as a clash between republican values of equality for girls and boys within the educational process, on the one hand, and retrograde Islamic oppression of females, on the other. Veiling, represented by the headscarves of the girls, appeared to many to be a manifestation of patriarchal tradition, a practice forced on them by their immigrant parents. It seemed that their parents would not allow them to pursue an education, mandated by the French state, unless they covered their heads in accord with Muslim values. However, the situation was more complex than a simple conflict between tradition and modernity, between religion and secularism. The girls consulted with Daniel-Youssof Leclerq, former president of the National Federation of Muslims in France and head of a group called *Integrité*. As the philosopher Seyla Benhabib points out, "[W]earing the scarf was a conscious political gesture on their part, a complex act of identification and defiance" (187). The French understanding of participation in the republic, of citizenship, rests on a belief in neutrality or universalism that in fact might be considered highly particular. Some analysts consider this a negative form of multiculturalism, one that seeks to achieve equality by subtracting differences, but in reality demands assimilation and acquiescence to a shared set of values by everyone in society. This is markedly different from a positive multiculturalism, such as that of Trinidad and Tobago, a state in which virtually every major subculture has a national holiday and many have state-supported schools. In Trinidad and Tobago, citizens understand that theirs is a complex and multicultural set of belongings, even though there are contestations over power and access.

Britain's population has different Muslim roots than France's, and it also engages in more discussion of multiculturalism as a goal, however imperfectly realized. Although Anglicanism is the constitutional religion of England, according to Index Mundi 2013, Britain is only 71.6 percent Christian (a mix of several denominations), with 2.7 percent of the population Muslim and 1 percent Hindu. The most recent debates in Britain have concerned the wearing not of the head covering, or hijab, but rather the head and face covering which leaves only the eyes visible, the niqab. Unlike the French laws, which are primarily ideological and cultural, the British debate is centered around practical issues, such as security and identification. Recently, a woman testifying in court was made to remove her niqab while testifying, though she was allowed to keep it on during the rest of the trial. Birmingham Metropolitan College passed a rule that all people on campus must have their faces visible, but it was withdrawn after major protests. Whereas the French seek to uphold secularism as a national value, the British affirm religious tolerance. When they do interfere with religious dress, the British are more concerned with preventing terrorist acts, with the practical fact of a hidden face. In fact, Britain has more surveillance cameras than any other society— one for every eleven people—so the covering of faces obviously interferes with what it believes is a legitimate public interest. Nonetheless, Britain seems to be moving more toward France's position on face veils. In September 2013, Prime Minister David Cameron said he would guide national debate on the topic. He does not advocate an all-out ban on the niqab or burqa, but he would support guidelines for teachers, judges, and immigration officials as to when they may require the removal of such face veils. Unlike President Sarkozy of France, Cameron reiterated that Britain supports the right of people to dress as they please in public spaces.

Western critiques of veiling practices within Islam are part of a tradition of using women's "oppression" in non-Western nations as a marker of civilizational inferiority and a justification for Western intervention. In the late twentieth century, for example, Western feminists took up the cause of female genital mutilation in Africa. Most recently, the United States used the Taliban's severe oppression of Afghani women as part of its rationale for going to war in Afghanistan. This is not to say that these practices are acceptable; rather, it is to point out that women's oppression might well be used, and in some cases is being used, to legitimate state actions that are actually about something else. In addition, focusing the spotlight on the wrongs of other societies can blind us to what is wrong in our own society. For American women, what is wrong in American society might include not feeling safe walking through a city at night, feeling deeply insecure about body image or appearance, or being subject to acquaintance rape on college campuses. It is always easier to see what is wrong in other societies than in one's own.

An article by the Muslim writer Nasrine Malik, posted on the website of *The Telegraph* (http://www.telegraph.co.uk/news/religion/10323303/I-was-forced-to-wear-the-veil-and-I-wish-no-other-woman-had-to-suffer-it.html), discusses the complexities of the issues surrounding the "veiling" of women in Islam in personal and detailed manner.

Social media such as Facebook are highlighting fashion trends within Islam as designers and fashion-conscious Muslim women experiment with colorful versions of the hijab and other traditional forms of dress. Some conservative Muslims critique the idea of drawing attention to oneself in public, even if modestly covered. The following links present examples of new fashions within Muslim dress:

"India: Remaking Modesty as a Global Fashion Statement," MuslimVillage.com (http://muslimvillage.com/2013/07/21/41386/india-remaking-modesty-as-a-global-fashion-statement/)

"Fashionable Niqabs Preferred by Muslims in India," MuslimVillage.com (http://muslimvillage.com/2014/03/03/50533/fashionable-niqabs-preferred-muslims-india/)

"The Veil Becomes a Fashion Statement," *Pacific Standard* (http://www.psmag.com/navigation/books-and-culture/the-veil-becomes-a-fashion-statement-8707/)

## Conclusion

Recent controversies over the dress of women in Islam highlight different issues in different settings, from Egypt to England. But they all illustrate the invention and reinvention of tradition and the fact that it is often women who are expected to be the bearers of traditions that reinforce cultural identity. This is part of the historical and cultural context through which the West and Islam view each other. Women often become symbols in nationalist and fundamentalist movements. While men participate in the global economy, women are expected to embody the "traditional" realm of domestic purity. This has been true of Catholic Ireland as well as Taliban Afghanistan. Thus many influential voices in the West have sometimes seen the hijab as a symbol of the oppression and seclusion of women, while many Muslim women have felt their coverings to be protective camouflage in public spaces. Some have seen them as secretive sources of power. In cases of insurgency, such as the Algerian War of the 1950s, women in burqas were able to conceal weapons and bombs under their

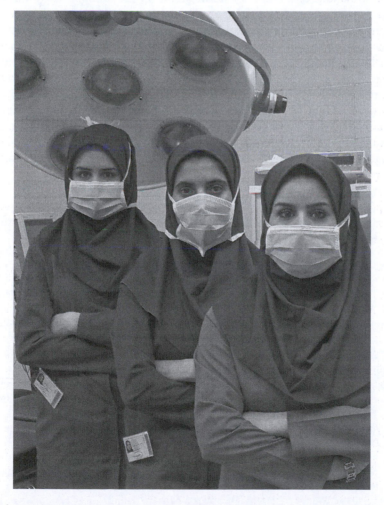

The picture shows three Iranian surgical technicians whose medical masks may suggest the wearing of the niqab although Iranian women's chadors cover only the head and the body.

*Source:* Wikipedia Commons. https://commons.wikimedia.org/wiki/File:Iranian_surgical_technologist_with_hijab_09.jpg

modest apparel. In more conservative societies, such as theocratic Iran after the 1979 revolution, encouragement of Western-style dress was rejected and the chador was mandated. In the past two decades in Europe, especially in France and the United Kingdom, the wearing of the veil by migrant populations has become a hotly contested practice, with many conflicting meanings and interpretations. The wearing of or refusal to wear the hijab by women in various places illustrates the arbitrary significance of cultural practices, the dependence of their meaning on local contexts, and the misinterpretation of them by groups with their own needs and agendas. The clashes in meaning and practice wrought by migration into Europe bring to the fore representational differences.

Feminist movements within Islam advocate both for and against conservative dress by women. And in fact, many, if not almost all, Islamic feminists make the point that Western perceptions of what it means to wear the hijab are biased and mistaken in seeing the veil as a mark of oppression. (See, for example, the writings listed at the end of this case study by Leila Ahmed, Asra Barlas, Fatima Mernissi, and Amina Wadud.) The currents and flows of Islamism, on the one hand, and Westernization, on the other, make a black-and-white view of these issues impossible. Multiple trends are going on both within majority Muslim nations and in non-Muslim ones. In 2013, for example, women in Algeria demonstrated in favor of their country's traditional colored robes and against Saudi-influenced black robes. Muslim women in a number of countries are designing brightly colored yet modest clothes, and fashionistas are blogging about them. These symptoms of globalized modernity may draw on the past, but they are thoroughly contemporary reactions to multiculturalism and imperialism—expressions of identity as difference. Surely the spread of stories, as well as analyses of controversies, about women's dress codes makes possible a greater understanding between insiders and outsiders and opens up a space that will make self-reflection de rigueur. This is a space that will promote respect, freedom, and education on all sides.

## References and Further Research

Afsaruddin, Asma. 2011. *Islam, the State, and Political Authority: Medieval Issues and Modern Concerns*. New York: Palgrave Macmillan.

Ahmed, Leila. 2005. "The Veil Debate—Again: A View from America in the Early Twenty-First Century." In *On Shifting Ground: Muslim Women in the Global Era*, edited by Fereshteh Nourale-Simone, 153–171. New York: The Feminist Press.

———. 2011. *A Quiet Revolution: The Veil's Resurgence, from the Middle East to America*. New Haven, CT: Yale University Press.

Badran, Margot, and Miriam Cooke, eds. 1990. *Opening the Gates: A Century of Arab Feminist Writing*. London: Virago Press.

Barlas, Asra. 2002. *"Believing Women" in Islam: Unreading Patriarchal Interpretations of the Qur'ān*. Austin: University of Texas Press.

Barlas, Asma. 2005. "Globalizing Equality: Muslim Women, Theology, and Feminisms." In *On Shifting Ground: Muslim Women in the Global Era*, edited by Fereshteh Nourale-Simone, 91–110. New York: Feminist Press.

Benhabib, Seyla. 2004. *The Rights of Zothers: Aliens, Residents, and Citizens*. Cambridge: Cambridge University Press.

Cochran, Kira. 2013. "The Niqab Debate: Is the Veil the Biggest Issue We Face in the UK?" *The Guardian*, September 16. http://www.theguardian.com/world/2013/sep/16/veil-biggest-issue-uk-niqab-debate.

Denari, Jordan. 2014. "Wait, I Thought That Was a Muslim Thing?" *dotCommonweal*, February 13. https://www.commonwealmagazine.org/blog/wait-i-thought-was-muslim-thing#/0.

Donohue, John J., and John L. Esposito, eds. 2007. *Islam in Transition: Muslim Perspectives*. New York: Oxford University Press.

Ernst, Carl W. 2003. *Following Muhammad: Rethinking Islam in the Contemporary World*. Chapel Hill: University of North Carolina Press.

Fawcett, Rachelle. 2013. "The Reality and Future of Islamic Feminism." *Al Jazeera*, March 28. http://www.aljazeera.com/indepth/opinion/2013/03/201332715585855781.html.

Johnson, Toni, and Mohammed Aly Sergie. 2014. "Islam: Governing under Sharia." In *CFR Backgrounder*. Washington, DC: Council on Foreign Relations, July 25. http://www.cfr.org/religion/islam-governing-under-sharia/p8034.

Mernissi, Fatima. 2011. *Beyond the Veil: Male-Female Dynamics in a Muslim Society*. London: Saqi.

"Reorienting the Veil: Veiling in East Africa." Chapel Hill, NC: UNC Center for European Studies. http://veil.unc.edu/regions/east-africa/.

Ruthven, Malise. 1997. *Islam: A Very Short Introduction*. Oxford: Oxford University Press.

Segran, Elizabeth. 2013. "The Rise of Islamic Feminists." *The Nation*, December 23–30. http://www.thenation.com/article/177467/rise-islamic-feminists#.

Sharp, Diamond. "Bridging the Disconnect: Unveiling the Hijab and Islamic Feminism." *GirlSpeak*. http://www.youngchicagoauthors.org/girlspeak/features_bridging_the_disconnect_unveiling_the_hijab_and_islamic_feminism_by_diamond_sharp.htm.

Wadud, Amina. 1999. *Qur'an and Woman: Rereading the Sacred Text from a Woman's Perspective*. Oxford: Oxford University Press.

———. 2006. *Inside the Gender Jihad: Women's Reform in Islam*. Oxford: Oneworld.

———. 2009. "Islam and Feminism." *The New Statesman*, April 22. http://www.newstatesman.com/blogs/the-faith-column/2009/04/sexual-equality-qur-feminism.

# 11

# "Keeping It Real": State, Corporate, or Underground Voices in Global Hip-Hop

In 1993, the scholar Paul Gilroy published *The Black Atlantic: Modernity and Double Consciousness*. The book examines the cultural and political geography established centuries ago by the Atlantic slave trade, whose transatlantic journeys created the African diaspora of today, connecting West Africa, Europe (primarily Britain), North America, and the Caribbean. The relationships between places, peoples, and cultures that grew out of the "Black Atlantic" are multidirectional. People, ideas, and cultural forms have traveled back and forth from their origins in Africa to the Caribbean and to London, Toronto, or New York and then circulated and developed in various locations. Gilroy uses the trope of the ship to focus on the centrality of both the Middle Passage and travel in the creation of modernity in the transatlantic world, a world in which black people and ideas are central. One of Gilroy's chapters focuses on black popular music as a public arena for expressions of human consciousness and debates on the nature of identity. The most recent genre he discusses, hip-hop, exemplifies the relationships among local, transnational, and global cultural practices, in this case produced out of black marginalization, but circulating throughout the world as a complex expression of resistance against oppression.

This pan-African historical backdrop helps to illuminate hip-hop as both a culture and a form of music. Because it is so multifaceted and widespread, this case study will focus primarily on hip-hop music and its circulation, ranging from Africa to the Caribbean to New York, and then back to Trinidad and Cuba, as well as the African nations of Ghana and Tanzania.

The evolution of global hip-hop illustrates the tensions between the local and the global as well as the agency of artists who have adapted it to new languages and locations, creating new hybrid forms of expression. But wherever hip-hop has spread, success in the form of commercial and government sponsorship has threatened the "authenticity" of the genre. And often the "conscious" or "underground" rappers who seek to "keep it real"—who strive for authenticity—are the ones whose content is explicitly tied to pan-Africanism and political critique.

---

**Key Elements of Hip-Hop**

**DJing**

In hip-hop, the DJ manipulates turntables to create the rhythms of the music—for instance, finding the break in the song and looping it over and over to form a long percussive break. The DJ's role is to create intensely rhythmic music that will energize a crowd and get them dancing. Following Jamaican influences, DJs initially used giant sound systems and often competed with other DJs.

### Turntabling, Dubbing, Scratching

These terms refer to manipulations of records by the DJ, which form the beat over which the rapper or emcee speaks or chants. Dub and hip-hop DJs use two turntables and a mixer; today, synthesizers and computers are often used.

### Sampling

The DJ uses portions of recorded songs, or "samples," with or without the words, as part of the hip-hop song; percussive breaks in recordings are used to create long rhythmic sections during which breakdancing takes place (this can also be done electronically).

### Emceeing, MCing, Toasting

These terms describe talking and chanting over rhythmic music, such as drumming, which in Afro-Caribbean traditions is sometimes traced back to the West African *griot*, or poet/historian. MCing in hip-hop derives from this tradition as well: the MC talks and chants over the rhythms produced by the DJ (the MC is equivalent to the rap artist).

### B-Boying, B-Girling, Break Dancing

These terms refer to a style of street dance performed often by "crews," or groups, during the long percussive breaks in hip-hop songs. This is sometimes done in competition with another group or, today, at formal competitions all over the world.

### Rap

A "rap" is a rhythmic and rhyming poem derived from spoken word poetry, which is spoken over the beat and sampling played by the DJ. Rap evolved into a number of subgenres, including commercially successful rap, gangsta rap, and conscious rap. *Commercial rap* is perceived as "selling out" to mass audiences and the interests of record companies, and its authenticity. *Gangsta rap* is spoken in the persona of gang members, drug lords, criminals, and pimps and is noted for being misogynistic and homophobic. *Conscious rap* usually takes critical stances about contemporary issues, often concerning the black and Latino communities or concerning the African diaspora. *Freestyle rapping* is done extemporaneously.

### Beatboxing

This is a form of vocal percussion, using the voice or other parts of the body to make rhythmic sounds. Some rappers combine beatboxing with verbal rapping.

## Transnational Roots of Hip-Hop: From West Africa to Black America, the Caribbean, and Back

At first glance, the beginnings of hip-hop, of which rap is one component, might be thought of as extremely localized. It began in the South Bronx, in New York City, in the early 1970s, at 1520 Sedgewick Avenue, home of DJ Kool Herc, now considered the founding father of hip-hop. The South Bronx at that time was a synonym for stereotyped urban decay, poverty, and hopelessness. Buildings were dilapidated, many of them burned out, empty, and windowless. Although everyone agrees that hip-hop was born in the block parties of this neighborhood, the Caribbean, and especially Jamaican, roots of the form are less well known. Underlying both the Caribbean and the South Bronx inventions of these musical forms are oral traditions brought across the Atlantic by enslaved Africans—traditions of storytelling and critique, of speaking truth to power, of call and response, and of drumming as accompaniment. A review of Dalton Higgins book *Hip Hop World* (as reviewed by Neil Armstrong (2009) in the Jamaican paper *The Gleaner*), notes the Caribbean connections of the earliest hip-hop artists: rapper Coke La Rock was born in Jamaica; DJ Kool Herc migrated to the Bronx from Jamaica; Grandmaster Flash, the first to incorporate "turntablism," is from Barbados; and Afrika Bambaataa, "godfather of hip-hop," is of Barbadian and Jamaican heritage.

> Various examples of early hip-hop are available on YouTube, including the following:
>
> Grandmaster Flash and the Furious Five, "The Message" (https://www.youtube.com/watch?v=PobrSpMwKk4)
> The Sugar Hill Gang, "Rapper's Delight" (https://www.youtube.com/watch?v=rKTUAESacQM; lyrics available at https://www.youtube.com/watch?v=tAnojTvyc0g)
> "NY77: The Rap Battle" (https://www.youtube.com/watch?v=2Bb5PHeA2n0&list=PLEBbObMwil-t0V-CwNiway4GMizvaGWQ4&index=9)

The sociologist Orlando Patterson's tracking of reggae music and transnationalism in his article "Ecumenical America: Global Culture and the American Cosmos" (1994) also explores these connections. Patterson uses Jamaican reggae to argue that global cultural interchange does not produce homogeneous Americanization, but rather that local cultures are being revitalized and influencing American culture. The new mixed forms of music are cultural hybrids or creolizations. This mixing is ongoing, pulling African retentions—aspects of culture that have survived through many generations (since Africans came to the Americas)—into new technologies and new political spaces. Jamaica's music has its roots in West Africa and the British Isles, but in the 1950s Jamaicans who worked on American farms brought back cowboy music and bluegrass to their island.

In addition, young men like Bob Marley and Peter Tosh sang American soul music at talent parades, but the Jamaicans adapted soul music by using more African rhythms, creating a new form, known as ska. Ska also developed into dub and rocksteady and then into reggae, played in dance halls, and it became popular not only with local Jamaicans but also with American tourists. Reggae also became associated with Rastafarianism, a religion that includes the idea of redemption as a return to Africa. Mass migration from Jamaica to Britain after World War II helped spread the influence of reggae to Britain and then to Europe, North Africa, and the rest of Africa, where it was fused with other musical influences. A second wave of Caribbean migration took place, this time to New York, following the 1965 Immigration and Nationality Act, which opened the United States to immigrants of color. Patterson argues that it was white middle-class youth who embraced reggae initially, and by the late 1970s, when black Americans embraced it as well, it emerged as rap, "the first popular American music to have an explicitly political lyrical content" (Patterson 1994, 108).

Information on the Jamaican roots of hip-hop and its relationship to reggae can be found on the following web pages:

"BBC—The Story of Reggae—Toasting & MCs," Jammin Reggae Archives (http://niceup.com/history/bbc/toastingsmc.html)

"Jamaican Music," Jamaicans.com (http://www.jamaicans.com/music/articles_reggae/when-did-reggae-become-ra.shtml)

In Jamaica, the working class could not afford individual record players, so entrepreneurs began renting out large sound systems and acting as disc jockeys (DJs). The DJs began to take an active role in manipulating the music, using their voices to make sounds and playing with the turntable, stopping and pushing it backwards, or "dubbing." Jamaican dubbing and toasting (talking and making sounds over the record) morphed into hip-hop's scratching and emceeing, or rapping. Lee "Scratch" Perry started using sound effects as well, mimicking the urban soundscape of guns firing, police sirens, and breaking glass. In Jamaica, two sound systems would compete with each other in the same space, with the DJs working the crowd. Similarly, in the Bronx, DJ Kool Herc started using two turntables at once to create breaks, or heavy percussive sections, in the music.

During the 1970s, sampling and drum machines became available and were incorporated into hip-hop music. B-boying, or break dancing, was done in the break sections created by turntabling. Break crews competed with each other, echoing the competition of gangs. Thus hip-hop, like its Jamaican antecedents, was born out of the grim challenges of urban poverty and oppression, offering entertainment, competition, opportunities for technical and artistic innovation, and a voice for consciousness raising and political critique. It included poetry, music, dance, and politics in perhaps the greatest efflorescence of black culture since the Harlem Renaissance of the 1920s. An early sign of the pan-African themes that reverberate through hip-hop was DJ Afrika Bambaataa's trip to Africa, which led him to transform his followers in the Bronx from a gang into the Universal Zulu Nation, a peaceful organization with branches around the world, including in France, Japan, Holland, Australia, South Korea, and South Africa. In 2012 Bambaataa was named visiting professor of hip-hop at Cornell University.

For information on the Zulu Nation and the history of hip-hop, visit the Zulu Nation website (http://www.zulunation.com/hip-hop-history/).

## The Perils of Commercial Success: Hip-Hop Controversies

By the early 1980s, hip-hop had expanded outside of New York through recordings, spreading transnationally as well as nationally. It also took on a variety of forms, including gangsta rap, popular rap, and conscious rap. The hip-hop created by DJs and MCs in the South Bronx in the early 1970s, like the music in Jamaican dance halls, was part of oral tradition and performance art, created and adapted to a particular moment in a specific setting, but once it was recorded it became fixed, and therefore consumable in many settings. This reproduction of live hip-hop tended to undermine its authenticity.

In an important 1936 essay titled "The Work of Art in the Age of Mechanical Reproduction" (https://www.marxists.org/reference/subject/philosophy/works/ge/benjamin.htm), Walter Benjamin analyzed the difference between an original painting and a mass-producible photograph. What he said can be applied to the difference between a live DJ's hip-hop performance and a recording. While something that is mass produced is more democratic and available to all, it also runs the risk of losing its "aura," or authenticity. Hip-hop created in specific locales is more like an original painting. From the mid-1980s to the early 1990s, hip-hop flourished with Afrocentric lyrics and innovative forms. Californian gangsta rap grew stronger and became extremely successful commercially. By the 1990s hip-hop became the dominant musical genre in the United States with performers like Public Enemy, Vanilla Ice, Dr. Dre, MC Hammer, and Snoop Dog, followed by Eminem and Jay-Z.

Earlier hip-hop artists created their own record labels or signed with small independent companies. But that would soon change. Both the popularity of hip-hop and the deregulation of the media industry—a process begun in 1996 when the Federal Communications Commission (FCC) began allowing cross-ownership among broadcast, Internet, phone, print, and other kinds of media—led to the buying up of small record companies by media giants. This new regulatory environment, strengthened by the FCC in 2003, would lead to massive conglomeration of the media industry. In 2016 there are three major record labels—Sony, Warner, and Universal—that control the music industry. As the large media companies took ownership of hip-hop production and consumption, commercial hip-hop became more homogeneous, foregrounding gangsta rap with its violent images and with bling-wearing black performers expressing misogynistic and homophobic lyrics with scantily clad women "shaking their booties." Women are represented as bitches and "hos." Critics argue that these negative stereotypes of black men and women are marketed to a primarily white audience to satisfy its ambivalent desires regarding the black population, while young men of color perceive these images as representing success and rebellion against an oppressive white establishment. According to the "Media Literacy" web page hosted by PBS's *Independent Lens* program, hip-hop generates $10 billion a year, and 70 percent of it is consumed by white males, while 90 percent of all producers and retailers of hip-hop are white-owned (http://www.pbs.org/independentlens/hiphop/literacy.htm).

> The Public Broadcasting Service (PBS) has a rich collection of resources on hip-hop and its relationship to black culture, some of which is available on these pages:
>
> "Black Culture Connection" (http://www.pbs.org/black-culture/explore/hip-hop/#.U347DHe2l8E)
> *Independent Lens* supplement to the film *Hip-Hop: Beyond Beats and Rhyme* (http://www.pbs.org/independentlens/hiphop/timeline.htm)

The commercial success of hip-hop, its global popularity, and its origins in resistance to oppression have led to numerous controversies, chief among them the commodification of gangsta rap. Whereas the original power of this kind of rap came from its raw expression of the unequal treatment of black men within the American criminal justice system, its commercial success has frozen it into something different. Instead of being a political critique of the predominantly white power structure, it has become a stereotyped expression of gangster lifestyles, such as drug lords drinking champagne and exploiting their "whores." Given the predominantly white audience for this pop gangsta rap, it has stopped being transgressive and satirical and has instead become a means for reinforcing white stereotypes about black males. There is a long colonial and racist tradition in the West of finding the "racialized Other" both alluring and repulsive. This derives from the psychology of colonization and racism. The colonizer takes the traits he or she is not allowed to express in society and projects them onto the racialized Other. If the colonizer or racist desires to be rational and law abiding, the Other is irrational, governed by emotions, and lawless. And, as many commentators have noted, colonizers who live in a sexually repressed society tend to project hypersexuality onto the Other. This psychology legitimizes the oppression of the Other as a dangerous force to be kept under control (see Kitwana 2005). Thus the commercial success of gangsta rap has encouraged its formulaic reproduction and discouraged alternative forms of expression within hip-hop from getting major play time.

---

**Feminist Critiques of Gangsta Rap**

The misogynistic lyrics of gangsta rap have not gone unchallenged by feminists, nor by artists in the hip-hop world itself. For instance, Rosa Clemente, an Afro-Puerto Rican self-styled hip-hop activist, feminist, and 2008 vice presidential candidate for the Green Party, has taken on the misogynist lyrics in popular rap. She critiques what she calls the "rap industrial complex," most recently in the form of rapper Rick Ross's promotion of rape drugs in the song "U.O.E.N.O.," which also includes a product placement for Reeboks. The women's rights group UltraViolet started a petition to get Rick Ross dropped from his Reeboks endorsement, which succeeded on April 11, 2013.

---

Tricia Rose's book *The Hip Hop Wars* (2008) takes up the negative aspects of hip-hop and how they have become prominent in mainstream culture. While she criticizes the dominance of gangsta rap, she also questions the way hip-hop is blamed as a causal factor in violence and misogyny. She argues that far from destroying American values, hip-hop represents them, especially the values of violence, sexism, and money. Rose makes the point that gangsta rap sells and that commercial rappers therefore stick to the successful formulas rather than critiquing violence against black people or the ways that the drug trade has harmed black and Latino communities. Presumably, to do so would not sell as well with the predominantly white audiences. Outside commercially successful recordings, "underground rap" and "conscious rap" do address serious political issues, just as mainstream hip-hop did in its early years. Rose also points out that the value and creativity of rap are denigrated by both supporters and critics of hip-hop. Thus Rose quotes the music and cultural critic Stanley Crouch's dismissal of rap on Oprah's town hall about hip-hop and BET News's *Hip Hop vs. America*, in which Crouch said rap is "Dick and Jane with dirty words." (Rose 2008, 217).

## Transnational Adaptations of Hip-Hop

Through videos and films of break dancing, as well as radio, pirated tapes, and records, hip-hop spread during the 1980s to most corners of the world. It became an important influence on popular music in Japan and Korea, in Western and Eastern Europe, and in many

African countries. But, as a number of scholars argue, hip-hop's influence is both global, as it spreads across oceans and national borders, and extremely local at the same time. Local traditions of both popular and traditional musics have fused with hip-hop, while local values, both cultural and state controlled, have influenced what types of messages will predominate in a particular place. Because global hip-hop is such a massive phenomenon, it is not possible to cover even a tenth of it here. Therefore, the rest of this case study will focus on the circulation of cultural influences through specific locales within the Black Atlantic, using the relationships among American hip-hop, Caribbean musics, and African hip-hop in Ghana and Tanzania. Omitted here are the important locations of the United Kingdom, France, the countries of North Africa, and Senegal, among others.

> For global examples of B-boying or break dancing, see the following YouTube videos:
>
> "Battle: Nutz Crew vs. Everest Crew" (https://www.youtube.com/watch?v=jZE13 iTEM5s)
> "Amazing Day—Final Battle—Morocco vs. Korea" (https://www.youtube.com/watch?v=2-b8rHkV6VI)

As mentioned earlier, the Atlantic slave trade, starting in the late fifteenth century and ending in the 1860s, forcibly moved millions of Africans of many different cultures and languages to the Americas. The African populations adapted to this new world, creolizing their languages, religions, and cultures by mixing with other Africans and by picking up influences from the indigenous peoples and the European colonizers who enslaved them. In addition to the process of cultural adaptation and mixing, members of the African diaspora retained a number of cultural practices and traditions, especially those deriving from oral traditions. Hybrid musical forms have developed out of drumming rhythms, call and response, and verbal play brought from West Africa. Within the English-speaking Caribbean, Jamaica and Trinidad have produced influential styles of music. Trinidadian calypso was popular in the big band era of the 1940s through 1960s, influencing in particular the dominant musical genre of Ghana, called highlife. As discussed earlier, Jamaican reggae had a major impact on world musics in the 1980s. Today Trinidadian soca and Jamaican dancehall compete with and influence each other.

Rap, in particular, can be seen as a close relative of the widespread African oral tradition of the praise song, a rhythmic form of poetry in which a litany of epithets (qualities of a thing or person being praised) is given to a deity, for instance, or trees, villages, or lineages. A poet—known as a griot—would recite the praises of a powerful chief and orally transmit the history of the clan. In some ethnic groups, each person is taught to recite the history of his or her extended family going back untold generations. Using call and response, the griot gives the specifics, and the audience chants a chorus or refrain. In some cases the epithets may be veiled or clever criticism, a prominent feature of Trinidadian calypso. Another word for Trinidadian calypso is *kaiso*, thought to come from the northern Nigeria Hausa word for "bravo," shouted in encouragement to the poet. In African American culture, the art of the clever insult is known as "signifyin'" or "doing the dozens." According to the scholar Henry Louis Gates Jr., in *The Signifying Monkey* (1988), "signifying" is the art of expression through clever figures of speech—from metaphor and irony to exaggeration and understatement. This kind of indirect speech is particularly useful among those subject to powerful others, as the enslaved Africans were.

More recently, as explored later, states in the post-independence period tended to control the content of African-derived popular music for the purposes of nation building, while economic liberalization led to both greater freedom of content and the forces of commercialization.

## Trinidad and Tobago

The African roots of both calypso and hip-hop become evident in their many parallel elements. Calypso has a much gentler sound than rap does, but its content can bite. Part of the events leading up to Carnival, the Trinbagonian version of the festival celebrated at the beginning of the Christian period of Lent, calypso has a long Afro-Trinidadian history. Calypsonians write and perform their songs of social and political critique in calypso tents, and on the Sunday before Ash Wednesday, which ends the Carnival season, they compete for the title of Calypso Monarch. Like hip-hop artists, calypsonians use soubriquets, or stage names, such as Black Stalin, Lord Kitchener, the Mighty Sparrow, Gypsy, Growling Tiger, Chalkdust, and Singing Susan. Often their calypsos include boasts about the singer's prowess and insults toward others. Hip-hop artists also boast, probably more excessively, about themselves and compete with each other in freestyle rapping.

During the period immediately before the 1962 independence of Trinidad and Tobago from Britain, and immediately after it, under the leadership of Prime Minister Eric Williams (1956–1981), calypso was harnessed to the state mission of building a unified nation out of a population that was extremely diverse but had two major subcultures: those whose ancestry was African, and those of Indian descent. Despite Williams's declaration on the occasion of independence in 1962 that there should be no more Mother Africa, no more Mother India, but only Mother Trinidad and Tobago, it was the Afro-Trinidadian traditions of Carnival, calypso, and steel band (or steel pan) that became *the* national traditions. Williams and his political party, the People's National Movement (PNM), created the Best Village competition to promote national artistic expression, especially in those arts that had been banned by the British colonizers, such as drumming.

In this effort to build a strong national identity, musical influences from outside traditions were discouraged, calypsonians living outside the nation could not participate in the Calypso Monarch competition, and calypsos that celebrated the nation tended to make it into the finals of the competition. By the 1970s, however, influences beyond the nation's borders, such as the Hammond B-3 organ, which was central to African American popular music, became a standard element of calypso music.

In the 1970s, soca (from a contraction of soul and calypso) evolved out of calypso, and today soca is the popular music of younger people. The calypsonian Lord Shorty (later Shorty Ras) developed soca by combining Indian tassa drums with calypso lyrics in order to make calypso more inclusive of the Indo-Caribbean population. Soca music is upbeat dance music, with fast rhythms; like dancehall and some hip-hop, it often includes directions for the dancers to perform certain actions. It is associated with "booty shaking," known as "wining" in Trinidad and Tobago, and the lyrics frequently use sexual double-entendres. Both soca and calypso followed the diasporic populations of the West Indies to New York, Toronto, and London; both are also popular throughout all of the Anglophone Caribbean. Although break dancing has found its way into music videos of soca musicians and some of their live performances on tour, "wining" remains the predominant style of dancing.

Trinidad's own music and dance styles have limited the influence of hip-hop seen so strongly in other parts of the world. Nonetheless, a fusion genre called rapso (rap plus calypso) was created by the calypsonian Brother Resistance. He raps about government corruption and social ills over calypso or soca beats. Today, 3canal has evolved rapso into a more techno beat. Brother Resistance views rapso as an anticolonial force that should be used to raise the consciousness of young people. He defines rapso as the "poetry of calypso" and "the rhythm of the word" and has an Afrocentric perspective on calypso and rapso, locating their roots in the role of the West African griot. Rapso maintains a strong stance against the dominance of party and wining lyrics in soca and in favor of what is called "conscious" or "underground" rap, with positive messages of pan-Africanism, respect, and solidarity.

For more information about rapso, see the following web pages and online reports:

"Brother Resistance and 3 Canal Rule Trinidadian Rapso," MTV News (http://www.mtv.com/news/820692/brother-resistance-and-3-canal-rule-trinidadian-rapso/)
"What is Rapso," *The Guardian* (http://www.guardian.co.tt/entertainment/2011/02/22/where-rapso)
"Brother Resistance: Biography" (http://www.brotherresistance.com/biography.htm)
Brother Resistance, "El rey del rapso" (https://www.youtube.com/watch?v=84MV0Ks8H5E)

## Cuba

Part of the Spanish-speaking Caribbean, Cuba has been a powerhouse of African-influenced music. Because slavery continued until 1886 and the colonial government in Cuba allowed Africans to maintain their languages and cultures, Afro-Cubans maintained a vibrant tradition of West African drumming, dancing, and spiritual practices known as Santeria. Prior to the 1959 Cuban Revolution, cross-fertilization between American big band music and Cuban rhythms was common. Whereas pre-revolutionary Cuba tended to marginalize its black population, Fidel Castro, the leader of the revolution and the country until his brother Raul took over in 2008, made Afro-Cubans central to the culture of the nation. The 1991 dissolution of the Soviet Union, upon which Cuba depended for oil and other products, led to the "Special Period" in Cuba, a time of harsh deprivation of material goods. Trucks and agricultural machinery sat rotting because no parts or gasoline to fuel them were available. In order to gain access to foreign exchange, Castro opened the Cuban economy to the U.S. dollar and to tourism, but in a manner still tightly controlled by the state.

Before the collapse of the Soviet Union, hip-hop was viewed with suspicion by the Cuban government, but young people were able to listen to it on radio stations based in Miami. The themes of deprivation and black identity appealed to Cuban youth, especially during the Special Period. Eventually, in 1995, the Havana collective of hip-hop artists called Grupo Uno organized the first annual rap festival in Cuba. The government began to allow rap to express constructive criticism of socialism and to highlight the narrative of African heritage in Cuba. Fidel had promoted the idea that nineteenth-century slave rebellions were the beginning phase of the Cuban Revolution, so the themes of conscious rap fit into this narrative, indigenizing rap to Cuba. In 1997 the Asociación Hermanos Saíz, a state organization for supporting young artists and writers, began funding the rap competition.

According to the music scholar and professor Geoffrey Baker (2005), it was after a 1999 visit to Cuba by Harry Belafonte (a Jamaican-American black activist and musician) that Fidel Castro created Agencia Cubana de Rap (Cuban Rap Agency). Through critiques of global capitalism and racism, Cuban rap could articulate a vision that served the interests of the Cuban state while also connecting with the urban poor suffering under globalization everywhere. The sociology professor Sujatha Fernandes's *Close to the Edge: In Search of the*

*Global Hip-Hop Generation* (2011) highlights the complex relationship between the Cuban state and a music that is meant to be rebellious and critical. Because Fidel represents revolutionary values and his leadership could not afford rebellion against the Cuban Revolution in the younger generation, he supported rap. In fact, it is arguable that he co-opted the music in the mid-1990s, just as Eric Williams exerted control over calypso competitions in the 1960s in the interests of nation building.

Meanwhile, outside of Cuba, a group of Cuban rappers in Paris came together to form a hybrid version of rap that drew on Cuban *son*, a mellow style of music repopularized by the *Buena Vista Social Club* CD (1997) and film (1999). *Son* had been immensely popular in the mid-twentieth century big band format, influencing many types of music, including Ghanaian highlife (though in Africa *son* was known as *rhumba*, an African-based Cuban dance music). However, rappers staying behind in Cuba wanted to distinguish themselves from those abroad by sticking to a noncommercial form of socially conscious rap. Authenticity, or "keeping it real," is central to hip-hop culture. That phrase, used around the world by "conscious" or underground rappers, refers to representing the gritty everyday realities of the inner city. In the Cuban case this is especially about the hardships of the Special Period.

Striking a middle position between the exiles in Paris and the conscious rappers at home, the successful Cuban hip-hop group Orishas was able to balance their representation of Cuban exoticism for international audiences with an "authentic" representation for the home audience. The name "Orisha" refers to the Yoruban word for spirits or deities, thus avowing the powerful connections between the African diaspora and African cultures on the continent. (The Yoruba people live in southeastern Nigeria; their religion remains prominent in a number of former colonies of the Americas, including Trinidad and Tobago and Brazil.) The musicology professor Lea Ramsdell argues that the Orishas' song "Represent" invokes the celebration of *cubania*, the mix of cultures that is the supposed essence of Cuba. While this strongly African-influenced mixture is true of Cuban culture, the reality is that black people are vastly underrepresented in the higher levels of the professions and state organizations. "Represent" mixes English with Spanish to connect with the American and transnational hip-hop cultures. Ramsdell emphasizes the ways that the song reinforces the presentation of Cuba as an island paradise where sexy women are available for the taking (and some money).

The economic situation in Cuba has forced the state to negotiate its way between its revolutionary commitments to socialism and solidarity, on the one hand, and its need to sell itself as a tourist commodity to gain dollars for trade, on the other. The U.S. trade embargo in place since 1959 has helped to establish Cuba as a visual icon of nostalgia: its 1950s American cars, 1980s Soviet cars, and peeling paint on colonial-era buildings, along with its beautiful mountains and beaches, create this aura. These images and the music that evokes them sell authenticity, but arguably they are highly commodified. Thus Ramsdell argues that the *cubania* of the album is packaged for tourist consumption, whereas the Orishas seek to create "authentic" representations of contemporary Cuba. This tension between "keeping it real" and being commercially successful for a wide audience plays out in every location where hip-hop takes root.

For an example of traditional Cuban *son* music, which influenced Ghanaian highlife and many other popular musics of the mid-twentieth century, see the YouTube video of La Familia Valera Miranda performing "Puro Son en Concierto," at https://www.youtube.com/watch?v=nVK5Hko0KWU.

A video of the Cuban hip-hop group Orishas song "Represent," discussed in the text, is also available on YouTube at https://www.youtube.com/watch?v=50kxtUSGMgg&list=RD50kxtUSGMgg.

## Ghana

Hip-hop spread to African countries in the 1980s and 1990s. Just as the Special Period in Cuba was a time of severe hardship, the 1980s in Africa were a brutal time economically. The International Monetary Fund (IMF) was imposing structural adjustment plans (SAPs) on debtor nations, which resulted in severely downsized civil service sectors and a shift from state ownership to private ownership of resources and production. Countries were pressured to channel resources into export products in order to earn hard currency. Societies struggled with high unemployment, lack of government support, and insufficient food and commodities. For many young people in Africa, American hip-hop communicated a "real" sense of urban poverty and racism, and it did so with attitude.

In Ghana, hip-hop–influenced music is called "hiplife," a fusion of international hip-hop and Ghanaian popular highlife music, which was dominant throughout the twentieth century. Ghana was led to independence from the British Empire in 1957 by Kwame Nkrumah, a proponent of African unity and pan-Africanism, which are often themes of "conscious" rap throughout the diaspora. Nkrumah studied in the United States from 1935 to 1945, earning degrees in divinity and philosophy and becoming part of a leftist group of multinational intellectuals, which included the Trinidadian C. L. R. James, a central figure in the African diaspora. While in the United States, Nkrumah learned about the Jamaican Marcus Garvey, who in the early twentieth century led black nationalist and pan-African movements and whose influence is present in some strains of hip-hop today. Nkrumah was critical of both capitalism and colonialism, and he sought alternatives in African culture to counter the destruction European rule and influence had wrought through the imposition of its religion and high culture. He was overthrown in a coup in 1966, but he still commands great respect for his visionary leadership. He also sought to unify the various ethnic groups within Ghana into a single national identity. The Ghanaian emphasis on national culture has made some people critical of hip-hop as a foreign import; thus its fusion with highlife and its commentaries on Ghanaian realities using local languages are especially important.

For an example of highlife music, watch the YouTube video "Classic Ghana Highlife Mix – Old School Mix" (https://www.youtube.com/watch?v=1xqA5-St6zU).
The trailer for the documentary *Living the Hiplife* is available on the Third World Newsreel YouTube channel (https://www.youtube.com/watch?v=qV3a4FKyTFk).

Highlife music developed in the 1920s along the coast of Ghana and Sierra Leone, mixing European music with Trinidadian calypso, Cuban *son* (called *rhumba* in Africa), and local African rhythms. The *clave* rhythm central to Cuban music is considered by ethnomusicologists to be common throughout African musics, and is specifically used in highlife. Ironically, it was brought to Cuba from West Africa, specifically from the area now known as Ghana and Nigeria. By the 1930s, highlife was divided into subgenres: a guitar-based, more African version based in the rural areas; a ballroom dance style for the elite; and a village brass-band style. Highlife was broadly influential in African music through the 1970s, when Congolese *soukous* (called *lingala* in East Africa) became popular in Kenya and Tanzania as the Congo entered into civil war and its musicians migrated. *Soukous* was also heavily influenced by Cuban *son* and Martinican/Guadeloupan *zouk*, which in turn were influenced by Congolese and other African musics. Thus Caribbean and African

American popular musics evolved out of African traditions brought over on slave ships and then returned as modern band music on recordings in the twentieth century to influence dance musics in Africa. Then, in a new wave of transnational diasporic influence, hip-hop flowed from the United States in the late twentieth and early twenty-first centuries to create new genres of local yet pan-African musics.

According to the scholar Jesse Weaver Shipley (2013), hiplife manifests these creolizations: it is a mix of hip-hop styles of rapping, beatmaking, and sampling over highlife music, traditional rhetoric using proverbs, and storytelling of the Akan, a West African people dating back centuries. It came to Ghana with Reggie Rockstone, a Ghanaian who had lived in London and gotten involved in the hip-hop scene there. International hip-hop appealed to Ghana's elite-urban youth in the 1980s, but hit a more popular audience as "hiplife" in the early and mid-1990s, when Rockstone arrived in Accra, the country's capital. Ghana's 1992 constitution mandated privatization of state-owned industries, opening up new media outlets. Radio stations were proliferating, giving airtime to new hip-hop artists, and cheap technology allowed young people to create new music themselves, without the mediation of a recording company. Thus hiplife lent itself to a celebration of entrepreneurship. After all, hip-hop artists create their personae—boasting about their prowess, competing with others—and they succeed through corporate sponsorship and recording contracts. As with American gangsta rap, rappers who start out as insurgent and marginal end up using product placements, showing off their diamonds and luxury cars, and owning businesses. In Ghana, for example, one of the first hip-hop competitions was sponsored by the multinational corporation Nescafe. An early group featured by Reggie Rockstone, called the Mobile Boys, was given a contract to perform an ad for Nescafe. Thus hiplife's indigenous developments were enmeshed with free trade, commodification, and corporate sponsorship.

While hip-hop was at first viewed as foreign, it quickly became infused with indigenous languages, highlife rhythms, and proverbs. Rappers often mixed many local languages within one song, reflecting the multilingualism of Accra. Shipley writes that Ghana is dominated by three musical genres: gospel, highlife, and hiplife. He believes the young are attracted to the cosmopolitan version of Africanness in hiplife. And, as always with hip-hop, it is defined as "real," a real representation of everyday life.

One of the differences between hip-hop in the United States and hip-hop in African societies is the significance of young people (primarily males) taking on a strong public voice. The dominant culture in the United States is youth oriented and individualistic, so it's not odd to see young people speaking out about politics or questioning authority. Gangsta rap even gave voice to those usually silenced in the United States: young men of color in the criminal justice system. Unlike the youth orientation in American society, however, elders hold the privileged place in most African societies, and young people must show respect for them. If rap lyrics resemble praise songs, then young rappers are appropriating a rhetorical role for themselves that is traditionally meant for highly respected elders. This violation of conventional age roles is especially shocking when young rappers criticize their political leaders. The hiplife scholar Halifu Osumare (2012) emphasizes the empowerment of black youth in the rebellious stance of hip-hop despite the global commodification of the music. Shipley, meanwhile, argues that Ghanaian rappers are less rebellious than those in other countries, such as Senegal, and more intent on earning respect. Yet to some degree the Ghanaian youth are being rebellious in seeking respect for their words in public spaces. In a 2014 residency at St. Lawrence University, in New York State, M.anifest, a contemporary hiplife artist from a highly educated Ghanaian family, argued that Ghanaian rappers have been commercialized from the beginning and are perhaps more interested in social commentary than in direct political debate.

Ghanaian hiplife artist M.anifest performs as part of his residency at St. Lawrence University in 2014. As noted in the case study, "hiplife" is a uniquely Ghanaian fusion of highlife music with hip-hop.

*Source:* Tzintzun V. Aguilar Izzo.

## Tanzania

Tanzania in East Africa has less direct historical connection with the Americas than Ghana and other West African countries do, but it has a thriving hip-hop culture—one connected to those of other East African Swahili-speaking nations, including Kenya and Uganda. Like Trinidad and Ghana, Tanzania emerged from colonialism in 1961 under a visionary socialist leader, Julius Nyerere. Nyerere was a strong advocate for equality and pan-Africanism. He fought for black majority rule in South Africa, independence for Zimbabwe, and the end of Idi Amin's dictatorial rule in Uganda. His "Arusha Declaration" of 1967 laid out the policy of his party (TANU) on "Socialism and Self-Reliance." However his core value of *ujamaa*, or family, resulted in the movement of tens of thousands of farmers into mixed-ethnicity collectives. Although huge resistance led to the destruction of many villages, Tanzania does not have the interethnic strife—aggravated by British colonial policies—that has plagued its neighbor Kenya.

Although Nyerere enforced single-party rule, he stepped down voluntarily as president in 1985, opening the way for neoliberal policies such as privatization and IMF-imposed structural adjustment plans. Under Nyerere, state censorship governed what could be recorded or played on the radio, and the state backed affirmative artists who supported it. As in many places, this led to the use of word play in popular music to avoid censorship. The scholar Alex Perullo (2011) points out that a long history of using hidden and double meanings exists in Swahili poetry and song. But when rap entered the country, privatization had led to the development of radio stations and recording studios that were not subject to the censor. The new economic system also made foreign goods available, such as American clothing and hip-hop publications. Initially, Tanzanian rappers used English, but they fairly quickly developed the ability to rap in Swahili and other local languages.

Shortly after economic and political liberalization transformed Tanzania, hip-hop followed. Hip-hop is prominent in slightly different forms in both Arusha, a city bordering Kenya on the north, and in the much larger former capital, Dar es Salaam. The Tanzanian hip-hop popular in Dar es Saalam is known as *bongo flava*. *Bongo* derives from the Swahili word for brains, while *flava* is the local pronunciation of the English word "flavor." The term was coined in 1996 by radio DJ Mike Mhagama. The "brains" part of the term refers to the cleverness and wit required for survival in Dar es Saalam on a daily basis. Rappers sing about problems of everyday life and their sociopolitical causes. Perullo, who characterizes *bongo flava* as a fusion of Caribbean popular musics and rhythm and blues, says many Tanzanian performers prefer the term hip-hop because they see *bongo flava* as too commercialized.

One of the most famous rappers is Professor Jay who told Perullo he was first drawn to the conscious rap of Public Enemy in 1989 through their shared blackness. Professor Jay's song "Ndio Mzee" (Yes elder) uses irony to critique Tanzanian politics. The Swahili word *mzee* is normally used as a term of respect in addressing elders. Tanzanian youth use the term ironically to address each other, but in the song Professor Jay represents an elder running for president who makes absurd proposals to fix Tanzania's problems. A sycophantic chorus keeps saying "yes, elder" to the absurd proposals. The *mzee* makes exaggerated promises to rid the country of poverty, to deliver water and milk through pipes to the whole country, and so forth. According to Perullo, the president of Tanzania, Benjamin Mkapa, used the wildly popular song in a speech, saying he did not want yes men in his government, thus showing he was in touch with popular culture and conferring a new stature on rap. In addition to attacking political issues, rappers speak about social issues such as the status of women and HIV/AIDS. Mr. II wrote the song "Chini ya Miaka Kumi na Nane" (Under the age of 18) empathizing with the plight of girls and women forced into sex work and then reviled by their community. The song prompted major public discourse on the situation of women. A couple of years later, female rappers took up the theme. One of them is Zay B, whose album *Mama Afrika* came out in 2002.

Another Tanzanian success story is that of X Plastaz from Arusha. The group incorporates Maasai (also Masai) language and deep chanting in songs like "Bamiza" and "Msimu Kwa Msimu." Jay Rutledge, the editor of the Rough Guides ethnic music series, arranged their tour of Europe and Latin America, and they recorded an album called *Maasai Hip-Hop* for a German record label. While the incorporation of Maasai language and artists into hip-hop is an extreme localization, their global success—as evidenced by the German production of their album and their attendance at the BET (Black Entertainment Television) Hip-Hop Awards dinner in 2009—paradoxically shows the marketability of indigeneity to transnational audiences. Often in hip-hop, locality, a feeling for place, is considered a key ingredient of authenticity. Although state censorship is no longer an important factor in the content of hip-hop lyrics, Tanzanian society does not approve of cursing or profanity. The values of Nyerere live on in a more subtle form, as the hip-hop community sees its role as raising the consciousness of the public.

For a selection of current *bongo flava* videos, go to http://bongoflava.net/.

For an example of a current *bongo flava* video, go to https://www.youtube.com/watch?v=HxNh5thLnAE/.

For information about X Plastaz, go to https://web.archive.org/web/20110718132958/http://www.xplastaz.com/

Mwenda Ntarangwi (2009), who writes about the regional hip-hop scene in East Africa, emphasizes the agency of hip-hop artists despite the challenges they face within their societies, especially those who come from lower-class backgrounds or marginalized areas. Ntarangwi emphasizes the ways the nation-states have been weakened by neoliberal constraints imposed from the outside, opening up East African countries to floods of foreign imports and diluting the nation's role as educator and socializer of youth. Hip-hop has created a space for young people to fashion themselves and to invent their own African identities within a transnational flow of discourses. Whereas the sociologist Sujatha Fernandes (2011) sees localization as the stronger pole of global hip-hop, Ntarangwi emphasizes its transnationalism, although this is an indigenized transnational sensibility. Among his many experiences with hip-hop in Uganda, Kenya, and Tanzania, he describes visiting the compound of the hip-hip group Ukoo Flani Mau Mau. There he found murals of Malcolm X, the Ethiopian emperor Haile Selassie (who is worshipped by Rastafarians), Bob Marley, the Kenyan freedom fighter Dedan Kimathi, Tupac Shakur, and Notorious Big. These figures reveal the group's pan-African framework, despite the fact that their name, "Mau Mau," refers to a very local war for Kenyan independence fought in the 1950s.

## Hip-Hop and International Relations

Many writers on hip-hop emphasize its rebellious self-fashioning and empowerment of youth facing injustices and restrictions in their societies. For U.S. males in urban ghettos who have thrust themselves onto the international stage and made millions of dollars through their records, their careers have indeed been empowering. Marginalized youth in the rest of the world have latched onto that vision and created new vibrant forms of rap music out of the African American models that were in turn created from African-based oral traditions.

Yet despite the initially transgressive gestures of hip-hop, both corporations and states have employed its power. As explored earlier, Trinidadian prime minister Eric Williams and Cuban leader Fidel Castro tapped into calypso and rap, respectively, for nation-building purposes, and Tanzanian president Benjamin Mkapa tapped into the popularity of "Ndio Mzee" to promise a noncorrupt administration. Recently the U.S. government has also exploited the transnational popularity of hip-hop to promote its interests. The U.S. State Department has used hip-hop in its American Music Abroad program. In 2000–2001, Toni Blackman was the first hip-hop ambassador from the United States, working with DJs and hip-hop communities in Senegal, Congo, and Guyana. The U.S. ambassador to France sponsored hip-hop conferences and in 2010 invited the controversial rap group K.Ommando Toxik to perform at his residence, to the displeasure of French authorities. In 2010 the State Department sent a group called Chen Lo and the Liberation Family to perform in Syria. *Forbes* magazine commented on these trends in an article entitled "Hip-hop Puts America in A Good Light through the State Department's Cultural Ambassador Program" (Blatt 2014). According to the World Hip Hop Market website (worldhiphopmarket.com), U.S. embassies use hip-hop to reach out to Muslim communities by supporting hip-hop groups representing "positive Islam." On the other hand, some European governments practice heavy surveillance of Muslim rap groups and prosecute them for inspiring violence. In 2011 the BBC blocked the words "free Palestine" in a track by British rapper Mic Righteous.

An article published in the respected journal *Foreign Affairs* calls hip-hop music "a new lingua franca for young people—especially marginalized young people—around the world" (Aidi 2014b). When asked why the State Department was sending hip-hop groups to perform abroad, then secretary of state Hillary Clinton told CBS News, "Hip-hop is America . . . . And so is jazz and so is every other form of music with American roots that tell a story" (Clinton 2010). Whether fully intended or not, the meaning of that statement is broad and powerful: to say that hip-hop is America, along with jazz, both rooted in African American culture, is to highlight the centrality of race and slavery in building America and in shaping American culture. Hip-hop also highlights the culture of free speech and critique. Clinton went on to explain that "we have to rebuild the image of our country, who we are as a people, where, you know, we are the most incredibly diverse, successful, freedom-loving people in the history of the world." The culture of free speech and critique is central to American culture, but it is also global, channeled through both underground critique and corporate circuits of production and consumption. Hip-hop's power as a set of modes of expression—through graffiti, break dancing, clothing and bling, and, most powerfully, rhythm and words—has been appropriated and embraced, and adapted and transformed, by youth all around the world to their own local purposes.

The website Hip Hop Diplomacy (http://hiphopdiplomacy.org/) presents case studies of rap's use in counterterrorism, as well as information on controversial arrests of rappers for alleged support of terrorism.

Hisham Aidi's article on "hip-hop diplomacy" is available on the *Foreign Affairs* website (https://www.foreignaffairs.com/articles/united-states/2014-04-16/hip-hop-diplomacy).

## References and Further Research

Aidi, Hisham. 2014a. "America's Hip-Hop Foreign Policy: How Rap became a Battleground in the War on Terror." *The Atlantic*, March 20. http://www.theatlantic.com/international/archive/2014/03/americas-hip-hop-foreign-policy/284522/.

———. 2014b. "Hip-Hop Diplomacy: U.S. Cultural Diplomacy Enters a New Era." *Foreign Affairs*, April 16. http://www.foreignaffairs.com/articles/141190/hisham-aidi/hip-hop-diplomacy.

Armstrong, Neil. 2009. "Hip Hop Book Taps into Jamaican Roots." *The Gleaner*, October 1. http://mobile.jamaica-gleaner.com/20091001/ent/ent1.php.

Baker, Geoffrey. 2005. "Hip Hop, Revolución! Nationalizing Rap in Cuba." *Ethnomusicology* 49, no. 3: 368–402.

———. 2006. "'La Habana que no conoces': Cuban Rap and the Social Construction of Urban Space." *Ethnomusicology Forum* 15, no. 2: 215–246.

Blatt, Ruth. 2014. "Hip-Hop Puts America in a Good Light Through the State Department's Cultural Ambassador Program." *Forbes*, February 26. http://www.forbes.com/sites/ruthblatt/2014/02/26/hip-hop-puts-america-in-a-good-light-through-the-state-departments-cultural-ambassador-program/.

Césaire, Aimé. 1972. *Discourse on Colonialism*. Translated by Joan Pinkham. New York: Monthly Review Press.

Charry, Eric, ed. 2012. *Hip Hop Africa: New African Music in a Globalizing World*. Bloomington: Indiana University Press.

Clark, Msia Kibona. 2007. "Africa: The Rise of African Hip Hop." *AllAfrica*, October 1. http://allafrica.com/stories/200710011449.html.

Clemente, Rosa. February 14, 2014 blog post. http://rosaclemente.net/nicki-minaj-young-money-records-remove-the-picture-of-malcolm-x-now/.

Clinton, Hillary Rodham. 2010. *Interview with CBS Sunday Morning's Tracy Smith*. Washington, DC: U.S. Department of State, June 15. http://www.state.gov/secretary/20092013clinton/rm/2010/06/143956.htm.

Fernandes, Sujatha. 2011. *Close to the Edge: In Search of the Global Hip Hop Generation*. London: Verso.

Gates, Henry Louis, Jr. 1988. *The Signifying Monkey: A Theory of Afro-American Literary Criticism*. New York: Oxford University Press.

Gilroy, Paul. 1993. *The Black Atlantic: Modernity and Double Consciousness*. Cambridge, UK: Harvard University Press.

———. 2011. *Darker Than Blue: On the Moral Economies of Black Atlantic Culture*. Cambridge, MA: Belknap Press of Harvard University Press.

Higgins, Dalton. 2009. *Hip Hop World: A Groundwork Guide*. Berkeley, CA and Toronto, Canada: Groundwood Books.

Kitwana, Bakari. 2005. *Why White Kids Love Hip-Hop: Wangstas, Wiggers, Wannabes, and the New Reality of Race in America*. New York: Basic Books.

Ntarangwi, Mwenda. 2009. *East African Hip Hop: Youth Culture and Globalization*. Urbana: University of Illinois Press.

Osumare, Halifu. 2008. *The Africanist Aesthetic in Global Hip-Hop: Power Moves*. New York: Palgrave Macmillan.

———. 2012. *The Hiplife in Ghana: West Africa Indigenization of Hip-Hop*. New York: Palgrave Macmillan.

Patterson, Orlando. 1994. "Ecumenical America: Global Culture and the American Cosmos." *World Policy Journal* 11, no. 2: 103–117.

Perullo, Alex. 2011. *Live from Dar es Salaam: Popular Music and Tanzania's Music Economy*. Bloomington: Indiana University Press.

Quinn, Eithne. 2005. *Nuthin' but a "G" Thang: The Culture and Commerce of Gangsta Rap*. New York: Columbia University Press.

Ramsdell, Lea. 2012. *Cuban Hip-Hop Goes Global: Orishas' A lo cubano*. *Latin American Music Review* 33, no. 1 (Spring/Summer): 102–123. http://utpress.utexas.edu/index.php/journals/latin-american-music-review#sthash.uXtZ19sF.dpuf.

Rose, Tricia. 2008. *The Hip Hop Wars: What We Talk about When We Talk about Hip Hop—And Why It Matters*. New York: Basic Civitas.

Saucier, P. Khalil. 2011. *Native Tongues: An African Hip-Hop Reader*. Trenton, NJ: Africa World Press.

Shipley, Jesse Weaver. 2013. *Living the Hiplife: Celebrity and Entrepreneurship in Ghanaian Popular Music*. Durham, NC: Duke University Press.

Smith, Tracy. 2010. "U.S. Diplomacy: Hitting the Right Notes." *CBS News*, July 4. http://www.cbsnews.com/news/us-diplomacy-hitting-the-right-notes/.

Weiss, Brad. 2009. *Street Dreams and Hip Hop Barbershops: Global Fantasy in Urban Tanzania*. Bloomington: Indiana University Press.

# 12

# Yoga in America: Competitive Sport or Spiritual Quest?

Globalization is often thought to impose cultural preferences and practices in one direction only: from the wealthy, powerful nations of the West—in particular the United States—to the developing nations of the Global South. Thus, for example, people in the English-speaking Caribbean worry about basketball replacing cricket (which is, ironically, a product of colonial influence), and Islamist leaders worry about the influence of Hollywood sexual mores on their populations. However, there are numerous examples that show cultural influences circulating in multiple directions. This chapter will explore yoga as a powerful cultural practice that has made the journey from India to most parts of the globe, in particular to North America. Focusing on "power yoga" and its antecedent, Ashtanga yoga, this case study will trace the transformation of yoga from a spiritual practice in ancient India to a fitness practice in modern North America.

There are many versions of yoga in the West today, ranging from a quest for spiritual insight to a class at the gym. Yoga was traditionally practiced under the tutelage of a guru, or master, but today it comes in many forms, affected by various social, cultural, and economic factors, which are often divorced from its spiritual roots in Hinduism. "Power yoga," while based in the traditional Ashtanga tradition, developed in the United States in response to American interests in fitness and spread to other, mostly Western, countries. The term "power yoga" was first used in the 1990s, though there is some debate over who coined the term. Beryl Bender Birch published a book, *Power Yoga*, in 1995, but several other Americans are associated with the term and the style of yoga, including Bryan Kest and Baron Baptiste. All of them were students of an Indian teacher, Sri K. Pattabhi Jois (1915–2009), a master of Ashtanga yoga, whose center of study and training is in Mysore, India. Thus, in North America today, yoga sits at a crossroads between a deep Indian heritage and culture, on the one hand, and an American preoccupation with competitive sports and fitness, on the other. Like other globalized cultural forms, it has been hybridized and adapted to a new environment, reflecting its new location more than its origins.

As a hybridized and globalized cultural tradition, power yoga exemplifies some of the controversies that surround the globalization of culture. Multiple issues are at stake in these debates. Some critics suggest that culture and tradition should remain pure and unmixed, and should reject any change as inauthentic. Others celebrate the new creations that result from the mixing of cultural practices and reject the idea that authenticity even exists. Still further, as new cultural forms enter globalized economic markets, some question whether ownership of, and profit from, an adopted cultural practice such as yoga is ethical. These complex issues—with power yoga as an informative example—will be explored in this case study.

## Background on Yoga: Its Origins and History

Before exploring the cases of Ashtanga and power yoga in contemporary North America, it is important to understand something about where yoga comes from and how it was transmitted to the West. Yoga developed on the Indian subcontinent about five thousand years ago. It is associated with Hindu religion (as well as Buddhism and the Jain religion), but Hinduism is itself a diverse set of practices and beliefs, articulated in a set of ancient texts written in Sanskrit: the four Vedas. The concept of *dharma*—rules of conduct, morality, law, or duty—is articulated in these texts. The word "Hindu" derives from the name of a river in the northwest (now Pakistan): the Sindhu, or Indus. The label "Hindu" came from contact with colonialism in India, first by Persians and then by the British. In recent history, a political party known as the Bharatiya Janata Party (BJP) has embraced a fundamentalist form of Hinduism as a national and ethnic identity in India, in contrast with Islam or Christianity. This politicized form of Hinduism attempts to define it as much more unified than the variety of Hinduisms would suggest. Hindus believe in one ultimate divinity that is manifested through multiple gods and goddesses. They also believe that the universe is both cyclical and eternal.

Just as Hinduism is multifaceted and its practices wide ranging, yoga is part of a complex cosmology or worldview, one in which humans seek to free themselves from the limitations of the physical body and to achieve enlightenment, or spiritual transcendence. According to this view, the material self (and the material world) is a kind of error or illusion that keeps us trapped in cycles of suffering. Most Hindus believe that people move through stages of reincarnation (*samsara*) based on *karma* (the consequences of one's actions, which can span different reincarnations), and their goal is to transcend this cycle of birth and rebirth by achieving liberation (*moksha*) from samsara and becoming one with ultimate divinity or consciousness. Yoga is a discipline or set of practices that can help the practitioner do this. It helps individuals achieve self-realization, true consciousness, or the transcendental self, known as *atman*. In this view, the ego, the self we think of as our identity, is false and limiting and responsible for all our suffering in the world.

While yoga's exact origins are subject to debate, it became codified through philosophical writings by the first century CE, when Buddhism and Jainism were flourishing along with Hinduism in South Asia. The earliest written systematization of yoga is Patanjali's Yoga Sutras, believed to have been written between 200 and 400 CE. Patanjali says that hatha yoga, his name for the physical poses of yoga (hatha yoga is often used as a generic term for yoga in the West), is the path to raja (higher or royal) yoga, which leads to the highest state of consciousness. Patanjali defined eight "limbs" of yoga practice:

> Through the practice of the different limbs, or steps to Yoga, whereby impurities are eliminated, there arises an illumination that culminates in discriminative wisdom, or enlightenment. The eight rungs, limbs, or steps of Yoga are the codes of self-regulation or restraint (yamas), observances or practices of self-training (niyamas), postures (asana), expansion of breath and prana (pranayama), withdrawal of the senses (pratyahara), concentration (dharana), meditation (dhyana), and perfected concentration (samadhi).
> (http://www.swamij.com/index-yoga-meditation-yoga-sutras.htm)

Thus the asanas, or poses (postures in the previous translation), of yoga are but one of the eight limbs. About the yoga poses, Patanjali says:

> 2.46.  The posture (asana) for Yoga meditation should be steady, stable, and motionless, as well as comfortable, and this is the third of the eight rungs of Yoga.

2.47. The means of perfecting the posture is that of relaxing or loosening of effort, and allowing attention to merge with endlessness, or the infinite.

2.48. From the attainment of that perfected posture, there arises an unassailable, unimpeded freedom from suffering due to the pairs of opposites (such as heat and cold, good and bad, or pain and pleasure).

(http://www.swamij.com/yoga-sutras-24648.htm)

While poses are central to the way Americans and other Westerners practice yoga, the idea that the poses should be effortless and that the yogi's attention should "merge with the infinite" are less common in the West. Another limb that is commonly practiced in the West is the control of breath, or *pranayama*. Generally, however, Western practitioners are not aware of the higher limbs, which have to do with virtues, self-restraint, and various levels of meditation.

---

### Some Common Yoga Terms

**asana:** poses
**dharma:** the way, or morality
**guru:** spiritual guide or teacher
**moksha:** liberation from reincarnation
**pranayama:** breath control
**samsara:** reincarnation
**vinyasa:** flow of poses

---

Another major text on hatha yoga is the fifteenth-century *Hatha Yoga Pradipika* by Svatmarama, which claims that the Hindu deity Lord Shiva described eighty-four asanas, of which the first four are essential. The first is a seated pose in which the yogi "gazes" into the "third eye," or space between the eyebrows. According to this text, the poses, or asanas, are the first step of hatha yoga, and each is associated with specific health benefits. According to this text, hatha yoga awakens *Kundalini* (literally the "serpent"—that is, the subtle energy coiled at the base of the spine) to move up the central energy channel along the spine. Breath control is practiced to awaken the serpent and open its path up the seven energy points, the *chakras*, of the spiritual body. The chakras are often pictured as a vertical series of lotus blossoms associated with specific colors, parts of the body, mind, and vibrations. The highest chakra is pure consciousness, and when Kundalini reaches this point, enlightenment is achieved. This is described as the union of Kundalini-Shakti (goddess energy) with Shiva (god). The universe itself is a manifestation of the interplay between Shiva and Shakti, consciousness and energy. The energy of Kundalini is typically blocked at the lower chakras, and yoga as a practice is meant to help the subtle energy of Kundalini move past the blockages. The three key blockages are at the root chakra, located at the base of the spine; the throat; and the third eye, representative of the mind.

---

For illustrations and explanations of the chakras, discussed in relation to Kundalini yoga, see the following web pages:

"Chakra Vibrations," SolAwakening (http://solawakening.com/chakra-vibration/)
"Kundalini Yoga," Advaita Yoga Ashrama (http://yoga108.org/pages/show/94)

Within the classical South Asian yoga traditions, the mind–body relationship is a central principle. The ultimate goal of classical yoga is spiritual: the achievement of liberation from reincarnation, hence a release from the physical body, and the attainment of oneness with ultimate consciousness. Nonetheless, bodily practices in the form of poses and other purification rituals are a pathway to the transcendence of the body. Hatha yoga can be interpreted as gaining control over the body before moving into the spiritual practices of raja yoga, which, as mentioned earlier, is considered by Patanjali to be the highest form. Patanjali wrote about yoga from a dualistic perspective, the view that matter (*prakriti*) and mind or consciousness (*purusha*) are two distinct entities—an idea comparable to, though not the same as, the Christian dualism of finite body and eternal soul. For Patanjali, the goal of yoga is to transcend the physical world and find unity with the consciousness that is God. Other classical versions of yoga, including those of Tantrism and Buddhism, by contrast, are nondualist. These philosophies believe that matter is dependent on consciousness and that the purpose of meditation or yoga is to achieve awareness of the illusory nature of the ego and the physical world.

## Hinduism and Yoga Move West

British colonization of India led to an interest in and the study of Indian history and traditions. In the nineteenth century, European and American thinkers were attracted to the ancient Indian texts that dealt with the mind or consciousness. In the United States, Ralph Waldo Emerson and Henry David Thoreau were influenced by Indian thought, as were the German philosopher Arthur Schopenhauer and the Anglo-Irish poet W. B. Yeats, among many others. They were looking for alternatives to Western religions and philosophies. In the early twentieth century, psychoanalytic thought was influenced by Hindu philosophies, and in the 1960s, as a counterculture developed in opposition to mainstream Christianity and the capitalist system, interest in Eastern philosophy and gurus grew.

Swami Vivekananda (1863–1902) is credited with bringing serious attention to Hinduism in the West, starting with his speech at the World's Parliament of Religions in 1893 in Chicago. He was well received by the thousands in attendance, as well as by the press, bringing a message of universal understanding. He opened the door for widespread interest in yoga in the West, teaching that the various versions of Hindu belief and practice are different paths to the same end. He also revitalized Hinduism and nationalism in British-ruled India. Paramahansa Yogananda (1893–1952) came to the United States in 1920 for a religious congress in Boston, founded the Self-Realization Fellowship Order to bring yoga to the world, and based it in Los Angeles. He promoted world unity and peace in many speeches and writings, and his book, *Autobiography of a Yogi*, has sold millions of copies and influenced many celebrities, including Steve Jobs, the founder of Apple. Yogananda practiced kriya yoga, which emphasizes pranayama (breath control) as described in Patanjali's Yoga Sutras. Yogananda describes kriya yoga as follows:

> The Kriya Yogi mentally directs his life energy to revolve, upward and downward, around the six spinal centers (medullary, cervical, dorsal, lumbar, sacral, and coccygeal plexuses) which correspond to the twelve astral signs of the zodiac, the symbolic Cosmic Man. One half-minute of revolution of energy around the sensitive spinal cord of man effects subtle progress in his evolution; that half-minute of Kriya equals one year of natural spiritual unfoldment.

(Chap. 26)

In 1924 the United States imposed strict immigration limits on Indians coming to the country, a policy that encouraged Westerners to travel to India to study with gurus. The limits were removed with the Immigration and Naturalization Act of 1965, which opened up immigration to people from non-European countries. This coincided with the counter-culture movement in the United States and helped foster the growth of yoga in the country. Mahareshi Mahesh Yogi's (1918–2008) Transcendental Meditation movement attracted millions around the world, including the rock group the Beatles. He popularized meditation for the sake of world peace, and in the 1960s he also promoted yoga as a pathway to enlightenment. A. C. Bhaktivedanta Swami (1896–1977) came to the United States in 1965 and established the Hare Krishna movement, the followers of which can still be seen today performing street chanting in Indian robes. Major celebrities became interested in Bhaktivedanta Swami's ideas, including George Harrison of the Beatles, who engaged in extensive conversation with him.

On George Harrison's and the Beatles' roles in popularizing yoga, see the following web pages:

"George Harrison's Spiritual Life," by Joshua M. Greene, *Hinduism Today* (https://www.hinduismtoday.com/modules/smartsection/item.php?itemid=1472)

"In His Own Words: George Harrison on Spirituality," Beliefnet (http://www.beliefnet.com/News/2001/12/In-His-Own-Words-George-Harrison-On-Spirituality.aspx#)

## Yoga Today

There are estimates that twenty million Americans and five million Europeans practice some form of yoga today; however, of these, only a small minority of these individuals are seriously interested in the spiritual goals of classical yoga. Most Westerners practice a version of hatha yoga. Some people simply seek physical exercise and therefore lean toward Ashtanga yoga or its derivative, power yoga. Others are seeking alternative forms of healing to those offered by Western medicine.

### New Age Hybrids of Non-Western Traditions

An example of the fusion of non-Western paradigms of health and healing can be found at the website Chakra Healing (www.Chakrahealing.com). It illustrates the way that various Eastern spiritual practices are intertwined—and confused—in the Western adaptation of yoga. On the site, you can see Chinese and Indian models of the body and the flow of energy, which are merged indistinguishably. It states that energy flows along *meridians*, which is a Chinese concept, and also flows through chakras, an Indian concept (mentioned earlier). It tells the reader that chakra leaks have to be patched to avoid losing "chi," or energy, another Chinese concept. The derivation of these concepts—whether Chinese or Indian—is not mentioned, leaving the user with an incomplete understanding of the practices being advocated.

For reliable information on the types of yoga practice in the United States and the West, the following source is useful:

- "Yoga Disciplines—Different Types of Yoga" (http://www.matsmatsmats.com/yoga/yoga-disciplines.html)

For images of yoga poses as used by Western practitioners, the following sources are useful:

- "Yoga Poses," *Yoga Journal* (http://www.yogajournal.com/poses/finder/browse_categories)
- "Bikram Yoga Poses" (https://www.bikramyoga.com/26-postures/)
- Ashtanga Yoga Poses (http://www.ashtangayoga.info/practice/cheat-sheets-pdf/)

The number of yoga styles in the United States and the West continues to multiply as the practice becomes more popular; the Yoga Journal describes twenty-one types (Cook 2007), and twenty types are listed on the web page "Yoga Disciplines—Different Types of Yoga" (http://www.matsmatsmats.com/yoga/yoga-disciplines.html). Most of these can trace their lineage through gurus to India. Among them are Iyengar yoga, which focuses on precise poses aided by props, such as blocks and straps. Bikram yoga, or, more generically, "hot yoga," is practiced in a room heated to over 100 degrees Fahrenheit. Kundalini yoga, whose purpose is to awaken "serpent" power, uses poses, breath control, chanting, and meditation. A newer form, Svaroopa yoga, is described as "yoga for the rest of us," meaning that a student does not need to be extremely fit or flexible to practice it. The founder of this type of yoga, Swami Nirmalananda, studied Kundalini yoga as well as hatha yoga and meditation. Svaroopa yoga focuses on opening the core spinal muscles for healing and illumination.

At the opposite end of the spectrum from Svaroopa yoga is Ashtanga, which, along with power yoga, is the focus of the rest of this chapter. Ashtanga yoga is the creation of Sri Krishna Pattabhi Jois (1915–2009). His guru, Sri T. Krishnamacharya, also influenced Iyengar and other influential teachers. Jois's Ashtanga Yoga Institute (established in 1948) was located in Mysore, India, and drew many Western students. Jois first came to the United States in 1975, returning in 1978 to California. Whereas hatha yoga focuses on the asanas, or poses, Ashtanga yoga is based on a "flow" through a series of poses coordinated with a particular kind of breath—that is, free breath with sound. The practice creates heat, which is supposed to purify the body and focus the mind. In Ashtanga yoga, a specific sequence of poses must be followed strictly. There are six main series of poses, but very few people get beyond the first one or two series. The sequences were allegedly laid down before the time of Patanjali in a Calcutta manuscript, but the manuscript has not been found. The Ashtanga student is supposed to practice six days per week, preferably at dawn, resting on Saturdays as well as the days of the full and new moon. The sequence of poses is vigorous and physically challenging, requiring a high level of fitness. The adjustments by the teacher can be painful and potentially harmful. For obvious reasons, this type of yoga appeals to competitive, achievement-oriented, and strong individuals. Among the celebrities who practice Ashtanga are Gwyneth Paltrow, Madonna, Sting, and Donna Karan. Because of its difficulty and its association with celebrities, Ashtanga yoga has a kind of elite cachet that some would consider inappropriate to the spiritual side of yoga.

**Power Yoga Illustrated**

An illustration of the fitness ethos of power yoga is evident in this advertisement from a power yoga studio in Buffalo, New York, following the style of Baron Baptiste:

We are not a spa. This is hard. We just want you [to] know that going in. You will not sit and relax. You stretch. And work. And push. And sweat. You will be renewed, but it will be up to you to make it happen. The body can do amazing things if the mind is willing. This will be the best workout you have ever had. And one of the hardest things you have ever done. The miracle isn't that you finish. It's that you have the courage to start. Welcome to Power Yoga Buffalo. (http://power yogabuffalo.com/)

Power yoga, which does not follow a set of series of poses, is an Americanized adaptation of Ashtanga yoga, suited to those who seek an athletic workout. Both Beryl Bender Birch of New York and Bryan Kest of Los Angeles, developers of power yoga, studied with Pattabhi Jois. Birch also studied Kundalini and Iyengar yoga. She traveled to India in 1974 in search of enlightenment, so she is no stranger to the classical tradition of yoga, but she has

In Yokosuka, Japan, Chieko Koymama conducts a yoga class in the hangar bay aboard the aircraft carrier *USS George Washington* (CVN 73) in February 2012. Illustrating the broad adaptations of yoga today, Koymama instructed both sailors and civilians on proper stretching techniques.

*Source:* U.S. Navy/Mass Communication Specialist Seaman Recruit Brian Abel/Wikimedia Commons. https://commons.wikimedia.org/wiki/File:US_Navy_120213-N-ZT599-068_Chieko_Koymama,_a_yoga_instructor_with_morale,_welfare_and_recreation_conducts_a_yoga_class_in_the_hangar_bay_aboard_the.jpg

embraced American pragmatism in adapting yoga to gym culture. And with her book, *Power Yoga*, published in 1995, she severed her relationship with Jois. As practiced and promoted by Birch, Kest, and others, power yoga is indeed quite distinct from its Ashtanga roots. Birch subsequently wrote *Beyond Power Yoga* (2000), in which she returned to the eight limbs of Patanjali's Yoga Sutras, asserting that power yoga was only the first level of Ashtanga yoga. She linked the seven subsequent stages to the seven chakras, thereby seeming to want to return to the fold of Ashtanga. However, in her next book, *Boomer Yoga* (2009), written for the aging baby boomer generation, she again espoused the more health- and fitness-oriented goals of power yoga.

> For a half-hour introduction to power yoga, see the video *Power Yoga with Bryan Jones*, available on YouTube (https://www.youtube.com/watch?v=hWhTRSUkxbY).

## Controversies Over Yoga Today

One consequence of the adaptation of power yoga to American gym culture is that many students who take a class believe they are practicing yoga but have no idea of the spiritual aims of the tradition. Indeed, many Americans who take yoga would be uncomfortable with the religious or spiritual aims of the practice. Numerous websites raise the issue of whether practicing yoga is equivalent to practicing the Hindu religion. This has been an issue in American public schools, where the practice of school prayer has been forbidden by the Supreme Court. It is also an issue in some British Christian church halls, where yoga classes have been held, and for Muslim and Jewish yoga practitioners. Parents in Encinitas, California, brought a suit to stop the teaching of yoga in their elementary schools, but the court ruled against them, arguing that the yoga being taught had been purged of its Hindu roots. The postures, based on Ashtanga, have been renamed in cute English-language terms for the children. For instance, the lotus pose (*padmasana*) is called "criss-cross applesauce." Ironically, it is Christian opponents of yoga who are publicizing its Hindu meaning and history for a public who sees it as a series of exercises with health benefits, such as stress relief. In another cultural twist, an alternative to yoga called "Praise Moves" has been developed for Christians to recite verses from the Bible while doing stretching exercises. Yet many Christians, ministers and priests included, think the practice of yoga, including its mental and spiritual benefits, can be reconciled with Christianity. They point out the fact that yoga was developed by three different religious groups in India—Hindus, Jains, and Buddhists—and that its roots are more philosophical than religious.

> For a discussion of the religious implications of doing yoga, read William Kremer's article "Does Doing Yoga Make You a Hindu?"
> (http://www.bbc.com/news/magazine-25006926).

Another kind of controversy surrounds the contemporary practice of yoga in Western countries, especially the United States: its relationship to commercial interests and capitalist values. Earlier generations of Westerners who embraced yoga's Hindu roots saw it as a kind of holistic practice that offered an antidote to Western materialism. The authority of yoga gurus has traditionally been passed down from one mentor to another, creating certain lineages with different emphases, but still with some assurance that traditional practices, and the meaning behind them, have been preserved. However, some high-profile leaders in different types of yoga practices have sought to brand their versions of yoga and copyright their approaches in hopes of garnering intellectual property rights for themselves and the yoga schools or authorities they represent. Bikram Choudhury, the founder of Bikram Yoga (performed in extremely hot rooms) has sought to copyright his approach for years, initially with some success. In 2011, however, the U.S. Copyright Office said it would not recognize copyright protection for the sequencing of yoga poses nor for the poses themselves (if they are traditional). The name "Bikram yoga" can be trademarked, but more generic names, like hatha yoga, cannot.

---

**And the Winner Is . . .**

Given the preoccupation with sports training and competition, perhaps it's not surprising that there's a push to make yoga an Olympic sport. In the run-up to the 2012 London Olympics, news outlets such as *Time* magazine and CBS News carried stories on whether yoga should become an Olympic sport. There is already a National Yoga Asana Championship. USA Yoga, which sponsors the competition, is headed by Rajashree Choudhury, the widow of Bikram Choudhury. According to their website, USA Yoga is a nonprofit organization formed for the purpose of developing and promoting Yoga Asana (yoga postures) as a sport. Choudhury defends the competition as being only about the poses and not about the eight limbs of yoga per se. Competitors perform seven poses in three minutes, five required and two poses of their choice. They are judged much the way a gymnast would be. Interestingly, both Bikram and Rajashree competed in asana competitions in India growing up, but she sees the Indian attitude toward these competitions as focused within the individual and not against the others. Most American yogis and yoginis (female yoga practitioners) who seek a spiritual alternative to American culture find this competitiveness so distasteful because it enmeshes yoga in the values they seek to escape.

---

With the growing popularity of yoga in the West, there has been an explosion of yoga-related commodities as well. Numerous brands of expensive yoga clothes, sold in catalogues such as prAna, Athleta, and Garnet Hill, have sprung up. One of more trendy brands, Lululemon Athletica, created a major scandal in 2013 when it came to the public's attention that their yoga pants were see-through and revealing. This led to a lawsuit by the company's stockholders. The pants were recalled, and the company lost $2 billion in market share. In April 2014 a judge dismissed the case, but the intense commodification of apparel to be worn in what was once a spiritual, anti-materialistic world tradition, seems highly ironic—an irony not lost on a lot of observers.

Over the past few years, several articles have been published in well-respected American media outlets criticizing yoga and its place in contemporary American society. These critiques, more from the left than from right-wing Christians, are often aimed at the upper-middle class and celebrity associations with yoga, especially Ashtanga yoga. One article in the *Huffington Post*, "Five Words That Do *Not* Belong in Yoga" (2009), was written by Lauren Cahn, a "recovering" Ashtanga follower who writes a blog called *Yoga Chickie*. Having become disenchanted with Ashtanga, she critiques it and its practitioners harshly in the article. According to her post, the five words that don't belong in yoga are "criminal" (as in breaking the strict rules and protocols of Ashtanga), "crank" (as in having your teacher or yourself crank your leg into position), "bad" (not being good at a pose), "cheating" (getting into a pose the wrong way), and "pain" (a good thing in Ashtanga yoga). As Cahn points out, most of these concepts go against the more traditional goals of yoga practice, helping to still your mind and bring inner peace and unity.

A much discussed 2012 article by William J. Broad in the *New York Times* was headlined "How Yoga Can Wreck Your Body." The article is a short version of a book on the same topic. The author himself severely hurt his back doing yoga, and he summarizes a number of medical studies claiming that yoga poses such as headstands can cause strokes and spinal damage. Some of this comes from teachers who are not sensitive to pupils' limitations or weaknesses and from what Cahn, in her *Huffington Post* article, refers to as cranking the body into extreme positions. Practices like Ashtanga are more prone to such injuries than ones that use props like Iyengar or Svaroopa.

Even more damning is a *Vanity Fair* article on the growing commercialized context of Ashtanga yoga. In "Whose Yoga Is It, Anyway?"(2012), Bethany McLean raises concerns about what has happened to the Ashtanga yoga "industry" since the death of Pattabhi Jois (referred to as Guruji by his followers) in 2009. Sonia Jones, a wealthy philanthropist from Greenwich, Connecticut, has partnered with Jois's daughter and grandson, Sharath, as well as Jones's friend, Salima Ruffin, to create a brand called "Jois yoga" and a corresponding line of yoga clothes. According to McLean, the community of Ashtanga teachers certified by Jois is unhappy about the apparent commercialization of their strenuous and disciplined practice. Sharath is now the only person who can certify a teacher of Ashtanga, and the teacher has to travel to Mysore in India, where Jois was based, to take the teacher-training class. McLean points to the Jois's family's negative attitude toward power yoga, which they view as a threat to the Jois style of yoga. On the other hand, a number of Ashtanga teachers certified by Jois told McLean that he always said yoga was universal and that his method came from the Patanjali Sutras. The commercial nature of the new Jois yoga is exemplified in their Encinitas, California, studio and boutique, which cost a million dollars to build, and by their website (http://joisyoga.com/), which advertises the clothing line and explains their philosophy.

> This Huffington Post article, "I Am So Much More Spiritual than You" (http://www.huffingtonpost.com/toni-nagy/stress-relief-humor_b_942383.html), offers a humorous take on the ways yoga has been adopted (or perverted) in the United States and other Western countries.

***

The transnational adaptation of yoga illustrates the value and power of cross-cultural exchange. It also shows, in an undeniably ironic way, the (perverted, some would say) application of the capitalist economic system—that is, the protection of intellectual property in terms of private ownership—to an ages-old tradition that could never be legitimately "owned" by any one person or entity. On the one hand, Americanized yoga offers an alternative path to holistic healing, stress relief, quieting the mind, and, for some, transcendence of the ego or perception of the divinity within themselves. On the other hand, it is simply another form of exercise that enhances flexibility and can be combined with Pilates for core strengthening. It can offer another way to achieve physical superiority alongside running races and triathlons. However, it's likely that most practitioners—or at least many of them—have learned more than physical poses and strength from their exposure to Indian philosophy and yoga. They have come to value peace and internal exploration, which often seems crowded out of American life from early in a child's life. Stilling the mind and turning inward seems even more valuable in a world where most people are attached to electronic devices and social media almost constantly. As those who fear Hindu indoctrination accompanying the practice of yoga argue, perhaps even those doing the poses as exercise will find some kind of peace and inner reflection entering their bodies unaware.

## References and Further Research

Birch, Beryl Bender. 1995. *Power Yoga: The Total Strength and Flexibility Workout*. New York: Simon & Schuster.

———. 2000. *Beyond Power Yoga*. New York: Fireside.

———. 2009. *Boomer Yoga*. South Portland, ME: Sellers.

Broad, William J. 2012. "How Yoga Can Wreck Your Body." *New York Times Magazine*, January 5. http://www.nytimes.com/2012/01/08/magazine/how-yoga-can-wreck-your-body.html?pagewanted=all&_r=0.

———. 2012. *The Science of Yoga: The Risks and Rewards*. New York: Simon and Schuster.

Cahn, Lauren. 2009. "Five Words That Do *Not* Belong in Yoga." *HuffPost Healthy Living*, August 3. http://www.huffingtonpost.com/lauren-cahn/five-words-that-do-emnote_b_250065.html.

Cook, Jennifer. 2007. "Find Your Match among the Many Types of Yoga." *Yogajournal.com*, August 28. http://www.yogajournal.com/article/beginners/not-all-yoga-is-created-equal/.

Feuerstein, George. 1996. *The Philosophy of Classical Yoga*. Rochester, VT: Inner Traditions.

Grossman, Samantha. 2012. "Should Yoga be an Olympic Sport?" *Time*, February 29. http://newsfeed.time.com/2012/02/29/should-yoga-be-an-olympic-sport/.

*Hare Krishna Home Page*. http://www.harekrishna.com/.

*K. Pattabji Jois Ashtanga Yoga Institute*. "*Biographies.*" http://kpjayi.org/biographies/k-pattabhi-jois.

Kremer, William. 2013. "Does Doing Yoga Make You a Hindu?" *BBC News*, November 20. http://www.bbc.com/news/magazine-25006926.

Lasater, Judith. 2007. "Beginning the Journey." *Yoga Journal*, August 28. http://www.yogajournal.com/wisdom/462.

McLean, Bethany. 2012. "Whose Yoga Is It, Anyway?" *Vanity Fair*, April. http://www.vanityfair.com/business/2012/04/krishna-pattanbhi-trophy-wife-ashtanga-yoga.

Moss, Rebecca. 2012. "Hold That Pose: Federal Judge Rules That Bikram Yoga Cannot be Copyrighted." *Village Voice*, December 19. http://blogs.villagevoice.com/runninscared/2012/12/hold_that_pose.php.

Peterson, Hayley. 2013. "The Sheer Yoga Pants That Lululemon Recalled Are Back in Stores and Selling for $92." *Business Insider*, November 12. http://www.businessinsider.com/lululemon-sells-recalled-sheer-pants-2013-11.

Svatmarama, and Brian Dana Akers, trans. 2002. *The Hatha Yoga Pradipika*. Woodstock, NY: YogaVidya.com.

Swami Satchidananda, trans. 2012. *The Yoga Sutras of Patanjali*. Yogaville, VA: Integral Yoga Publications.

Transcendental Meditation. http://www.tm.org/enlightenment. USA Yoga. http://www.usayoga.org/.

Wright, David, Ben Newman, and Lauren Effron. 2012. "Bikram Yoga Guru Reaches Settlement in Copyright Suit." *ABC News*, December 3. http://abcnews.go.com/Business/bikram-yoga-guru-reaches-settlement-copyright-suit/story?id=17869598.

"Yoga Poses as Olympic Sport: Is That a Stretch?" 2012. CBS News, February 28. http://www.cbsnews.com/news/yoga-poses-as-olympic-sport-is-that-a-stretch/.

"Yoga Sutras of Patanjali." SwamiJ.com Yoga Meditation. http://www.swamij.com/yoga-sutras.htm.

Yogananda, Paramahansa (Swami Vivekenanda). 1946. *Autobiography of a Yogi*. New York: Philosophical Library.

# 13

## Global Solidarity Movements: Palestine, Tibet, and Beyond

Solidarity is the most fundamental building block of what many scholars have called "globalization from below," or the process of creating grassroots linkages and movements in response to pervasive global hierarchies and injustices. While there is nothing new about people using feelings of solidarity to inform political action, the emergence of new media and information technologies in recent decades has altered the conditions of possibility for solidarity movements and for the efforts of powerful actors to respond to such movements. Any attempt to understand contemporary solidarity movements, therefore, must not only place them in historical context, but also examine how they are embedded in the changing dynamics of globalization itself. In other words, to adopt Raymond Williams's famous terminology from British cultural studies, solidarity movements always include both residual and emergent elements.

But what is solidarity itself? At its core, solidarity is a human impulse that combines a number of principles:

- Common humanity: The belief in the value of nurturing connections across the social divisions that are created and exploited by dominant social groups.
- Hope: The belief that another, more just world is possible.
- Collective action: The belief that dominant social structures can be transformed from the bottom up.
- Unity of struggles: The belief that because "injustice anywhere is a threat to justice everywhere," as Dr. Martin Luther King Jr. put it, the pursuit of global justice requires solidarity with other struggles.

Solidarity is thus a political commitment grounded in a specific kind of social relationship, one based on mutual responsibility rather than exploitation, passive interaction, or charity. Solidarity is about working together across lines of difference to support those who are struggling for social justice and, by extension, create a better world for all. Given that narratives of globalization often focus disproportionately on the actions of states and other elite actors, it is important to pay attention to solidarity movements that operate at the grassroots level. Doing so can help us construct what might be called a "people's history" of globalization.

### Solidarity and Solidarity Movements: A Brief History

Some of the earliest and most influential examples of global solidarity movements were truly "universalist" in their orientation, consciously seeking to act beyond and against the national borders separating vulnerable groups. For these movements, the struggle was assumed to be located everywhere, and the constituency was potentially enormous—it might, for example, include all workers, all women, all people of African descent, or even all humans. Scholars have explored at great length these forms of internationalism and their connection with specific political frameworks (e.g., socialism, communism, anticolonialism, antifascism, feminism, Afrocentrism, liberation theology) and geopolitical and geocultural formations (e.g., the United Nations, the Non-Aligned Movement, the Socialist International, the Islamic *ummah*). The political commitments animating these universalist movements remain profoundly influential today even as the movements themselves have evolved in response to changing political conditions and critiques (e.g., the postcolonial critique of feminist universalism).

Since the early 1990s, new solidarity movements have emerged in response to relatively local struggles that are seen by many to have a global significance, even if the struggle itself is not universal in the sense that, say, the women's movement once claimed to be universal. The technologies associated with time-space compression—primarily transnational networks of high-speed transportation and information exchange—enable such local struggles to rise to the global level, entering the political consciousness of people in all corners of the globe. One early prophetic case was the Spanish Civil War (1936–1939), which drew thousands of volunteers (known as *brigadistas*, after the "International Brigades" to which they belonged) from outside Spain to defend the country's first democratic government against the fascist forces led by General Francisco Franco.

More recently, four struggles grounded in different parts of the world are noteworthy for having generated strong corresponding movements of global solidarity. The connections among them reveal important aspects of how solidarity movements fit into the larger picture of globalization. First, the struggle for Tibetan liberation from Chinese rule has grown from a local independence movement starting in the late 1950s into a global cause, a process that has gone hand in hand with the transnational diffusion of interest in Buddhism. Second, the struggle against apartheid in South Africa was a focus of global activism throughout the 1970s and 1980s. Anti-apartheid activists sought to bring economic pressure on the South African government, drawing on existing bonds of Third World solidarity but also on traditions of protest associated with the civil rights movement in the United States. Third, in the same year that South Africa held its first democratic elections (1994), indigenous activists in Chiapas, Mexico, launched what became known as the Zapatista revolt in response to the inauguration of the North American Free Trade Agreement (NAFTA). The movement quickly achieved global notoriety thanks to its close connection with the emerging issue of neoliberal restructuring and its effect on indigenous people and other subaltern groups. Finally, a significant increase in solidarity activity with the Palestinian liberation struggle has emerged since the outbreak of the second Palestinian intifada (uprising) in 2000, leading most recently to a South Africa–inspired focus on boycott, divestment, and sanctions (BDS) as a strategy for pressuring Israel to change its policies toward the Palestinians.

While there are important differences between the universalist movements and the more recent ones just mentioned, both types of solidarity movements seek to make connections between the local and the global. The universalist movements provide a global language through which to make sense of local conditions (e.g., in the case of the labor movement), whereas the more recent movements often provide a local language through which to make sense of global conditions (e.g., in the case of the Zapatista movement). The World Social Forum (WSF), launched in 2001 in Porto Alegre, Brazil, provides an instructive illustration of the relationship between the local and global. Often described as a "movement of movements," the WSF seeks to serve as a kind of umbrella movement, enabling activists to maintain a productive balance between unity and diversity, the local and the global, the universal and the particular. Seeking such a balance is a key concern of all contemporary solidarity movements.

## Social and Cultural Elements of Solidarity Movements

In his influential article "Disjuncture and Difference in the Global Cultural Economy," Arjun Appadurai argues that the present era of globalization is marked by "a new role for the imagination in social life" (1996, 31). He further contends that the increasing speed and complexity of global flows lead to new opportunities for people to reimagine the world as they see and experience it via their own complex social locations and angles of vision. Solidarity movements fit into this picture because they challenge us to imagine new kinds of connections, rethink the constructed boundaries between Self and Other, and envision alternative futures. Appadurai's related concept of "scapes"—areas of human life and interaction—can help us pinpoint some of the most important social and cultural elements of contemporary solidarity movements. Each of the five types of scapes discussed in his article (ethnoscapes, technoscapes, financescapes, mediascapes, and ideoscapes) and also discussed in Chapter 3 of this volume can be seen in the operation of these movements.

Many of the local struggles that inspire global solidarity movements are marked by intense forms of deterritorialization. As discussed later, this is particularly true in the case of settler colonial situations, where the creation of a new settler society is predicated on the displacement of the indigenous population. The resulting forms of geographic and social dislocation—diasporas, expulsion, labor migration, political exile, rural dislocation, and so forth—are key factors generating what Appadurai calls ethnoscapes, and these in turn become defining features of the new solidarity movements described earlier. It is impossible to imagine such a movement today without the prominent role played by people on the move, whether South Africans or Tibetans in exile or international volunteers going to Gaza or Chiapas to lend direct support to the struggles there.

Transnational activist networks (TANs) such as the WSF or networks of human rights activists are examples of ethnoscapes in action, with individuals from diverse backgrounds collaborating in organizations, on university campuses, in the streets, and in all the other spaces traditionally associated with civil society. In addition, the use of virtual spaces by solidarity movements for organizational purposes, combined with the growing use of social media and other technologies of accelerated communication for purposes of bearing witness and sharing information with the public, suggests the operation of technoscapes. The same technologies, of course, are also available to governments, corporations, and other institutions to which solidarity movements are often responding.

The presence of financescapes can be seen when solidarity movements adopt tactics of economic pressure, such as boycotts and divestment, to further their goals. In doing so, they take advantage of the networked nature of the global economy, knowing that as they target key companies and industries, the very connectedness of the system will help spread the ripple effects of these actions. In some cases, boycotts represent a form of cultural activism connected with mediascapes, such as when prominent artists express their solidarity by refusing to perform in a particular country (e.g., apartheid South Africa). Similarly, major cultural events such as benefits (e.g., the annual Tibet House US Benefit Concert), pop songs (e.g., 1985's "Sun City"), and documentary films (e.g., 2012's Academy Award–nominated *5 Broken Cameras*) can play a significant role in solidarity movements by using the mass media to promote awareness of the conditions faced by disenfranchised groups.

### Examples of Cultural Activism

Information on the annual Tibet House US Benefit Concert, which is held at Carnegie Hall in New York City, can be found on the Tibet House website (https://tibethouse. us/benefit-concert/).

"Sun City" is a famous example of what is sometimes called "charity rock." Many versions of the song, written by Steven Van Zandt and recorded by Artists United Against Apartheid, can be found on YouTube.

Information about the movie *5 Broken Cameras*—including notes from the film-makers and how to view the movie—can be found on the Kino Lorber website (http://www.kinolorber.com/5brokencameras/).

The idea of mediascapes can also help us understand why many solidarity movements come to be defined in the popular imagination by iconic images and personalities. The Dalai Lama, for example, is the symbol most widely associated with the struggle for Tibetan liberation (despite the fact that he has not taken a position in favor of Tibetan independence), just as Nelson Mandela became a global icon for his role in the anti-apartheid movement and South Africa's subsequent transition to majority rule. The leaders of the Zapatista movement were clearly aware of the importance of mediascapes, choosing to cultivate a mysterious image of rebellious anonymity symbolized by their leader, Subcomandante Marcos, who is regularly portrayed wearing a ski mask.

The global circulation of these iconic images reveals the existence of powerful ideoscapes that shape people's ideas about power, resistance, and the possibilities for social change. These ideoscapes are made up of more than just images, however. They also include words and phrases, narratives and chronologies, categories and intellectual frameworks—in short,

Musician Harri Stojka and his band prepare to perform at a 2012 Europe for Tibet solidarity rally held in Vienna, Austria. The Dalai Lama addressed the gathering, which drew several thousand people to Vienna's Heldenplatz Square.

*Source:* Wolfgang H. Wögerer/Wikimedia Commons. http://commons.wikimedia.org/wiki/File:Vienna_ 2012–05–26_-_Europe_for_Tibet_Solidarity_Rally_011_Harri_Stojka_and_band,_soundcheck.jpg

an endless supply of material through which meaning can be created and re-created. For all of these reasons, a close look at the social and cultural elements of global solidarity movements can help us understand something important about how grassroots activism generates new ways of imagining and organizing the world.

## Local Struggles in a Global Context

The struggle for Palestinian rights has emerged in recent decades as a global symbol of resistance, a magnet for solidarity activism, and a key theme in the larger global justice movement. Palestine's relatively small size, in other words, is far outstripped by its growing transnational significance. Examining how Palestine fits into larger global processes can help us see how all of the contemporary solidarity movements under consideration here (Palestine, South Africa, Tibet, and Chiapas) are connected with one another and how they all reveal the operation of the scapes discussed earlier.

The basic historical and political outlines of what Edward Said called "the question of Palestine" are well known and demonstrate that this "question" has always been a global question, affecting the lives of people on the ground in and around Israel/Palestine but also being shaped by global processes and, in turn, producing effects that reverberate throughout the world. Seeking to respond to an ongoing climate of anti-Semitism in nineteenth-century Europe, the Zionist movement sought to create a national home for the Jewish people in Palestine. In carrying out this project, it borrowed from the attitudes and practices associated with European imperialism and colonialism in general, and settler colonialism in particular (see later). The indigenous Arab population of Palestine was ultimately displaced in large numbers, with roughly 800,000 becoming refugees either in the West Bank and Gaza (controlled by Jordan and Egypt, respectively) or in surrounding countries during the violent process that culminated in the creation of the State of Israel in 1948. This near-destruction of Palestinian society, an event referred to by Palestinians as the "Nakba" (catastrophe), produced the territorial and demographic space for a majority-Jewish state in the immediate aftermath of the Holocaust while ironically beginning a new diaspora—that of the Palestinians.

> To get a sense of the cultural and social impact of the Nakba on Palestinians, it is helpful to know something about the society that was broken apart through the creation of the State of Israel. For a useful online guide to the lives of Palestinians before the Nakba, see the web page "Before Their Diaspora" on the website of the Institute for Palestine Studies (http://btd.palestine-studies.org/).

Israel expanded its territorial reach when it captured the West Bank and Gaza during the 1967 Arab-Israeli War, creating an additional outflow of Palestinian refugees. Since that time, benefiting from high levels of U.S. financial and diplomatic support, it has created dozens of Jewish-only settlement colonies in these conquered territories, along with the infrastructure to support them. Palestinians in the West Bank and Gaza have lived under Israeli military occupation for decades, subject to state-sponsored land confiscation, house demolitions, mass arrests, and bureaucratic harassment. Palestinians living inside Israel, despite making up roughly 20 percent of the overall Israeli population, have been second-class citizens in a state that defines itself in explicitly ethnoreligious terms as the state of the Jewish people and that makes a basic legal distinction between Jews and non-Jews. Palestinian resistance to the settler project has taken a variety of forms, ranging from peaceful protest (e.g., in response to rural land confiscation) to mass rebellion (e.g., in the 1987 popular uprising known as the "intifada") to armed struggle (e.g., in the form of guerrilla attacks and suicide bombings).

Most scholarly and other public discourse has used an international relations paradigm to construct Palestine as the site of a "conflict" between two equal parties (Israeli Jews and Palestinians). In addition to downplaying the obvious power imbalance between the two groups, such a frame privileges the role of states and elites in seeking and carrying out the solution to the "conflict." An international relations perspective also fits smoothly with official Israeli discourse, which seeks to frame the issue in a state-centric way as a problem of national defense, national security, and anti-terrorism. By contrast, the Palestine solidarity movement looks at the issue from an indigenous perspective, constructing it as a human and civil rights problem, and as part of a wider struggle against the effects of a series of global structures and processes, three of which are especially salient in this context: settler colonialism, apartheid, and neoliberalism. The movement emphasizes the role of transnational, grassroots activism in changing public opinion, putting pressure on states and elites, and creating new political realities.

The concepts of settler colonialism and apartheid provide some context for understanding the longstanding bonds of solidarity between Palestinians and black South Africans. (Some would argue that settler colonialism is also relevant to the case of Tibet, where Chinese settlement since 1950 constitutes one of the main grievances of the Tibetan independence movement.) What makes settler colonialism distinct from other forms of colonialism (e.g., the British in India or the Dutch in Indonesia) is that settler colonizers set out to create a new, permanent society in place of an existing, indigenous one. In other words, settler colonialism is about more than temporary, small-scale settlement for the purpose of exploiting labor and resources; rather, it is about the permanent structural transformation of the society and territory in question. Politically, settler projects are grounded in the desire to negate indigenous sovereignty, a goal that is typically pursued through the wholesale displacement (and sometimes the near elimination) of the indigenous population; they are built upon what the anthropologist Patrick Wolfe calls a "logic of elimination" (2006, 387).

In recent years the study of settler colonialism has emerged as a distinct interdisciplinary field drawing on scholarship in history, anthropology, cultural studies, indigenous studies, and other fields. For more information on how scholars are approaching the study of settler colonialism, see the journal *Settler Colonial Studies* (http://www.tandfonline.com/loi/rset20#.VISHycmy7f0).

The Voortrekker Monument in South Africa, created to memorialize the Afrikaner settlers whose "Great Trek" outward from the Cape of Good Hope expanded the frontiers of white settlement in the nineteenth century, reveals some of the cultural connections among settler projects. The monument includes images of covered wagons and women wearing bonnets, recalling the westward expansion of white settlers in North America. For more information, see the official Voortrekker Monument website (http://www.vtm.org.za/).

The term *apartheid*, originally used to describe South Africa's formal system of racial separation and discrimination between 1948 and 1994, has come to be used in a number of other contexts in recent years. Given the settler-colonial similarities between South Africa and Israel/Palestine, it is not surprising that solidarity activists are now using the term regularly to characterize how Israel's control of Palestine involves structures of hierarchy and privilege based on racial/ethnic and religious identity—structures that also recall the years of Jim Crow segregation in the United States. The 2001 World Conference on Racism, held in South Africa, symbolized these linkages by providing a platform for discussing Palestine as a racial justice issue. Strong supporters of Israel reject such comparisons, insisting that Israel is a unique case because of the history of anti-Semitism and Arab opposition to Israel's existence as a Jewish state.

Use of the term by solidarity activists calls our attention to the fact that settler colonial projects create societies that are multicultural, but also sharply marked by racialization (the process of promoting and enforcing the political, legal, and social importance of racial categories within a context of domination or structural inequality). As a result, solidarity movements, such as the movement against South African apartheid in the 1980s or the current movement supporting Palestinians, tend to be oriented toward the democratic transformation of the existing multicultural society rather than the taking of state power. The desire to transform that society into something truly democratic has led to a focus on the "one-state solution": a single state for all who live in Israel/Palestine.

Significantly, this shift has coincided with the involvement of growing numbers of Jewish activists (especially those belonging to the younger generation) in the movement, as Jews are forced to choose between Zionism and their commitment to universal human rights. The one-state solution puts the solidarity movement somewhat at odds with the older Palestinian independence movement, led by the Palestine Liberation Organization (PLO), which modeled itself on the classic, Third World–style anticolonial struggles in places like Algeria. The movement to support Tibet has faced a similar challenge of negotiating between the desire for formal political independence and the need to fight for human and civil rights, in this case within the context of Chinese rule.

> The anticolonial struggle in Algeria was led by the Front de Libération Nationale (FLN), which sought to eject the French colonial presence from the country. The highly influential 1966 film *The Battle of Algiers* chronicles the FLN's struggle beginning in 1954, when its first armed insurrection began, to Algeria's independence in 1962. Information and scenes from the film can be found at the Criterion Collection website (http://www.criterion.com/films/248-the-battle-of-algiers).

Interestingly, the post-1994 era in South Africa reveals how even a successful anti-apartheid struggle cannot guarantee fundamental socioeconomic transformation, since the application of neoliberal economic policies often serves to reinforce (or even intensify) old patterns of inequality. For this reason, solidarity activists emphasize that the local struggles they support are directly connected with the broader global struggle against the impact of neoliberalism. In South Africa, for example, activists have focused attention on how neoliberal restructuring has produced what the sociologist Andy Clarno calls "an unprecedented growth of 'surplus' or 'disposable' populations: permanently unemployed, too poor to consume, separated from the means of subsistence, and abandoned by the neo-liberal state" (2008, 187). This development, Clarno argues, is closely related to the "proliferation of walled enclosures" and the gradual militarization of police power and other structures of social control aimed at maintaining the conditions for capital accumulation (163). Similarly, many scholars have noted how neoliberal restructuring has undermined the country's public health system at a time of growing HIV/AIDS infection rates.

The Zapatista rebellion in Chiapas was launched explicitly in opposition to a key piece of neoliberal restructuring (NAFTA), which it sought to portray as an assault by undemocratic forces, allied with the U.S. and Mexican governments, against indigenous people and the poor more generally. For the Zapatistas, resistance to neoliberalism is a deeply cultural issue, since it is about defending traditional ways of life, habitation, agriculture, and social organization. This orientation helps reveal why solidarity activists view neoliberalism as a close cousin of settler colonialism and apartheid, with all three serving to promote the interests of global and local elites through the disruption and destruction of indigenous societies. Rather than seeing indigenous communities as "behind" their more "developed" counterparts, these activists see indigenous communities as the test subjects for a new set of capitalist social arrangements that are being imposed on everyone.

## The Scapes of Solidarity

A closer look at the case of Palestine reveals the complex operation of Appadurai's scapes, while also opening up more connections with other solidarity movements. A good place to begin is with ethnoscapes. Palestine is embedded in several overlapping networks of solidarity, each of which has its own history and its own cultural and political dynamics. The core of the Palestine solidarity movement is made up of Palestinians themselves, along with Jewish activists who are opposed either to Zionism itself or to Israel's treatment of Palestinians. Thus, while the movement continues to attract growing numbers of people who belong to neither of these groups, it is the ethnoscapes associated with the Palestinian and Jewish diasporas that are most fundamental to the movement's character. Each of these diasporas has its own particular history, its own internal forms of organization and solidarity, and its own complex relationship to Palestine as a political cause.

In the years following the Nakba, Palestinians nurtured ties of family, village, region, and nation in order to keep alive the hope of return, survive economic hardship, and promote the appreciation of Palestinian culture, both externally and among Palestinians themselves. Over time, these linkages enabled wide-ranging forms of political association and activism, both independently and in connection with the PLO and other groups. The most recent manifestations of global solidarity with Palestine build on these efforts in the diaspora while also connecting with the intense forms of political organization happening on the ground in Palestine. For Arabs who feel a strong sense of pan-Arab identity and pride, the "loss" of Palestine in 1948 makes Palestine a primary focus of pan-Arab solidarity. Palestine has also generated high levels of pan-Islamic solidarity, particularly after the September 11, 2001, attacks and the declaration of the U.S.-led "global war on terrorism," with many Muslims viewing Palestinian victimization as emblematic of wider patterns of violence and injustice affecting Muslims in places like Bosnia, Iraq, and Afghanistan.

An additional network of solidarity stems from Palestine's central role in the history of Christianity. For many Christians, concern for the protection of holy places such as Jerusalem and Bethlehem dovetails with concern for the status of Palestine's small but vibrant Christian population. These concerns produce forms of solidarity that are driven not only by religious devotion but also often by faith-based commitments to social justice. To a greater extent, similar commitments form part of the other solidarity movements under study here, from the prominent role of Christian clergy such as Archbishop Desmond Tutu in South Africa, to the identification of international Buddhist communities with the Tibetan struggle, to the important role of liberation theology and Catholic activism in supporting Latin American liberation movements.

Before looking at Jewish solidarity with Palestine, it is worth noting that Zionism itself has functioned for more than a century as a kind of global solidarity movement seeking to mobilize people, financial resources, and political support for its project of building and maintaining a Jewish state. In this case, of course, the object of solidarity is not Palestine but Israel; Palestine appears as an object of negation rather than affirmation. Jews make up the primary constituency for Zionism, with sacred places such as the Western Wall in Jerusalem providing a focus for Jewish solidarity. At various points, however, Zionism has also drawn on the support of a range of non-Jewish groups. These include volunteers who were drawn to the socialist (but also racially exclusionary) ethos of the Israeli kibbutz (collective farm); Western liberals who saw Israel as an underdog story during its early years; and the governments of other settler states, most notably the United States, where expressions of admiration and support for Israel are common in official political discourse. Most recently, support for Israel by conservative, evangelical Protestant groups, including those known as "Christian Zionists," has surged. Ironically, some of these groups themselves have anti-Semitic elements, choosing to support Israel for theological reasons connected with biblical prophecies of Armageddon and the second coming of Christ.

The "ethnoscape" model becomes more complex and more powerful when the deep history of Jewish solidarity with Palestinians is considered. Indeed, it is as old as the Palestinian cause itself: some of the most prominent public voices on the issue have been major Jewish intellectuals such as Noam Chomsky and Judith Butler. Efforts to broaden the base of Jewish solidarity with Palestinians have long been limited by the strong ideological forces working to promote Jewish loyalty to Zionism and the State of Israel. As a result, Israeli or other Jews who work in support of Palestinian rights have often done so at great personal cost, facing strong forms of censorship and moral condemnation from within the Jewish community. Over time, however, a wider space for Jewish dissent has opened as discussions about "post-Zionism" have gained traction. Early steps in this direction included the growth in peace activism during and after Israel's 1982 invasion of Lebanon, the emergence of an Israeli draft resistance movement, and the work of human rights groups such as B'Tselem and Women in Black. The current global solidarity movement with Palestine features significant numbers of Jewish activists, including those in Israel (e.g., in the Israeli Committee Against House Demolitions) working directly alongside Palestinians in the West Bank and Gaza and those working outside (e.g., in organizations such as Jewish Voice for Peace).

One defining feature of the new wave of Palestine solidarity activism is the participation of international activists in nonviolent direct action (NVDA), a strategy and set of related tactics grounded in theories and histories of pacifism, civil disobedience, anticolonial resistance, and labor activism. The creation of the International Solidarity Movement (ISM) was a key step in pushing this trend forward. Formed by Palestinian and Jewish activists in 2001, the ISM has brought many international volunteers to work with Palestinians struggling against Israeli domination. ISM activists and their counterparts in groups such as Christian Peacemaker Teams (CPT) have used NVDA to support Palestinian farmers suffering vigilante attacks by Israeli colonists, document abuses at military checkpoints and peaceful demonstrations, and stand with Palestinian families facing house demolitions or the loss of agricultural land.

The regular flow of activists in and out of Palestine during this period constitutes its own small ethnoscape, recalling the long tradition of religious pilgrimage to the Holy Land, as well as other histories of "political tourism" and solidarity activism, such as the aforementioned *brigadistas* in Spain and the Freedom Riders who went to the southern United States to work for racial justice during the civil rights movement. While direct action by internationals did not play a major role in the anti-apartheid movement in South Africa, the Zapatista movement has been able to build upon older networks of solidarity (including the work of progressive Christian activists to support Central Americans struggling against

Palestinians and international activists take part in a solidarity march in Ramallah in response to attacks carried out by the Israeli military in 2002. The attacks caused severe damage to Palestinian infrastructure, as seen in the background of the photo.

*Source:* Diego López Calvin.

U.S.-backed military dictatorships in the 1980s) in order to draw internationals to Chiapas. Study abroad programs and tours organized by groups such as the Mexico Solidarity Network have also played a key role in promoting on-the-ground connections between local and international activists there.

Information about the advocacy and solidarity groups mentioned in this section can be found at these websites:

B'Tselem—The Israeli Information Center for Human Rights in the Occupied Territories (http://www.btselem.org/)
Christian Peacemaker Teams (http://www.cpt.org/)
ICAHD-USA (http://icahdusa.org/)
International Solidarity Movement (http://palsolidarity.org/)
Israeli Committee Against House Demolitions (http://www.icahd.org/)
Jewish Voice for Peace (http://jewishvoiceforpeace.org/)
Mexico Solidarity Network (http://mexicosolidarity.org/)
Palestinian BDS National Committee (http://www.bdsmovement.net/)
Women in Black (http://womeninblack.org/vigils-arround-the-world/europa/israel/)

Also, a series of documentary films made by Just Vision explores the role of NVDA in bringing together Palestinian, Israeli, and international activists who share a commitment to social justice. For more information and excerpts from these films, visit the Just Vision website (http://www.justvision.org/).

Closely related to the use of NVDA is the importance of witnessing and citizen journalism as methods of documenting what is happening in conflict areas. Given the tendency of many mainstream Western news media outlets to internalize dominant Israeli categories and narratives when discussing Palestine, this kind of independent voice can have a transformative effect on audiences who are hearing alternative perspectives for the first time. Whether using personal blog sites (LiveJournal, WordPress), established social media platforms (Facebook, Twitter, Flickr, YouTube), or Palestine-specific sites (Electronic Intifada, Palestine Monitor), activists have made heavy use of new technologies to upload and circulate images, videos, and firsthand accounts. Appadurai's mediascapes and technoscapes are thus central to the new wave of solidarity with Palestine. The success of solidarity activists in circulating their message has led the Israeli state to take extraordinary measures to prevent them from entering the country. Like most governments, however, they have discovered that it is ultimately very difficult to exert the kind of message control that was possible prior to the social media era. The best the state can do, as in the case of the Gaza flotilla project launched by solidarity activists in 2008, is create its own narrative and try to undermine competing narratives—in short, engage in ideological struggle on a playing field that is more level than it was in the past.

Examples of Palestine-specific independent media sites include the following:

Electronic Intifada (http://electronicintifada.net/)
Palestine Monitor (http://www.palestinemonitor.org/)
We Are Not Numbers (http://www.wearenotnumbers.org/)

---

### The Gaza Flotilla

The Gaza flotilla project, launched by solidarity activists to draw attention to the ongoing Israeli siege of Gaza, became an object of international controversy when the Israeli military attacked one of the flotillas sailing for Gaza in 2010. Both the activists and the military attempted to influence the narrative surrounding the event by releasing their own video and other testimony. More information about the incident and its aftermath can be found in the following documents and web pages:

- "The Gaza Flotilla at the Frontlines of Web 2.0: Interview with Curtis Brown," Institute for Palestine Studies (http://www.palestine-studies.org/jps/fulltext/42395)
- "Israeli Military Fighting for the Narrative, Online," *The World Post* (http://www. huffingtonpost.com/yermi-brenner/post_690_b_683695.html)
- "Q&A: Israeli Deadly Raid on Aid Flotilla," BBC News (http://www.bbc.co.uk/ news/10203726)
- *Report of the International Fact-Finding Mission to Investigate Violations of International Law, Including International Humanitarian and Human Rights Law, Resulting from the Israeli Attacks on the Flotilla of Ships Carrying Humanitarian Assistance*, United Nations Human Rights Council (http://www2.ohchr.org/ english/bodies/hrcouncil/docs/15session/A.HRC.15.21_en.pdf)

---

Financescapes play an important role in the Palestine solidarity movement as well. As activists have begun to use the concept of apartheid to describe the separate and unequal relations between Palestinians and Israeli Jews, they have naturally turned to the example of the South African anti-apartheid movement and its successful use of economic pressure to produce political transformation. During the 1980s, at the height of the South African government's repression of the country's black population, global solidarity activists were able to bring significant pressure on the government by pushing universities and other institutions to divest from companies doing business in South Africa. When combined with other tactics, including cultural boycotts and state-level economic sanctions, these measures dramatically raised the moral and financial cost of maintaining the apartheid system.

With this model in mind, many activists working in solidarity with Palestine have embraced the boycott, divestment, and sanctions (BDS) framework created in 2005 by a group of nongovernmental organizations in Palestine. BDS activists have worked to support an academic and cultural boycott of Israeli institutions; encouraged divestment by universities, churches, and pension funds from companies such as Motorola and Caterpillar that profit from the Israeli occupation; and lobbied governments to place economic sanctions on Israel. Given the highly polemical nature of the Israel/Palestine issue, the BDS movement has faced significant obstacles, but there is no question that when combined with the larger wave of Palestine activism, BDS has helped shift the public debate while educating a new generation of activists. It also dovetails with a wider interest in divestment among student activists, most notably those working on climate change and environmental justice issues.

It should be clear from this discussion that the new wave of solidarity with Palestine is about more than building a social movement; it is also about transforming what "Palestine" means for global audiences. This is where the fifth of Appadurai's scapes comes into play: ideoscapes. In the years after 1948, Palestine was initially associated with defeat and with the plight of refugees, who were often constructed as voiceless objects of charity. As Palestinians began to speak up for their rights more forcefully, the very concept of "Palestine" began to provoke intense ideological controversy, with strong supporters of Israel seeking to delegitimize Palestinian political claims by associating Palestine with terrorism and anti-Semitism. In a similar way, the apartheid government in South Africa regularly sought to define black resistance as terrorism and to portray its own violence as a necessary response grounded in self-defense. Here it is worth noting that when the idea of "terrorism" emerged as an object of academic study, public concern, and counterinsurgency policy starting in the early 1970s, many of the voices dominating discussion of the issue were from settler colonial states, including the United States, South Africa, and Israel.

For their part, Palestinians and their global supporters have used a variety of strategies over the years to counter these negative portrayals. Through its dominance of Palestinian politics from the late 1960s through the 1990s, for example, the PLO sought to locate Palestine within a different ideoscape by constructing an image of revolutionary strength and determination. This approach is perhaps best symbolized by Yasser Arafat's 1974 appearance before the UN General Assembly, when the PLO leader announced that he was bringing both an olive branch (a symbol of peace) and "a freedom fighter's gun." The PLO's decision to embrace the strategy of armed struggle boosted its revolutionary credibility in the eyes of some, but also made it difficult for Palestinians to separate themselves entirely from the ideoscape imposed upon them by Zionism, particularly when Islamist groups began carrying out suicide attacks against Israelis during and after the first intifada. The intifada, however, also began a process of creating a new picture of Palestinians as a youthful people seeking liberation through largely nonviolent strategies of civil resistance. The image of the young stone thrower, a staple of intifada news coverage, effectively turned on its head the biblical story of David and Goliath, which had previously helped Israel portray itself as the underdog in relation to its Arab neighbors.

In fact, nonviolent struggle has always been an everyday reality for Palestinians, and it has constituted the core of their liberation movement. What is changing, with the help of the new wave of solidarity activism, is the ability of Palestinians to promote an ideoscape that is consistent with that reality. This new ideoscape, which emphasizes powerful concepts like democracy and human rights, continues to exist within a larger discursive universe that includes other, competing understandings of "Palestine," not least the post-9/11 discourse of terrorism. For some Muslims who are sympathetic to militant Islamist politics, Palestine may represent a faith-based call to arms or a symbol of anti-Muslim violence supported by Western governments, or both. Meanwhile, for secular activists on the left, Palestine may symbolize heroic resistance against the forces of global injustice, or may simply be a "cool" cause with which to identify. The popularity of the Palestinian kaffiyeh (headscarf, also spelled keffiyeh), whose basic design has been translated into many colors and mass-produced for sale on street corners in many cities across the world, demonstrates how easily an artifact associated with a concrete, local struggle can be turned into a political (or even apolitical) fashion statement. In short, the kinds of flows associated with globalization continue to shape how the idea of "Palestine" enters into other cultural contexts at a time when political solidarity with Palestinians continues to grow.

## The Future of Global Solidarity Movements

The movements for justice in Palestine, Tibet, South Africa, and Chiapas share an important characteristic: their ability to appeal to external audiences who feel both a commitment to supporting a "local" struggle and a belief in that struggle's larger, global significance. To borrow a phrase from the anthropologist Arturo Escobar, we can say that each of these movements is "place-based, yet transnationalized." Such movements typically arise out of a need to resist particular forms of disruption and deterritorialization associated with imperial expansion, colonization, and neoliberal restructuring. Yet they do so, in part, by taking advantage of the interconnectedness associated with modern globalization, especially its technologies of transportation and communication. What can these examples tell us about the future of global solidarity movements?

First, we can expect that we will continue to see movements seeking to protest the ongoing impact of settler colonial projects, and that such movements will be increasingly linked with one another via technology and the bonds of solidarity. The Idle No More movement, which arose among First Nations people in Canada in late 2012 in conjunction with a widely publicized hunger strike, is an excellent example. Social media helped the movement quickly catch the attention of global solidarity activists, demonstrating the continuing capacity of settler colonialism to produce new forms of resistance. Given that such resistance represents a threat to the dominant political and economic order, it is also likely to provoke growing state surveillance, repression, and criminalization of solidarity activists.

A second set of lessons to be learned concerns issues of voice, cultural authenticity, and cultural translation. The ethnoscapes, technoscapes, and mediascapes discussed earlier combine to create a situation where many voices can be part of the conversation surrounding a given solidarity movement. These include not only local voices (e.g., of Tibetans), but also diasporic voices and the voices of internationals who wish to join the struggle. The speed and ease with which all of these voices can be in dialogue intensifies a dilemma that has long been associated with social movements: Who speaks for the struggle? For example, if there are thousands of people marching all over the world with signs saying "We are all Zapatistas," does that mean that anyone can speak for the people of Chiapas? Similarly, as local struggles continue to rise to the global level, activists will increasingly face the problem of how to help people in radically different circumstances make sense of the movements they support and what it means for them in their own local context. In the case of Palestine, for example, activists in a variety of places have picked up and used the term "intifada" to describe their efforts to oppose their own local injustices. At what point do such efforts at cultural and political translation cross the line from solidarity to irresponsible appropriation?

These issues become even more complex in light of the fact that Internet technologies now make it easier than ever for people to misrepresent themselves and their identities. Given the political intensity surrounding Palestine, and the Middle East and Islam more generally, it is not surprising that impersonating Palestinians and Muslims in cyberspace in an effort to undermine or discredit the work of solidarity activists has become a problem. Nor is it surprising that political, economic, and military elites are increasing their efforts to respond to solidarity movements with high-tech surveillance tactics. In other words, the same technologies that may aid activists in networking, planning actions, or strategically maintaining anonymity may also be used against them by others. For all of these reasons, it is clear that questions of representation in solidarity movements—who is authentic, who has the right to speak for whom, who may possess and share information, and so on—will only become more urgent and complex in the future.

Finally, to return to the initial theme of this case study, if globalization is going to mean something other than the globalization of hierarchical social relations, then solidarity movements will continue to be necessary and will continue to capture the imagination of people across the world. At the same time, the critical issue of global climate change introduces the possibility of solidarity movements that focus less on specific human communities and more on the planet itself. This suggests the emergence of new ideoscapes that may alter in fundamental ways our very understanding of solidarity.

## References and Further Research

Appadurai, Arjun. 1996. "Disjuncture and Difference in the Global Cultural Economy." In *Modernity At Large: Cultural Dimensions of Globalization*, 27–43. Minneapolis: University of Minnesota Press.

Barghouti, Omar. 2011. *BDS: Boycott, Divestment, Sanctions: The Global Struggle for Palestinian Rights*. Chicago: Haymarket Books.

Carey, Roane, and Jonathan Shainin, eds. 2002. *The Other Israel: Voices of Refusal and Dissent*. New York: W. W. Norton.

Clarno, Andy. 2008. "A Tale of Two Walled Cities: Neo-Liberalization and Enclosure in Johannesburg and Jerusalem." In *Political Power and Social Theory*. Vol. 19, edited by Diane E. Davis and Christina Proenza-Coles, 159–205. Bingley, UK: Emerald Group.

Collins, John. 2011. *Global Palestine*. London: Hurst.

Corrie, Rachel. 2008. *Let Me Stand Alone: The Journals of Rachel Corrie*. New York: W. W. Norton.

Davies, Andrew. 2009. "Ethnography, Space, and Politics: Interrogating the Process of Protest in the Tibetan Freedom Movement." *Area* 41, no. 1: 19–25.

Desai, Ashwin. 2002. *We Are the Poors: Community Struggles in Post-Apartheid South Africa*. New York: Monthly Review Press.

Escobar, Arturo. 2004. "Beyond the Third World: Imperial Globality, Global Coloniality and Anti-Globalisation Social Movements." *Third World Quarterly* 25, no. 1: 207–230.

Featherstone, Mike. 2012. *Solidarity: Hidden Histories and Geographies of Internationalism*. London: Zed.

Freire, Paolo. 2009. *Pedagogy of the Oppressed*. 30th anniversary ed. Translated by Myra Bergman Ramos. New York: Continuum.

Ganguly, Meenakshi. 2001. "Generation Exile: Big Trouble in Little Tibet." *Transition* 10, no. 3: 4–25.

Guelke, Adrian. 2005. *Rethinking the Rise and Fall of Apartheid: South Africa and World Politics*. New York: Palgrave Macmillan.

Halper, Lezlee Brown, and Stefan Halper. 2014. *Tibet: An Unfinished Story*. Oxford: Oxford University Press.

Hart, Gillian. 2002. *Disabling Globalization: Places of Power in Post-Apartheid South Africa*. Berkeley: University of California Press.

Keck, Margaret, and Kathryn Sikkink. 1998. *Activists beyond Borders: Advocacy Networks in International Politics*. Ithaca: Cornell University Press.

Khabnabish, Alex. 2008. *Zapatismo beyond Borders: New Imaginations of Political Possibility.* Toronto: University of Toronto Press.

Love, Janice. 1985. *The U.S. Anti-Apartheid Movement: Local Activism in Global Politics.* New York: Praeger.

Marcos, Subcomandante. 2001. *Our Word Is Our Weapon: Selected Writings.* Edited by Juana Ponce de León. New York: Seven Stories Press.

McLagan, Meg. 2002. "Spectacles of Difference: Cultural Activism and the Mass Mediation of Tibet." In *Media Worlds: Anthropology on New Terrain*, edited by Faye Ginsburg, Lila Abu-Lughod, and Brian Larkin, 90–114. Berkeley: University of California Press.

Said, Edward. 1979. *The Question of Palestine.* New York: Times Books.

Sandercock, Josie, ed. 2004. *Peace Under Fire: Israel/Palestine and the International Solidarity Movement.* London: Verso.

Santos, Boaventura de Sousa. 2006. *The Rise of the Global Left: The World Social Forum and Beyond.* New York: Zed.

Stohlman, Nancy, and Laurieann Aladin. 2006. *Live from Palestine: International and Palestinian Direct Action against the Occupation.* Cambridge, MA: South End Press.

Thorn, Hakan. 2006. *Anti-Apartheid and the Emergence of a Global Civil Society.* New York: Palgrave Macmillan.

Wolfe, Patrick. 2006. "Settler Colonialism and the Elimination of the Native." *Journal of Genocide Research* 8, no. 4: 387–409.

# 14

## Conclusion to Case Studies

This book has provided an introduction to the emergent field of global studies through a focus on how the interdisciplinary approaches employed in the field can illuminate key social and cultural processes associated with globalization. Beginning with an overview of the field itself and of essential debates surrounding these processes, the book then features nine case studies designed to represent the breadth and depth of global studies work by showing how concepts and theories can be put to use in a variety of ways.

In order to see how these case studies illustrate the distinct strengths of a global studies approach, it is useful to return to the overview provided in Chapter 1. In particular, the importance of six characteristics of global studies identified in that chapter can be seen throughout the case studies:

1. Global studies is an emergent and integrative field of knowledge that includes both interdisciplinary and transdisciplinary elements. It builds upon and synthesizes the work of traditional disciplines while also seeking to build a new intellectual architecture that is appropriate to a world marked by the intensive and extensive impact of globalization. This integrative approach extends to the realms of epistemology (how knowledge itself is understood) and methodology (how knowledge is pursued).
2. Global studies is about viewing the world in terms of what might be called the "multi-scaled relationality" of global processes. That is, its primary focus is on complex global-local dynamics whose effects are unevenly distributed across scales, spaces, and social groups.
3. Global studies begins from the premise that contemporary global processes cannot be fully understood without examining their deep historical roots. Further, it affirms that the social and cultural elements of these processes are always interwoven with their political and economic elements.
4. In identifying particular processes to investigate, global studies scholars rely as much on thematic foci (e.g., a focus on migration, violence, or identity) as they do on traditional geographic and disciplinary categories.
5. Global studies seeks to support ongoing efforts to challenge and transcend Eurocentrism, the systematic privileging of viewpoints, narratives, and categories derived from Europe. It does so, in part, by prioritizing a bottom-up angle of vision that makes a special effort to view global structures and relationships from the margins, that is, from the perspective of ordinary people who are often erroneously constructed as passive objects of history rather than as active participants in processes of social change.
6. Finally, global studies is deeply shaped by intellectual traditions for which the critical analysis of knowledge structures themselves goes hand in hand with the critical

analysis of the social world. For this reason the emerging field of global studies bears the imprint of other interdisciplinary currents such as critical theory, cultural studies, gender and sexuality studies, post-structuralism, postcolonialism, and world-systems theory.

The first case study, "Global News Media: From the BBC and CNN to Al Jazeera and TeleSUR," offers a thematic focus on how the rise of large media outlets based in the Global South is changing the global news media landscape. Situating these developments in relation to the political economy and history of the global media system, the chapter reveals both the long-term cultural influence of European imperialism and the evolving role of the media in an era of rapid global transformation. In the process, it illustrates the value of a transdisciplinary approach to a set of phenomena that spill across disciplinary and geographic boundaries. The chapter's theoretical emphasis is on the politics of representation: how structures of power (in this case, overlapping structures of geopolitical and media power) shape the social construction of reality and the way individuals and communities see the world. Both Qatar-based Al Jazeera and Venezuela-based TeleSUR are examined in detail in order to illustrate the different regional forms that challenges to Northern media hegemony can take.

The second case study, "Indigenous People and Intellectual Property Rights," examines the ways people define themselves as indigenous, or attached to a specific place and ecosystem, in a world characterized by the migrations of vast numbers of people. The global-local dynamics explored in this case study are multileveled: today's indigenous groups resort to globalized means of communication and activism in order to learn from each other and gain leverage from world opinion in fighting various forms of exploitation—national, corporate, and transnational. This analysis is set against a historical backdrop and considers how the exploitation of indigenous people's resources and marginalization of their political status goes back deep in time, especially in the Americas. Today they face a new threat: the appropriation of knowledge they have used for millennia to grow food and to heal themselves through their detailed knowledge of their local ecosystems. Ironically this knowledge of local ecosystems was initially devalued by European colonizers, but in recent decades, through activism against climate change and against Eurocentrism, indigenous knowledge has become prized by the dominant culture. This has led to patenting of indigenous plants by transnational corporations that are in turn protected by global intellectual property rights agreements.

The third case study, "NGOs, Humanitarianism, and the Cultural Construction of Global Hierarchy," explores the cultural dynamics surrounding the growing role of civil society, particularly nongovernmental organizations (NGOs), in responding to the world's need for humanitarian assistance. From a global studies perspective, it is important to understand how these contemporary forms of transnational assistance are shaped by longstanding patterns of geopolitical and cultural power that have established racialized and gendered ideas of who is "needy" and who is empowered to "help." The chapter demonstrates the strong influence of postcolonial and other forms of critical theory that challenge Eurocentric knowledge structures and interrogate the relationship between knowledge and power. These dynamics are illustrated through an analysis of several recent examples of humanitarian campaigns that have provoked widespread debate over the continuing imprint of global hierarchies and the role of social media in both reinforcing and challenging these hierarchies.

The fourth case study, "Climate Change and Changing Global Imaginaries," illustrates why the field of global studies features such a strong and distinctive commitment to epistemological diversity and triangulation of multiple viewpoints when considering any global issue. The enormity of the challenge posed by anthropogenic global climate change requires urgent and effective global responses, but the way people understand both the problem and the potential solutions is inevitably shaped by forms of knowledge and consciousness that are culturally specific. Drawing on the interdisciplinary theoretical concept of cultural "imaginaries," the chapter reveals that these cultural structures have always been diverse, and that this diversity remains a significant factor today as humans seek effective political strategies to combat the impact of climate change. Specific examples covered in the chapter show the remarkable range of creative ways in which artists, activists, and communities are responding to this global problem.

The fifth case study, "Transnational LGBT Identities: Liberation or Westernization?," examines the complex local-global dynamics involved in the transformations—conceptually and in practice—of gender and sexuality. The chapter examines a selection of local constructions of same-sex erotic relationships and their engagement with histories of colonization, past and present. In particular the Western notion of gender and sexual identities is juxtaposed with older, local ideas about third genders and fluid sexual roles. In highlighting the range of local perspectives on gender and sexuality, the case study questions the Eurocentric reification of identity as a primary category of being and examines the unquestioned Western concept of gay identity as one relating to liberation. At the same time, the influence of Western homophobia and anti-sodomy laws on former European colonies is examined: in the end the diversity of genders and sexual practices and their interrelationships has to be balanced against a more universal practice of human rights.

The sixth case study, "The Islamic Veil and the Global Politics of Gender," is a transdisciplinary examination of the hijab, or Islamic head covering: it explores the meanings of the hijab, or Islamic head covering, from the perspective of local-global narratives, as well as through historical and geographic lenses. The chapter considers the pre-Islamic origins of veiling in various cultures to its role among minority groups in Europe to its status in several predominantly Muslim nations. There are deep and different histories through which the practice of veiling has traveled: from being a local custom to one viewed as a central signifier of Islamic faith. Even within predominantly Muslim nations, its meaning has shifted historically—in Turkey, Iran, and Egypt, for example, it was supplanted by "modern" Western dress for much of the twentieth century. The Iranian revolution then imposed it by law, while in other countries it is having a resurgence. In Europe, Muslim women struggle to be allowed to cover their heads and faces in public spaces. This case study illustrates the multiple meanings and functions of the hijab depending on local contexts, but those local contexts are often a reaction against global Eurocentric paradigms of modernity imposed by hegemonic powers. Nonetheless in all these contexts it is women who are expected to be the symbolic bearers of local cultural identities.

The seventh case study, "'Keeping It Real': State, Corporate, or Underground Voices in Global Hip-Hop," examines the pan-African circulation of African musical traditions through hip-hop, a globalized genre with very local roots and styles. As a form of global popular culture, hip-hop struggles to maintain its authentic spirit of protest and resistance even as it has been appropriated by corporate sponsorship and co-opted for nation-building purposes. In addition to the global-local dynamics explored here, the case study frames hip-hop in terms of its historical roots. Its deepest influences can be traced back to the role of the griot in West Africa and to the rhythmic music brought by enslaved Africans to the New World. Through enslavement, emancipation, and oppression, the African-descended peoples of the Americas used verbal and rhythmic forms to keep alive their dignity and their cultural identities in resistance against assimilation to Eurocentric cultures. The case study traces various hybrid forms of Afro-Caribbean music from Jamaica and Trinidad as they morph into the beginnings of hip-hop in the Bronx, spread outward again, and return to African nations such as Tanzania and Ghana.

The eighth case study, "Yoga in America: Competitive Sport or Spiritual Quest?," examines local-global dynamics of a cultural phenomenon—yoga as practiced in the West—and critically analyzes it against Western economic and social processes. It looks at the tensions between the local, ancient practices of yoga as part of the Hindu quest for spiritual enlightenment and the increasingly globalized, commodified practices of yoga today, especially in the United States. Unlike many other globalized cultural practices, yoga moves from the East to the West through the contact zone created by British colonization of India in the eighteenth and nineteenth centuries. Many European and American writers and intellectuals were fascinated by Hinduism and Buddhism and by the early twentieth century were beginning to study yoga. But in 1965 the United States changed its immigration laws, allowing much greater access for non-Europeans. The counterculture movements of the sixties also popularized Indian spiritual practices, and since then numerous schools of yoga have been created and trademarked to protect the profits of their founders. A particularly American form of yoga, power yoga, is described in the chapter.

The ninth and final case study, "Global Solidarity Movements: Palestine, Tibet, and Beyond," uses a transdisciplinary approach to understand what is a quintessentially transnational process: the role of global solidarity movements in supporting locally grounded liberation struggles in places such as Palestine, Tibet, South Africa, and Mexico. Such struggles invariably emerge out of long-term historical processes of colonization, capital accumulation, and state building that form an essential context for all global studies work. The chapter employs anthropologist Arjun Appadurai's influential concept of global "scapes" to explore what solidarity movements can tell us about transnational flows of people, information, images, identities, and forms of violence and resistance. In this sense, the case study provides an opportunity to consider how globalization operates through multiple channels across multiple scales, creating the conditions not only for connections at the level of elite groups and institutions, but also at the grassroots level of social movements and ordinary people.

The selection of the book's case studies is designed to affirm and illustrate the flexibility of global studies approaches and their ability to reveal the connections among diverse examples. Global studies is ultimately about weaving together perspectives, disciplines, theories, and methods in the interest of understanding the forces and processes that constitute our contemporary world. This orientation enables both breadth (in terms of making connections across the various case studies) and depth (in terms of the level of integration present within each individual case study). It is this combination of breadth and depth, pursued in ways that deliberately stretch across geographical and knowledge boundaries, that distinguishes global studies as an exciting and emerging field of study. With this in mind, the book has sought to do at least two things simultaneously: to model the specific kinds of focused analysis found in the field of global studies, and to provide a diversity of examples so that students can build their own connections and begin to imagine conducting their own global studies research.

# Index

*Note: Page numbers in italic indicate a photo on the corresponding page.*